FOOTPRINTS IN THE SNOW

JULIE HILL lives near Chichester with
her husband, Kevin, and their two children.
This is her first book.

FOOTPRINTS IN THE SNOW

How Science Helped Turn Tragedy to Triumph

Julie Hill

PAN BOOKS

First published 2000 by Macmillan

First published in paperback 2001 by Pan Books

This edition published 2007 by Pan Books
an imprint of Pan Macmillan Ltd
Pan Macmillan, 20 New Wharf Road, London N1 9RR
Basingstoke and Oxford
Associated companies throughout the world
www.panmacmillan.com

ISBN 978-0-330-45325-7

'Tomorrow I'm Going to Rewrite the English Language' by Lois Keith,
reprinted on page v, is used by permission of The Women's Press Ltd.
From *Musn't Grumble – Writing by Disabled Women*, edited by Lois Keith,
first published in Great Britain 1994 by The Women's Press Ltd,
34 Great Sutton Street, London EC1V 0LQ.

1 3 5 7 9 8 6 4 2

A CIP catalogue record for this book is available from
the British Library.

Typeset by SetSystems Ltd, Saffron Walden, Essex
Printed and bound in Great Britain by
Mackays of Chatham plc, Chatham, Kent

Visit **www.panmacmillan.com** to read more about all our books and to buy
them. You will also find features, author interviews and news of any author
events, and you can sign up for e-newsletters so that you're always first to hear
about our new releases.

To absent friends

Tomorrow I am going to rewrite the English Language.
I will discard all those striving ambulist metaphors
of power and success
And construct new images to describe my strength.
My new, different strength.

Then I won't have to feel dependent
Because I can't stand on my own two feet.
And I'll refuse to feel a failure
When I don't stay one step ahead.
I won't feel inadequate if I can't
Stand up for myself
Or illogical when I don't
Take it one step at a time.

I will make them understand that it is a very male way
To describe the world.
All this walking tall
And making great strides.

Yes, tomorrow I am going to rewrite the English Language
Creating the world in my own image.
Mine will be a gentler, more womanly way
To describe my progress.
I will wheel, cover and encircle.
Somehow I will learn to say it all.

'Tomorrow I'm Going to Rewrite the English Language',
Lois Keith, 1994

Contents

Acknowledgements

THERE ARE countless people whose kindness and professionalism have contributed to my progress and therefore to this book. I am indebted to them all. Not only friends and family members, but those who have dedicated untold amounts of time and energy to the experiment that is me. Special thanks must, of course, go to my family – Kev, Mum, Dad, Nathan, Daniel, Neil and Bridget – and to the team that has made all this possible, Tim, Nick, Peter, Viv, Duncan, Tony, Davids Grundy and Rushton, and all the wonderful nursing staff at the Duke of Cornwall Spinal Treatment Centre, Salisbury. Friends Angie and Andy and Alan and Ann deserve special mention, along with Julian Alexander of Lucas Alexander Whitley, and Malcolm Brinkworth and Bennetta Adamson of Touch Productions. Janine Catterall has also been a star. My final thanks go to Wendy Holden, who somehow managed to get right inside my head, bullied me into getting my homework in on time and created an amazingly comfortable environment which enabled memories to come flooding back with alarming clarity.

Anyone wishing to make a donation should contact:

THE BACK-UP TRUST
The Business Village
Broomhill Road
London SW18 4JQ
Tel: (020) 8871 1805
www.backup.org.com

and

The INSPIRE Foundation
Spinal Treatment Centre
Salisbury District Hospital
Salisbury SP2 8BJ
Tel: 01722 336262 X2465
www.inspire.demon.co.uk

ONE

Darkness

THERE IS a lot that I can remember about that night. Unfortunately. Like the sensation of flying through the night sky, seconds after losing control, my legs and arms flailing weightlessly. The car from which I had been flung in that split second of destiny was twirling and spinning likewise in the air behind me, its headlamps flashing crazily around the sky like searchlights, after we had both hurtled headlong up a steep bank and lunged onwards through the hedgerow and into space. Loud music filled the air – the car stereo was still blasting away with the pounding music of Chris De Burgh. As the world beneath me turned upside down, I heard the words I shall never forget: 'Don't pay the ferryman, Don't even fix a price, Don't pay the ferryman, Until he gets you to the other side . . .'

There was a loud thump and a sudden silence as the car crashed to the ground first, the force of the impact cutting its engine, stilling the music and blacking the headlights seconds after they had illuminated a shadowy corner of the ploughed field into which we had both been somersaulted. Gone too was the scream of metal fracturing under stress. There was a newer kind of silence, an eerie stillness after my body landed with a sickening crump seconds later and lay, skewed awkwardly on the ground, facing up at the stars.

It was pitch black and a dreadful torpor pervaded my body. For several seconds, I thought that I was dead. To say I was terrified wouldn't do justice to the ice-cold fear that gripped my heart in those first moments, waiting for sensation to return. I was completely numb, winded, and rigid with the horror of my new situation as question after question raced through my mind. How could I have been so stupid? I had my whole life ahead of me. I had two small children, for God's sake. How would they cope without me? I had lost my specs and was blinking hard to focus in the gloom, wondering what would happen next if this was it – death. Was this it? Was I doomed to lie like this, cold and lifeless in the darkness, for eternity?

'Oh, God!' I wailed, my breath forming a cloud of mist above me in the cool night air. As I heard my own voice, its sound seemed to trigger the first waves of pain which began to wash over me, and I realized with tremendous relief that I must be alive to be feeling so many agonizing sensations. With that realization also came the shocked recognition that I was very seriously injured.

'Christ, I've really done it this time,' I thought sheepishly, as all the other bumps and scratches in my fairly accident-prone life flashed briefly before me – the time I had been dazzled by the headlights of another car and ridden my moped into a ditch; the broken arms and legs caused by spills from bicycles and trees when I was a kid. But here I was now, twenty-eight years old, a working mother with a husband, a massive mortgage and increasing responsibilities – and however hard I tried, I couldn't feel my legs.

Fear rose up from the pit of my stomach and engulfed me, as the pain in the middle of my back became almost too much to bear. It was excruciating – worse than anything I had ever experienced before, even childbirth. It was a persistent, throbbing pain, hot and angry, which refused to subside. And still the darkness and the silence overwhelmed me. I began to panic. Maybe I'd made a mistake. Maybe I *was* dead and this was hell; this was how I was destined to spend eternity. I wasn't religious, never had been, but I suddenly found myself praying to some unknown God for mercy, begging for release from the nightmare in which I found myself. I had never felt more lonely in my life. 'Help! . . . help me, please!' I called – with the greatest effort, opening my mouth to cry out. The high-pitched shriek that emerged bore little resemblance to any sound I recognized as mine. There was desperation in that voice – it was the cry of a little girl, frightened and alone in the dark.

Again I called out into the inky blackness, staring up at the twinkling moonless night and willing someone, somewhere, to answer my prayers. But even if I was still alive, it was late at night and I knew I was miles from anywhere. I could lie here all night unnoticed.

My ears strained eagerly for a response. But there was nothing, just the whisper of leaves in the hedgerow and the rhythmic ticking and hissing of the car's engine as it settled groaningly into its muddy crater. But then I heard, or thought I heard, a distant sound, a voice from nowhere. Tears of relief and joy – someone was approaching, on the other side of the hedge, trying to beat their way through towards me. 'Keep shouting!' the voice encouraged in the distance. 'Where are you?' another voice called. It was two women.

'Over here! I'm over here!' I managed weakly, my voice breaking with emotion. 'Please, hurry! Help me.' My eyes were trained keenly upwards, straining to see something at the edge of my limited view, desperate for some human contact. Peering into the darkness until my eyes began to smart, I blinked only when a shadowy figure finally arrived and knelt beside me. That first touch of a hand in mine, the first sight of a blurred face looking down at me, induced such a surge of emotion that my tears came faster, and the shock and relief snatched my breath away.

'Now, now, don't cry,' the woman kneeling over me pleaded, stroking my cheek tenderly with the back of her hand as the other woman hovered anxiously in the background. Her voice sounded soft and comforting, like a hot milky drink late at night. Her hands were warm and plump. She was my angel of mercy – just having her by my side, talking to me, reminding me that I was alive, seemed to lessen the pain. 'It's all right,' she soothed. 'I'm here now. Help is on its way.' Her name was Helen; that was all I knew, all I needed to know at that moment, and everything was going to be all right. She told me so.

It was with some contrition that I realized that my saviour was the very same woman who, only a few minutes earlier, I had been cursing at out loud as she dawdled along in front of me down the B2178, the country lane that runs between East Ashling and my home village of Rowland's Castle, near Portsmouth in

Hampshire. It was 10.15 p.m. on Wednesday 11 April 1990, two days before the Easter Bank Holiday week-end, and I was driving home to my husband Kevin and our two sons, Nathan, six, and Daniel, four. It had been a long and busy day. My demanding new job as a sales representative for a local drinks wholesaler had involved me in ferrying some senior members of the local Ladies' Licensed Victuallers' Association to and from their annual shindig – a day out at the Goodwood races on the South Downs, with lunch and a party in nearby Chichester afterwards.

I had enjoyed the lunch, gone home to pick up the kids, dropped them off at my mum's, and then returned to my clients. I'd told Kevin I hoped to be home around eight o'clock, but some of the ladies had enjoyed their day out a bit too enthusiatically, ending up on the brandy, and they needed to be driven home. As their local sales rep, it was good public relations for me to stay on and volunteer my services as a chauffeur.

When I had last called Kevin from the phone box at the Castle pub in Chichester at nine to tell him that I would be later still, he had not been at all happy. He didn't like me doing this job in the first place – he knew we needed the extra income to pay for our smart new house and the rising expenses of a young family, but he resented the hours I worked and felt threatened by the nature of the job. I loved it, though. In spite of the nuisance of the occasional late night, it did me a power of good after years of being stuck at home with the children. I had a new self-esteem and confidence in myself that I would never have thought possible.

Part of his response had been to give in his notice at his old firm and take on a new, better-paid job as a senior accountant with another company, Julius Meller Toiletries in Portsmouth, a position which had been confirmed just one week before and which he was due to take up in three weeks' time. The new job would, he hoped, mean better long-term security and a chance for me to do a job he considered, well, less demanding. Kevin had watched me grow from the naive teenager he had married ten years earlier into someone he no longer recognized, going off in my power suits and company car to socialize with flirtatious pub landlords, and he hated it.

His final, sullen words to me the night of the accident were: 'I'll probably be in bed when you get home.' Then he hung up, and I dreaded the brooding, silent treatment I knew would be waiting for me as soon as I opened the front door and crept guiltily upstairs to our bedroom.

Turning the key in the engine of my blue Vauxhall Cavalier estate after I had dropped off my last passenger, my mind was miles away. I knew I had to get home as quickly as possible and try to make my peace with Kevin as best I could. I hated going to sleep with an argument brewing; it was something I always tried to avoid. Coupled with my anxieties about his reaction were my ongoing concerns about my job. I had only been in it for ten weeks – my three-month probationary period was nearly up, and I wasn't sure I had yet brought in enough new sales to justify the company keeping me on. I had been made redundant from two other jobs previously and I knew that if it happened a third time it would really hurt, especially losing a job I enjoyed so much. Kevin didn't seem to understand my viewpoint at all. He was too busy nursing his wounded pride to see that I needed to do everything I could to keep the bosses sweet.

I don't even remember putting my seat belt on as I pressed the play button on the stereo-cassette and set off from the outskirts of Chichester with a squeal of tyres, just as Chris De Burgh started to sing. It was a clear, cold night, fine and dry, and there was little traffic after ten o'clock. I chose the back road from Chichester because it was the route I was most familiar with. I drove along that road every day – it was a short cut, a pretty winding lane through villages and across open countryside – avoiding the busy A27. My mind was buzzing with everything I had to do the next day – cook breakfast, make Nathan's sandwiches, drop Nathan off at school, take Daniel to my mum's, deliver the two barrels of beer and the crate of lager rattling around in the back of the car, do the food shopping for the forthcoming long weekend, buy the boys their Easter eggs, prepare supper and – last, but by no means least – try and appease Kevin yet again.

Ten minutes into my journey, I was making good time and feeling a bit happier about what would face me when I got home. Kevin would be all right, with a bit of smooth talking and ego-stroking. We had some friends, Colin and Carol, coming down from Scotland for the weekend, something we had both been looking forward to for ages, and I knew he wouldn't carry his moodiness on into what promised to be such a happy event. Colin was a colleague of his, and Kevin was all for maintaining the image of an idyllic home and family life, even if sometimes that picture wasn't quite the truth.

It wasn't that our marriage was on the rocks exactly,

but we had certainly drifted apart of late. Having the kids had made a big difference to our social life and standard of living, and Kevin was working even harder to try and pay for everything. Much as I adored the boys, I had often felt bored and trapped at home after years of working full-time in a variety of jobs, and I had to readjust my sights as far as all the things I had hoped to achieve were concerned. Going back to full-time work had been my idea, and at first Kevin had approved. But when the challenges of the new job changed me from the mousy housewife and mother he had come to take for granted into a feisty career woman with my own money and ambitions, he quickly did a U-turn, and his negative attitude had recently driven a wedge between us. It was nothing I couldn't handle, I felt, and I had never considered the possibility that we might split up. But the more he resented me working and staying out late, the more I resented the aggravation he gave me about it.

Approaching the tight bend in the centre of the village of East Ashling at a good pace and with nothing in front of me, I was making good time and hoping to be home before Kevin had gone to sleep. But rounding the bend, I was annoyed at having to dip my headlights and apply the brake as I suddenly came up behind two cars, sticking closely to each other and to the irritatingly restrictive thirty-mile-per-hour limit. Frustrated by their rigid adherence to the law when I was in such a hurry, I tapped my fingers on the steering wheel impatiently in time to the music, and waited for my chance to overtake. Chris De Burgh's voice filled the car and his words matched my mood: 'It was late at night on the open road, Speeding like a man on the run, A lifetime spent preparing for the journey . . .'

I started to sing along, but then I'm afraid my temper got the better of me. 'Oh, for God's sake, get a move on!' I yelled at the two drivers idling along in front of me, their tail-lights obscuring my view. I became more and more angry. 'What are you waiting for?' I shouted, seeing from the speedometer that they had now dropped to twenty-six miles an hour although they had just passed a road sign informing them that the speed limit was now sixty.

Familiar with the road, I knew that just a few hundred yards further on, past a long line of poplar trees, there was a nice straight stretch of tarmac where I would be able to overtake both cars easily, as long as there was nothing coming the other way. Straining to the right and seeing no oncoming headlights, I seized my moment, shifted down a gear and stepped on the gas, revving the noisy two-litre engine. I had always been a bit of a 'girl racer' and, in an attempt to demonstrate my irritation at the slowness of my fellow road-users, I deliberately over-revved to let them know that I meant business. Accelerating away easily, I flew past the first car, a Vauxhall Nova. The driver flashed her headlights at my impatience, but I didn't care.

The music was spurring me on, egging me on to take both cars, to complete my single manoeuvre in style. I'd show those slow-coaches how to drive. I even smiled to myself with satisfaction as I nipped in between the two cars and prepared to take the next before easing in at a slight angle so as to return to my side of the road. This was the new me, the go-getter in a company car with an attitude to match. I had everything – a good job, a clever husband, a nice house and two great kids. Nothing was going to stand in my way. 'It was late at night on the open road, Speeding like a man on the run, A lifetime spent preparing for the journey . . .' Chris De Burgh was right. I *had* spent my life preparing for this journey, and as I returned home to my near-perfect family to resume my place in my near-perfect world, everything felt good.

But just as I was about to overtake the second car, a Morris Marina, before nipping back on to my side of the road, fate intervened. Something went very wrong with the car and, in an instant – less than a heartbeat – I found myself no longer in control. As I fought frantically with the steering wheel, the road ahead of me inexplicably dipped below my horizon and all I could see out of the windscreen was black sky. My near-perfect world was about to spin crazily off its axis. Everything I had known up to now was to end, and a new, imperfect world was about to begin. I didn't know it then, but at that critical moment when I was at the very height of my smug complacency, when I was driving too fast and had the least control, one of my front tyres had burst.

Within the space of a few heart-stopping moments after the car veered off the road, I encountered my next bit of bad luck. Exactly at the point where I left the road there was a large, natural hump in the grass verge – the only one like it for several hundred yards. This bumpy launch pad sent the car (and me) onwards and upwards, over a steep bank, through the top branches of a thick hawthorn hedge and on towards a field. As I hurtled through the air, twisting and spinning, the driver's door was thrown open and I somehow parted company with the vehicle, landing a few seconds later at great speed on the unyielding earth, my lower spine bearing the brunt of the fall.

With an irony that I could not have imagined, the woman at the wheel of the leading vehicle, the very driver whose existence I had cursed minutes earlier, was now my only link with the world outside my excruciating and strangely blurred existence. This angelic presence at my side was comforting me and stroking my hand and telling me that my perfect world was still intact, when I knew deep down that she was lying. I was in shock, desperate to believe that she was speaking the truth and to retain some sort of control in a situation that seemed so unreal. I began gabbling instructions. 'Please telephone Kevin,' I told the woman whose face I could barely make out, reciting the number, 'and tell him what's happened.' She nodded and squeezed my hand, as if she knew who Kevin was. 'He'll need to call my mum and dad and get them to look after the boys for the night,' I prattled on. 'I'll probably have to stay in hospital for a day or two.' She nodded again, less vigorously this time, but still didn't move from my side as I closed my eyes to picture my sons tucked up asleep under their Thomas the Tank Engine duvets, surrounded by their fluffy toys and dreaming of opening the brightly coloured foil on their Easter eggs at the weekend.

I still can't quite conjure up Helen's face, and in a way she has taken up an almost mystical place in my memory. Softly spoken and kind, she seemed an ethereal presence, an almost heavenly creature there beside me in those twenty minutes it took for the ambulance to arrive, summoned by the driver of the other vehicle who had run back down the road to get help. Strange as it sounds, I became very close to Helen in those frozen instants before anyone else arrived. At this moment of tremendous crisis I bonded with her, and I still feel deeply emotional about her and what she did for me, something I was unable to thank her properly for at the time.

She could clearly see that I was in agony and did all she could to keep my mind off the pain. 'Tell me more about your family,' she encouraged, in her clear, calm voice. 'What are your sons' names?' She urged me to talk, to tell her all about Kevin and the boys and my home life. She knew that she had to try to keep me conscious. Several times I had almost drifted off, and she had gently shaken me, asking me question after question, never appearing to tire of my rambling, incoherent answers.

Against all the odds, she made me feel at ease, and before long I found myself telling her all about myself – my job, my family, the friends who were coming for the Easter weekend. 'I hope they'll still come,' I added, 'I don't want to spoil their visit.' She did all she could to reassure me, telling me over and over that the ambulance would be with us any minute and that I was not to worry, everything would be all right. I peered up into the dark shape from which her voice came and willed myself to believe her.

Although I felt conscious and lucid, I must have been more stupefied than I realized, because the first time I was aware that there were people there other than Helen was when a sudden bright light shone on us both which seemed to herald a flurry of activity and noise. The light was coming from the back of an ambulance which had appeared at my side, and its rear doors had been opened in readiness to receive me. The interior lights illuminated Helen, me and the rough clods of earth on which I lay sprawled. The ambulance had apparently been driven up into the field as close as possible to where I lay, and then reversed into position for easier access, although I have no recollection of any of that happening.

Squinting at the sudden change of light, I looked around and was struck by the sheer numbers of people silhouetted all around me – policemen, firemen, paramedics, people with telephones and torches and radios, all talking at the same time and seeming to jockey for position. Alarmed by their sudden presence and for the first time strangely self-conscious, I became aware of the weirdest, and increasingly distressing, sensation in my lower body. I somehow felt, lying there flat on my back and unable to move, that my legs were up in the air and bent at the knees as if still in a sitting position. If that was so, then I must have been baring my knickers to the hordes of strange men now gathered around me. I was wearing my work clothes – a green corduroy calf-length skirt, a white blouse and a little waistcoat, and leather boots. I found myself wishing I had a pair of trousers on.

Unable to move or lift my head to see for myself what position I was in, I asked Helen – whose hand I was still tightly clutching – for her help. 'Please put my legs down,' I pleaded, 'they're in the air, put them down.' But she continued to smile and pat my hand and tell me not to worry, and I became even more upset when she did nothing. It was scaring the hell out of me that I couldn't move my lower body or feel my legs normally. That was when the fear really started to set in.

I was still unable to see much more than a blur because of my missing specs, and I began to plead with the people milling around me to find them. 'My glasses, I need my glasses, I can't see anything,' I wailed, the panic rising again. I was shocked and confused, and I became inexplicably concerned about some cash that I knew had been in my skirt pocket, but which I was afraid might have been lost in the accident. 'I've lost some money,' I cried breathlessly. 'Please look for it. I need it for tomorrow.' I also remember asking one of the policemen who was now permanently at my side if he thought my car was an insurance write-off. 'Please tell me it isn't,' I begged him. 'My job's far from safe as it is.' I don't remember his answer. All I could hear were voices and revving car engines and yells from the nearby road, all competing with the sound of my heartbeat thumping in my ears.

But my main concern, and the thing I kept on and on about, continued to be the position I thought I was lying in. I was bordering on the hysterical about it. 'My legs, please lay them down,' I urged a green-suited paramedic who was injecting something into my arm for the pain as his colleague carefully secured a neck brace under my head. 'Please, listen to me, I want you to do something about my legs.' Neither man took a blind bit of notice, and I felt like screaming at them out of frustration and fear.

More and more dark figures closed in around me, peering down into my face as I struggled to speak and catch my breath. One lifted my eyelids with his thumbs and shone a thin beam of light into each of my pupils. 'Vital signs good,' he said to his colleague. 'She's still conscious.' Their faces melded together, until I felt as if there was a vast crowd staring at me, enjoying my embarrassment, ignoring my cries for help. As the medical team bustled around me, preparing to lift me on to a special spinal board and into the back of the ambulance, Helen – the only presence that had remained constant, whose hand I had been gripping throughout – was gradually pulled away, her fingers slipping from mine.

That is when I started to panic big time, calling her name and sobbing uncontrollably. 'Helen, Helen, don't leave me. Helen!' I screamed, terrified of what the future held for me away from her calming influence. But she was gone, now just another anonymous face in the crowd, slipping quietly away into the darkness, back to her car and her life, leaving me to face a new and alarming world on my own.

Weeping, inconsolable at the departure of the gentle escort who had guided me through limbo before I entered what felt like the place of the damned, I was now flanked by shadowy figures and lifted out of the dark underworld of the field. I squeezed my eyes shut against the tears and the pain as I was gingerly carried over to a bright hole – the back of the ambulance, with its glaring lights and clinical whiteness. A plastic oxygen mask was lowered over my face, sending me into a complete panic, until a paramedic pinned my arms down and told me to try to stay calm. Staring up into a pair of crystal-blue eyes, I suddenly found myself breathing very fast and feeling incredibly hot and clammy.

As my senses started to heighten with the oxygen, all I could smell in my nose and the back of my throat was beer – sweet, sickly beer – and it made me feel very sick. I briefly wondered what had caused the smell, then I realized that the barrels of beer and all the bottles of lager in the back of the car must have shattered and spilled when it hit the ground. I must have stunk like a brewery. The waves of pain washing over me were now accompanied by waves of nausea, and I felt for a while as if I had lost all control of myself – emotionally and physically. I had never felt so sick, but I couldn't vomit. I looked up into the eyes of the paramedic above me and mentally pleaded with him to make me better. Everything seemed so completely removed from reality. I felt as if I was under water, drowning slowly, and only half-seeing, half-hearing what was going on around me.

As my breathing slowed slightly and my senses cleared, I began to appreciate where I was and what was happening. 'You've been in a road accident and we're taking you to hospital,' the paramedic was telling me, speaking very deliberately so as to make me understand. His face appeared to blur and clear alternately, and I wondered why the ambulance was driving so very slowly, first out of the bumpy field, and then along the main road. There was no siren wailing, no flashing blue light, no apparent sense of urgency to get me to hospital. The paramedic took my hand and told me not to worry, and as he did so I began to calm a little, thinking that if the ambulance wasn't in any hurry, it must be because I wasn't too badly injured. Perhaps Helen had been telling the truth all along.

Slightly less distressed and better able to comprehend my situation, my overriding concern again became the position that my legs were in – they felt so strange; it was almost as if I knew they must be lying flat, but my brain was telling me that they were still in the position they had been in when I was driving. Again and again, I tried to tell the paramedic through my oxygen mask to lay my legs down, to spare my embarrassment, but

like all the others before him he didn't seem to hear
me.

By the time we reached St Richard's Hospital in Chichester, I was feeling decidedly woozy. It felt warm and
safe in the slow-moving vehicle and all I wanted to do
was to go to sleep. I was still in a great deal of pain, but
whatever they had injected me with at the scene of the
accident had taken the edge off it, thankfully, and made
me very drowsy. Just as I was about to drift off, the
ambulance doors were suddenly flung open and more
bright lights and cool air flooded in.

Again I found myself surrounded by strangers, and
my heartbeat increased with my rising fear and panic.
They were all staring down at me and talking about me
as if I wasn't there. In spite of my reluctance to be
moved from my new safe haven, they lifted me on to a
trolley and wheeled me inside, quickly ushering me into
a cubicle and drawing the curtains so that they could
all take a closer look at the strange creature who had
been delivered into their midst. After a brief discussion
amongst themselves, the curtains were thrown back and
I was wheeled to the X-ray department, where I was
slotted into a spot below a huge monstrosity of a
machine. Feeling very close to tears again, I shut my
eyes as it took my photograph.

The next twenty minutes or so were a muzzy blur,
as I was wheeled back to another curtained cubicle and
examined by yet more strangers, their foreheads fur-
rowed, their voices half-whispers. People were talking
to me and about me, but I couldn't hear properly. No
one would listen to me about my legs being in the air,

and I had never felt more isolated. A kindly policeman I recognized from the scene of the accident appeared at my bedside, and I was relieved to see his face – until I realized he had come to breathalyse me. It was something he was legally required to do, especially as I stank of alcohol, and he tried to make it as easy as possible for me in the circumstances. Thankfully, a prosecution for drink-driving was not something I'd have to worry about, he assured me before he left rather sheepishly.

The next time someone I recognized appeared within my limited view, my tears erupted and I lost control. It was Kevin, and as he leaned over me, his ashen face close to mine, I sobbed hysterically. My dad, Norman, was with him, equally pale and dark-eyed, and I could hardly bear to meet his gaze over Kev's shoulder. Ripping the oxygen mask from my face, I blurted out: 'I've really messed up this time.' Woken from his sleep by a phone call from the police just twenty minutes earlier, he looked ghastly. He did his best to comfort me. 'Don't worry, it'll be fine. I'm here now,' he said over and over again, his moustache bristling familiarly against my cheek. They were words I'd heard not long before, lying in the field with Helen at my side, but the look in his big brown eyes did nothing to soothe my anxiety. When the strangers returned and tried to remove him and Dad from the curtained-off cubicle to examine me further, I screamed at them to let my family stay. I had lost Helen, and now Kevin's hand was being prised from mine. The more distressed I became, the more upset he was; my father stood trembling helplessly on the sidelines, his hand to his mouth. I pleaded with the nursing staff to let Kevin stay. I begged him to put my legs down, but he kept telling me they were fine, nothing was wrong.

By the time Kevin had eventually been pushed away and the doctors had given me more drugs to calm me down, I could barely remember who or where I was. 'Tell me if you feel this,' they kept saying, holding up what looked like a large sharpened hat-pin so as to show me what they were planning to do with it at the foot of the bed. Just before I began drifting off into a deep but troubled sleep, I wondered why they hadn't bothered to prick me with the pin anywhere, after all. Perhaps they'd changed their minds.

The rest of that night was a dense fog of pain and mental distortion. I was transferred three times from one trolley to another and finally to a bed in the maternity unit (the only spare bed available), but I was barely aware of my surroundings apart from sudden moments of intense clarity and discomfort. Each time they moved me from one ward to another, the trolley seemed to bump over every vent cover in the floor, jarring my back and causing tremendous pain. When I was finally laid on a blanket to prevent pressure sores, the sheepskin it was made of made my skin itch relentlessly. And the pain in the middle of my back had not gone away – in fact it had worsened – and in my twilight state all I could feel was the searing sensation above my waistline, coupled with the unbearable itchiness.

The following morning there seemed to be a new parade of pale faces in the room peering down at me, this time tearfully. Kevin, Dad, Mum, Kev's mum, my brother Neil, his partner Bridget. Every time I opened my eyes, everyone within my field of vision seemed to be behaving very emotionally and I didn't really understand why. My brother and I had never really got on and yet there was something about his eyes, the way he looked at me now, that seemed softer, more special, as if he really cared for me after all. I felt frightened and confused.

I don't remember much else about those next few hours, apart from the sight of a doctor in a white coat standing at the foot of my bed saying that Stoke Mandeville Hospital was full but he had found me a bed at the Duke of Cornwall Spinal Treatment Centre at the Salisbury District Hospital on the outskirts of the city. He said a helicopter scrambled from Biggin Hill would be taking me there later that day. Smiling weakly through my muzziness, I told Dad croakily: 'I've always wanted to go in a helicopter.' Somewhere in the background, I heard Mum break down again.

They cleared the small gravel car park at the back of the hospital for the helicopter to land at four o'clock that afternoon. Fire engines and police cars stood by as the air crew brought it down safely. Strapped to a trolley and wheeled outside, I felt the wind on my face from the rotors, and gripped Kev's hand tighter still as I was loaded on to a special stretcher, cushioned in an air bag which had been inflated to my exact shape so as to buffer me against the fifty-mile flight. The paramedics slid me into an incredibly claustrophobic hole deep inside the aircraft which left me completely unable to see what was going on. The only consolation was that Kev came too, wearing headphones so that he could talk to the paramedics on board and give them my full medical history.

Although I was still very poorly and in a great deal of pain, I felt nothing but relief at leaving St Richard's. The chief paramedic on board was apoplectic when he learned from Kev how many times I had been moved around and that I hadn't been given proper pain relief. He gave me some morphine instantly. The air crew seemed amazingly efficient and composed, and I felt that I was in the care of people who knew exactly what they were doing and who were taking me to a place where they had the expertise to make me better. As soon as they had patched me up, I could go home and see Nathan and Daniel, the two people I had most wanted to see but who, for some reason, had not been brought to visit me at the hospital.

As the helicopter finally took off, lifting us high above the bustling town of Chichester in a flurry of wind and noise, all I could focus on was getting home to the boys and getting back to normal as quickly as possible. I truly believed that I had had a very lucky escape. I could so easily have been killed on that road; I could have lain in that field and breathed my last. But I hadn't. I was alive. My little accident had been a lesson to me to slow down and not to take things for granted. The sooner I got home and was back on my feet, the better.

TWO

Dawn

THE WORLD and his wife were waiting to greet me at the hilltop spinal unit of the Salisbury District Hospital: sixteen medical staff, all lined up in their white coats, their heads bowed against the dust being whipped up by the rotor blades. I had survived the journey between the two cities without major incident, and the pilot had apparently given me what they call 'the Queen's landing' – the type given to HRH so that she doesn't feel a bump.

Rolled out into the bright sunshine from my dark and airless corner of the cabin, I was again separated from Kevin, and the waiting doctors and nurses helped to carefully transfer me to a trolley and wheel me into the modern red-brick building on the edge of the city suburb of Odstock. 'This is Julie Hill, a transfer from St Richard's, Chichester. She's been involved in an RTA in which she was thrown from her car,' the helicopter paramedic recounted to the doctor as they conducted their formal hand-over. 'Her BP is stable at 130 over 70, her pulse is 73, she's had a crush injury to her spine, her conscious levels are good, but no response to stimuli below T9 as yet.' He continued to relay my vital statistics in that special medical code that means little to anyone outside the profession.

Closing my eyes in embarrassment and shame as they fussed and fiddled all around me, I heard the first friendly voice. 'Hi, Julie, my name's Claire and I'll be one of the people who'll be looking after you for a while,' the woman told me in a cheery and distinctive New Zealand accent. I opened my eyes and looked up into the smiling face of a plump, sparkly-eyed redhead, her hair cut short, who squeezed my hand reassuringly and made me feel instantly more relaxed. She would be my new Helen, I decided, smiling weakly and squeezing her hand back, clinging on to it like a drowning woman clasping a fragment of shipwreck debris.

Clamped into a neck brace, unable to see where I was going or register anything very much above the general pain and confusion, I was briskly whisked off to 'Avon', the eight-bed acute ward which forms the core of the unit. Then I was ushered away behind another set of brightly coloured curtains, where a six-man team of nurses and orderlies expertly swung me into a bed and tucked me in under crisp white cotton sheets. Abandoned for a while behind the curtains, I felt suddenly frightened and alone again. Something was very wrong, but I couldn't figure out exactly what. The drugs they had given me made me feel very dopey and numb, but it was more than that. Apart from the continual pain in the middle of my back, I still had little sensation elsewhere. Try as I might to concentrate my mind and remain focused on my new environment, I felt as if I was floating somewhere several feet above my head.

His eyes dark and heavy and his fingers nervously

stroking his moustache, Kevin looked just as afraid when the curtains were pulled back to reveal him standing there awkwardly, unsure of what was now expected of him. I could see the fear in his face whenever I caught sight of him off guard. We had hardly said a word to each other since the accident and although he had never left my side, squeezing my hand and trying to reassure me with the usual platitudes, I was always too spaced out to respond. Shuffled aside now, while the medical team returned to attend to my needs, he was directed rather brusquely to the door and left alone in the corridor to wait for my mum and dad to arrive.

Suddenly feeling the need to sit down, he found a chair and slumped there with his head in his hands for a moment, still trying to take in all that had happened in the last few hours. Less than a day ago, his world had been completely normal. He was happily married with a wife and two kids, a good job and an even better one lined up. He had a nice house, a company car, and a comfortable level of income. Sure, there were the odd differences of opinion between him and me, but he too felt it was nothing serious. Once he had started in his new job and the bigger salary started to kick in, he felt confident of persuading me to take a different role, one that didn't involve me in the drinks industry, being out in the evenings and away from home.

But what on earth did the future hold now? he wondered. Where would the events of the last day and night leave him, and me, in terms of our family? Looking up after a few minutes to see if my parents were there yet, Kevin suddenly noticed that the corridor was littered with empty wheelchairs. They were everywhere, their alien shapes reflected in the polished lino. Further along the corridor several recently disabled patients wheeled themselves to and from their rooms. Kev suddenly felt surrounded. Gasping to catch his breath, he felt physically winded. For him, that was the moment of impact – as real and final as the sickening crump I had heard when I landed in the field. Shaken to the core and completely alone for the first time in eighteen nightmarish hours, he found himself trembling from head to toe and blinking back the tears.

Life for me remained pretty much a blur for the next three days as the drugs I was given took me to Cloud-cuckoo-land and left me floating there. Nurses would come and go, along with the odd white-coated doctor, but Kev and my parents stayed constantly at my bedside, their expressions fixed and grim. In spite of my discomfort and the confines of the position I had been laid in, banked up with pillows, I slept a great deal, my dreams busy and confused. Through the grogginess of my waking moments I gradually began to acclimatize to the noisy hustle and bustle of the place in which I now found myself. All thoughts of rest and quiet in hospital were instantly dispelled – there was never any peace. Day and night, there was the sound of talking and machinery and strange electronic noises. If I hadn't been on the drugs, I don't know how I would have been expected to sleep.

Unable to do anything but lie slightly to one side, a pillow under my restricting neck brace and another under my knees, I was on high doses of morphine and diamorphine and not aware of anything very much except Kevin, who kept telling me that I was going to have some sort of operation soon. Four or five people came to my bed every few hours to turn me so that I didn't get pressure sores, which can be fatal for someone in the condition I was in, but their interference only irritated me. That, and the fact that the tube up my nose and into my stomach was really bugging me. As often as I pulled it out, moaning, the nurses shoved it back in, until one of them got really cross with me. 'Julie, you must stop doing that,' she scolded, pulling my hands away once more. 'We think you may have damaged your liver, spleen and kidneys in your car accident and we need the tube to drain off any poisonous fluids.' I had almost forgotten about the accident, and was unaware of most of my circumstances, least of all that I had tubes up every orifice, including a catheter for my bodily fluids. I was still unable to feel anything below my waist.

Kev was my mainstay in those first few days; always there, holding my hand, by my side when I woke and still there when I dropped off to sleep again. I had no concept of time – it felt as if I had been there for years – and the drug-induced stupor made me feel quite comfortable staying that way. People came and went, their voices and faces swimming in and out of my dreams – my mum, dad, other close family members, the nurses I was coming to recognize. All I wanted to do was sleep. I felt as if I could sleep for ever, and when anyone or anything woke me up I considered it a nuisance.

Apart from Kevin's constant presence, I became vaguely aware of another permanent fixture, the patient in the bed next to me, far to the right-hand edge of my vision. I couldn't see her because of the orange curtain between us, but I heard people talking to her and gathered that her name was Becky. Occasionally, I heard her voice – it was young, the voice of a teenager, and it sounded subdued and afraid. Several silent figures sat or stood around her bedside day and night, but that was all I was able to take in. I was so very tired, and my back hurt so badly when the drugs started to wear off that my main priority was to keep as still as was humanly possible, waiting for my next dose and for things to get better.

By now it was Easter Saturday, and instead of being home with my family, entertaining our weekend guests (who were forced to cancel their trip), I was doped up to the eyeballs and still in hospital, impatiently waiting to be 'fixed'. I wondered what was taking the doctors so long. I have a vague recollection of a surgeon standing at the foot of the bed at one point, distinguishable to me by his blue surgical clothes and a face mask hanging loosely around his neck. He had clearly come straight from the operating theatre to talk to Kevin. I was a big fan of the television drama *Casualty* and the scene reminded me of something from that. The surgeon was telling Kevin what he was planning. 'Julie only broke one bone in the accident, but it was a pretty important one,' was all I heard him say. I honestly didn't care what the surgeon did as long as it didn't hurt too much and that afterwards I could be rid of some of the infernal tubes. Sleepily, I wondered which bone I had broken.

Within the hour, I was woken from my slumbers by the sensation of being gently manhandled on to a trolley and wheeled out of the ward by green-clad porters. Kevin was there too, and he never let go of my hand the entire journey down the long corridor. I could only stare up at the ceiling, mesmerized by the bright lights rolling past overhead as we moved gradually towards the operating theatre. 'Take care, love. See you later,' Kevin whispered in my ear, his face buried in my hair, just before he finally let go of my hand. I could only sort of murmur something to him – I don't remember what – as my fingers slipped from his. The double doors of the operating theatre opened and closed behind me as I was wheeled in for what was to be a highly complicated operation on my spine.

Once I was fully anaesthetized and in position, lying on my right side, the consultant orthopaedic surgeon, a man called John Carvell, began by cutting a 'zipper' up my back, peeling open the skin, muscles and tissue to reveal the affected area. He then fixed two nine-inch metal rods, known as Harrington rods, on to my damaged spine, before using a bone graft to fuse things together, encasing the rods in strips of bone cut from my left hip.

Mr Carvell was an experienced and respected practitioner, one of the best in the business. I was very lucky to be under his knife. Known as 'JC' by the hospital staff – and not just because they were his initials – he had done this sort of operation hundreds of times before and he knew exactly what he was doing. I didn't know it at the time, but I couldn't have been in better hands, even if one minor aspect of the procedure was later going to threaten everything I hoped to achieve. Being an Easter Bank Holiday weekend, there was no chance of getting new supplies of medical equipment in, and when Mr Carvell searched his stocks he discovered that the only Harrington rods he had were nine inches long, when he really wanted seven-inch ones. Unable to find replacements, he went ahead and inserted the nine-inch ones anyway, resolving to shorten them later if they caused me any problems.

The operation took more than five hours, and all that time Kevin paced the corridor outside my ward, anxiously waiting for news. Mum and Dad stayed home with the children, chain-smoking. They and Kev had always got on and were fond of each other, maintaining a respectful level of affection for the last thirteen years. Dad, a naval engineer until he retired, would take Kevin for the occasional pint and share a joke; Kev would offer to help my mum out when my father was away. Now, with their nerves frayed to breaking point and their minds filled with all the dreadful possibilities of what my accident could mean for me and for every one of them, they were circling each other warily, each wondering how the others would react.

My father fetched cup after polystyrene cup of insipid tea and coffee each time he came to the hospital to give Kevin moral support, and my mum was spending a lot of her time looking after the children and waiting for a phone call. Kev, barely able to speak to either one of them, sat with his head in his hands feeling as if he was on the verge of a nervous breakdown, wondering what he had done to deserve such a fate.

By the time I eventually emerged from the operating theatre, I was considerably weaker and again in the 'at risk' category. I was taken to a recovery room, wired up to all sorts of cardiac and blood pressure machines and monitored closely until I began to show signs of coming to. Then I was wheeled back to Avon ward, which was to be my new home. The very first thing I was aware of when I finally woke up from the anaesthetic was the intense pain, worse even than the pain I'd experienced before. It was scorching, all across my upper back, like a red-hot poker being inserted and then twisted around and around. Every inch of me that had been tampered with throbbed, and it was all I could do to stop myself screaming.

The pain brought me to my senses quickly. It immediately dispelled any hopes that my car accident might have been nothing but a horrible nightmare and that I was about to wake up in my own bed at home, with the world I had known up till then completely safe and intact. Kevin was still at my side, ever the anxious husband, listening to my groans with an anguished expression on his face. Help was regularly on hand in the form of a nurse bearing morphine, but I was soon to learn that the doses were measured out so as to be not quite high enough to stop the pain, only lessen it to the level just below screaming point. Flat on my back and completely helpless, I was unable to do anything but endure my situation as best I could. But there were times when it felt totally unendurable. Poor Kevin had to put up with my constant carping and crying, and my useless pleas for him to get me something to end the misery.

The nurses who had been assigned to me – Claire, Paula, Andrea, Avril and Katrina – were well accustomed to the likes of me and dealt with me admirably, ignoring my pitiful appeals for more pain relief and sticking strictly to the 'one shot every four hours' rule. As a consequence, in those first few days I became obsessed by the clock on the wall, watching each second ticking by, waiting for my next 'fix' of morphine. I'm sure I came close to understanding what it must be like for a junkie, totally dependent on drugs. Nothing else mattered, all other events were forgotten or ignored – just the urgent need to feed the habit. My ward sister and chief 'supplier' by then was a wonderful New Zealander called Mo. She was tall with long dark hair, extremely efficient and good at her job, and she had a wicked sense of humour, but she could be very sister-like and brash. It was not by chance that she was placed in charge of the drugs cabinet, and she used to do a sprint past my bed between doses in case I started begging for more. I was quite pathetic, I am now ashamed to admit. I had a very low pain threshold and was in agony for much of the time, crying out like a baby when most of my fellow patients seemed to remain still and uncomplaining, especially my neighbour, Becky.

The nights were the worst. In the eerie silence of the early hours I would lie awake, fighting mentally to concentrate on anything but the spasms that racked my broken body. The morphine worked very well in the first hour after a shot and all but knocked me out, but as it began to wear off the pain slowly increased, and with it came the hallucinations of the befuddled. Some were frightening, others just weird, and all so real, so truly lifelike that it is still hard to believe that they were figments of my drugged imagination. My most regular night-time visitor was a little pixie, a colourful garden gnome ten inches high, who sat on the edge of a large glass vase of flowers next to my bed and chuckled every time I looked at him.

I was surrounded by flowers – friends, family, colleagues, even publicans had all sent bouquets. Unable to visit me because of my poorly condition, they had expressed their sympathy and sense of helplessness with vast arrays of bright-red roses, purple chrysanthemums, white lilies, daffodils and freesias. Looking up at my giggling pixie through the vivid flower-bed that had sprung up all around me, I imagined myself as a pixie too, and together we romped around our little garden all night long, with the flowers gently bending their heads to talk to us.

In another amazingly realistic vision, the air vent in the ceiling above my head suddenly started to change shape, and before I knew it it had turned into an upside-down pool of water, with concentric ripples running across it. I called Claire, my Kiwi nurse, over with an urgent wave of my hand. 'Is everything all right?' she asked, a concerned expression on her face as she bent over me.

'No,' I told her in a slurred voice. Pointing to the ceiling, I added: 'You really should get someone to take a look at that . . . It's turned to water.' She nodded and smiled, tucking me in, and no doubt making a mental note to reduce my medication.

The air vents continued to feature regularly in my hallucinations. The one right above my head also had the irritating habit of turning into a lift shaft, with lights deep up inside it, which kept ferrying people I knew down through the ceiling to visit me. Neil, my brother, seemed to be in charge, standing guard at the lift door while, one after another, people I had known all my life – old schoolfriends, workmates, boyfriends and relatives – wandered in and out of my head.

But the fantasy was the easy part. It was the reality I was starting to have problems with. Gently weaned off my drugs in those first few days, still in pain but increasingly more lucid as I slowly surfaced to full consciousness, it gradually began to dawn on me where I was and why. As I lay awake at night, rewinding, pausing and replaying the events of the previous week, I came to the chilling realization that something was not just wrong, but terribly wrong. Previously, I had been unable to appreciate the extent of the damage I might have done to myself and I'd clung to the certainty that I'd eventually make a complete recovery and go back home as normal, but I now spent hour after hour carefully piecing together in my mind all the fragments of conversations, the snatched memories of events and the medical team's words.

There had been Kevin's fixed and frightened smile, Mum's tearful face, Dad's sorrowful eyes, the unexplained delay in seeing the children, the nurses' constant chatter of 'rehabilitation' and 'milestones', and the surgeon's final farewell after the operation. The way things went in the ward was never to think beyond the next couple of hours, to stick to the here and now. I was constantly being given goals to achieve, to do with how my wounds were healing and how quickly I could start to do certain things for myself. I had progressed well and was passing the hurdles quickly, but still no one had said anything to me about getting up and going home. It took several nights of agonizing and deliberating, but by the end of the second week I came slowly, painfully, to the dreadful truth.

And it was this: the safe, sure, able-bodied life that I had known for twenty-eight years had been severed in a single moment – the moment my body had landed on the unforgiving surface of a roughly ploughed field that fateful night. While Chris De Burgh strained his lungs and sang the words: 'It was late at night on the open road, Speeding like a man on the run, A lifetime spent preparing for the journey . . .' my own journey had ended. Spinning and twisting and flailing in the air after parting company with my car, I had fallen into the unknown abyss of serious spinal injury and was never going to walk again.

I, Julie Hill, was never going to walk again.

Just forming the words in my head set my heart pounding in my chest, and my breathing came thick and fast. Tears started up and I squeezed my eyes tight shut against the flow. In a single rash moment of impatience and stupidity, I had completely ruined my life, and my family's life. I was going to be a burden to everyone, completely dependent on other people for the rest of my days. Kevin would probably leave me – or, if he stayed, it would only be out of some noble sense of obligation. The children would grow up with the social impediment of a wheelchair-bound mother. I was a useless cripple. Disabled. Damaged goods. It was a terrible mental adjustment to have to make and I allowed the waves of self-pity to engulf me in a flood of tears.

Hearing my stifled sobs, Claire, my faithful nurse, was suddenly at my side, holding my hand and asking what was wrong. Opening my eyes and fixing her with a glare, I sputtered: 'Is this it? Am I going to spend the rest of my life paralysed?' The words I had been thinking for so long now came out in a headlong rush. I sucked in my breath and held it as I waited for her answer. She was my last chance. Only she could bring me back from the petrifying brink of the pit I saw opening up in front of me.

Claire bowed her head and inhaled deeply before making her reply. When her gentle eyes locked with mine, they had a new sadness in them that said it all. I was seeing the look of pity for the first time; a look I had never knowingly seen directed at me before, but one that I knew I would continue to see for the rest of my life. She spoke softly, her words chosen carefully for their ambiguity. 'It's very likely,' she said. 'But no one can really say.' I pressed my head as far back into my pillow as I could and blinked at her, horrified at the full impact of her response.

'There are no definites in this world,' she added quickly, in what I suspected was a well-rehearsed speech. 'People respond differently to all sorts of different treatments, and who knows what might be around the corner?'

I shook my head silently, the tears coming fast again. I didn't care what might or might not be possible in the future – I wanted something to happen for me, and now. I wanted her to tell me it had all been a dreadful mistake, that I had badly misread the signs in my confused mental state, that the operation had been a great success and I would be able to walk out of the hospital in a few weeks' time. This couldn't possibly be happening to me, could it? Not to *me*? Julie Hill?

Claire barely left my side for the rest of the night and did all she could to help me through those first few hideous hours of realization. She had obviously been in this situation many times before and she seemed to know exactly what to say. She never stopped talking. She told me how full and active my life could be, how she knew of tetraplegics – people paralysed from the neck down – who had travelled the world, climbed mountains and even entered the Olympics. 'I know you might find this hard to believe right now, but you're actually very lucky,' she assured me, as I continued to shake my head in horror. 'Your break was low in the back and you'll almost certainly have the full use of your upper body.'

She told me that it was time to focus on my ability,

not on my disability. 'Your family says you have a wonderful sense of humour, Julie, and that you'll be able to get through this together.' I swallowed hard. Of course. They all knew. Kev, Mum, Dad. It all made sense now. The pity I had seen in Claire's eyes, just for that first instant. I had recognized it from the looks on the faces of my family. It was Neil, my brother, who had shown it first, at St Richard's. I simply hadn't known what it was until now.

'Oh God, no. Oh God,' I wailed, biting on my fist to keep myself from losing control completely. My mind flashed up dreadful images of the future – waiting at the school gates in a wheelchair with all the other mums whispering and staring down at me; Kevin wheeling me into a cinema and having to sit at the end of the row while I blocked the aisle; the children asking me sheepishly if I wouldn't mind not coming to see them in the Christmas play to spare their embarrassment. I would have been better off dead than alive like this, trapped in a living death.

I cried until there were no more tears left to cry, and all the while Claire just carried on talking. Breathless from sobbing, I lay back on the pillow and began to listen to her calming words, trying desperately to wring every drop of comfort from them. 'However awful your situation seems, you have to understand that it could have been so much worse,' she said. 'There are five tetraplegics in this ward and only three paraplegics. You are one of the lucky ones. Think of your sons, think of their future. You have two wonderful children, Julie, who love you and are expecting you to come home, which you will. Be grateful that you have them – and

Kevin. Be grateful that you haven't suffered the injuries that someone like Becky has.'

Focusing for the next few days on Becky and her tragic situation helped me enormously. Claire made me begin to appreciate that no matter how dreadful my own position or how awful the loss I had suffered, there was always someone far worse off than me. Seventeen-year-old Becky was a former championship swimmer. She had fallen asleep at the wheel of her car while driving to an early-morning practice session and had gone off the road at a roundabout. She wasn't wearing a seat belt and was thrown from the car, her head and neck smashing against the edge of a kerbstone as she landed. The injury she suffered snapped the spinal cord in her neck and she was permanently paralysed below the break. Now, here she was, lying in bed next to me, flat on her back, her arms and hands outstretched on splints in the crucifix position to prevent them from contracting into claws, unable to move anything but her head.

Yet in all the days she had been there, during all the times I had been crying out in pain and misery, I had never once heard her complain. Realizing that humbled me. Compared to Becky, I *was* lucky. Lucky to be alive in the first place and to be a paraplegic in the second. However desperate my own position appeared to be — and at times it seemed unthinkable — it *could* have been so much worse. I told myself that over and over again. Once in a while, I even allowed myself to believe it.

But in spite of all Claire's comforting and advice, and the salutary thought of Becky's sad predicament, I have to say that the following few days were some of the hardest I have ever had to bear. I lay on my bed silently, drifting with the tides of my moods, sometimes up, sometimes down, always emotionally fragile. When I was at my best I tried to take comfort from all the positives, to thank my lucky stars for my family, for my mum and dad, and for the happy, carefree life I had led before the accident. There was a lot to be thankful for. I'd married well and Kevin and I had a good standard of living. We were reasonably secure financially, and the boys were healthy and in a good school. None of that should change.

When I was at my worst, I was eaten up with anger, frustration and overwhelming self-pity. I thought of all the time I had wasted, not getting on with life when I had the chance. I had been a real 'couch potato' before the accident, giving up my teenage sports and flopping in front of the television most nights. I smoked and drank too much, I had put on weight after the boys were born and was generally pretty unfit, factors that would now affect my health enormously. I had been complacent, not realizing many of my youthful ambitions – to go on a really adventurous African safari, to go skiing, and to tour the waterways of England and Europe with Kev. Whatever happened now, those sorts of chances seemed lost to me for ever and the bitterness of that thought began to eat into me.

One night, after another day of platitudes and cheerful reassurance from the nursing staff, I lost control completely. What the hell did *they* know? They could still walk. I was sick and tired of people stalling me, reminding me how much I had yet to face, months of physiotherapy and rehabilitation before I could even start to think about going home. I was to take it 'stage by stage', everyone said, carefully avoiding the now very inappropriate expression 'step by step'. So many normal, everyday expressions were now suddenly out of bounds – standing on your own two feet, walking tall, making strides, kicking yourself. I didn't know which was worse, hearing them said and realizing that they no longer applied to me, or watching someone squirm as they registered their *faux pas* and tried desperately to backtrack.

During another particularly memorable night of wallowing self-pity, I let myself dwell too long on something that had been bothering me from the start, but that I hadn't previously felt able to raise – my sex life. 'How on earth are Kevin and I ever going to make love again, what with all my tubes and a complete lack of sensation below my waist?' I howled at the long-suffering Claire. 'I no longer even feel like a woman.' I felt as if I had completely lost touch with my own sexuality, and the idea of lying in bed next to my husband again both appalled and frightened me. I could just about stand the look of pity in his eyes whenever he came to visit me in hospital, but I couldn't stomach imagining the look of revulsion on his face when he first lay on top of my unfeeling carcass and tried to make love to me amongst the catheters and urine bags.

Gently, oh so kindly, Claire told me that it was not something I would have to worry about immediately. 'Your sex life will rebuild and grow over time,' she assured me. 'You'll learn to please each other in different ways, using the parts of your body that are still fully functional. You'll discover the joys of giving Kevin pleasure, unselfishly, and you'll take comfort from the fact that you can still hold each other in your arms, cuddle, kiss and have oral sex.'

Wiping my nose with the back of my hand, I tried hard to focus on what Claire was saying, to collect and store away each precious crumb of comfort she was offering. The trouble was, every time she said the word 'sex' it came out as 'six' because of her strong New Zealand accent, and in the end I just couldn't help it and burst out laughing when she referred yet again to 'oral six'. Laughing back at me, delighted to have somehow lifted my mood, Claire wondered what she had said that was so funny. I started to tell her, but was overcome by such a fit of the giggles that I couldn't speak for crying tears of laughter. It was the first time I had laughed in ages and it felt so good to be finding some humour in a subject that at that moment was so distressing, so vital to my future mental and physical well-being, that it had made me file that particular problem away until it was absolutely necessary to raise it.

Armed with what seemed to be the liveliest sense of humour on the ward, and bolstered by Claire, the other staff and new-found friends all around me, I slowly began to get my head around the idea of my future life as a paraplegic. It wasn't going to be easy, it would be the toughest thing I had ever had to cope with, but as I had no choice in the matter, it was something I was going to have to face up to sooner rather than later. And the sooner I began to cope, the sooner I could go home and start to piece together the shattered fragments of my life.

It was very much later that I learned that my disability was something poor Kevin had been forced to face up to weeks earlier. On the night of the accident, he had been warned to expect the worst and had stayed at St Richard's Hospital with my father until five o'clock in the morning. He had only gone home to get a change of clothes and to see the children. Waking them early to break the bad news, he knelt down in front of them and held each of their hands. 'Mummy's had an accident and she's in hospital being looked after by the doctors and nurses. She's all right, but she's going to stay there for a little while. When she's better, I'll take you to see her – OK?'

Pale and pensive in their pyjamas, the children nodded and quietly got on with their day. They were too young to recognize the strange look in their father's eyes or to notice the tremor in his voice. Kev hoped to God they were too young to understand any of it.

Bleary-eyed and exhausted after a shower and a hasty breakfast, Kev and Dad returned to the hospital at eight o'clock, just three hours after they had left, and were almost immediately taken to a consulting room to speak to a specialist. Neither of them had slept a wink since the first phone call from the police had woken Kev the previous night at eleven.

Kev's hands trembled as he took the first damning X-ray of my spine from the hands of the consultant. Holding it up against the light, he could see immediately that my backbone was completely severed, cut clean across, taking the spinal cord with it. The two bone ends had shifted and overlapped with the force of the impact – which was why they had needed to be readjusted and pinned together with the Harrington rods. I was a full two inches shorter than I had been before the accident.

'It's a very serious injury, and an irreparable one,' the doctor told the two men. His tone was brusque and businesslike. He had obviously identified Kevin as someone who wouldn't want him to beat about the bush at such a critical moment. 'Even in the best-case scenario,' he added, shaking his head, 'I can say with some certainty that you can forget about your wife ever being able to stand or walk again.'

Kevin swallowed hard as the surgeon spoke; all the colour drained from his face and he felt as if his knees would buckle under him. A sudden crashing noise startled him and made him look round. My father had passed out with the shock and was slumped in a crumpled heap on the floor.

THREE

Brilliance

T HE MONTH of my accident, April 1990, was a worrying one for Nick Donaldson and Tim Perkins, two of the biomedical engineers whose pioneering work was later to mean so much to me. With a combined experience of thirty-two years, they were part of a small team of dedicated technical staff based at the Institute of Psychiatry and University College London, who devoted their lives to improving those of others less fortunate than themselves. The trouble was that in 1990, with the imminent retirement of their director and mentor, they had no idea whether they would receive enough government funding to carry on their work.

The two men had first met in 1976 when Nick, then aged twenty-three and recently graduated from Trinity College, Cambridge, with a BA in engineering and electrical sciences, joined his father Peter Donaldson at the neurological prostheses unit run by Professor Giles Brindley at an annexe of the Institute in Denmark Hill, south London. Professor Brindley, a lively and versatile academic neurophysiologist and an acknowledged pioneer in his field, was the head of physiology there. He had set up the new prostheses unit in 1972 after persuading the Medical Research Council (MRC) to fund him. Among his existing staff was Tim Perkins, a bright young physics graduate from Bristol University.

The chief aim of the unit was to harness the wonders of electronics technology for the benefit of the disabled. Their plan was to explore and develop the relatively new field of micro-electronic stimulation by surgical implant to try and improve the lives of those whose own, natural, stimulation systems had failed them. As far back as 1791, a scientist called Galvani had observed that the legs of frogs could be artificially stimulated with a small electric charge. Various experiments on all sorts of animals, but mainly cats and dogs, were carried out over the following decades. In the 1950s, great advances in transistor technology allowed radio control of such trials, but since then there hadn't been much real progress in developing the technique.

Professor Brindley, the only son of a widowed GP, and a former reader in physiology at Cambridge, had been fascinated for a long time by the potential of micro-electronic stimulation, particularly with a view to helping the blind. He had examined the theory of eye and brain function, experimenting with animals and digesting all the medical literature on the subject, from the First World War to modern-day Canadian reports. By the autumn of 1964, he fully expected someone to be able to create, sooner or later, a surgically implanted neurological device which, using state-of-the-art micro-electronic gadgetry, might be used as a sort of mini jump-lead between a tiny camera and the brain to artificially stimulate vision in the blind.

When the first stimulator implants were used in

animal experiments – culminating in the perfecting and implantation of the first cardiac pacemaker in 1960 – it was a great moment in biomedical engineering. Giles Brindley was among the many excited scientists and engineers who made sure they found out all they could about the new techniques. But investigating further only made him increasingly aware of the many pitfalls in micro-electronic devices for surgical implant, the chief ones being to do with their design and materials and the rate at which they caused infection in the patient. His concerns brought it home to him, though, that as no one else seemed to know that much about implant-making either, no one was better placed to attempt the first visual implant than he was.

Giles Brindley first approached the MRC to see if it would consider funding him for such an experiment, but it turned him down. Unfazed, the small, bespectacled academic set to work in his spare time, working alone in the university's physiology laboratory, often late into the night. After several months, he came up with a unique device that resembled an elongated rubber skull-cap. It was an electroneural visual prosthesis, something that few people in the world, at the time, even considered a possibility. Supported financially as well as intellectually by Alan Hodgkin, the acting head of his department and a leading physiologist himself, Giles Brindley managed to get a grant of £900 in 1965 to continue his work. With only one technician working for him, he perfected his device until it was finally ready to be tested a year later.

When he went to seek the advice of Arthur Lister, his former mentor at the London Hospital, Giles Brindley knew that what he had to ask was a tall order. He needed someone who would agree to have major invasive surgery

done chiefly for the sake of others and not for themselves. (He had never once suggested that the implant
would benefit the volunteer very much at this embryo
stage.) The only satisfaction would be the knowledge
that, by offering themselves for research, the volunteer
would be helping push back the scientific frontiers.
To Giles Brindley's amazement, Arthur Lister had good
news for him. 'I think I know just the patient,' he told
him enthusiastically. 'A fifty-four-year-old experienced
nurse who's been blinded by glaucoma.' His hunch was
right. The woman immediately agreed to become their
guinea-pig and a surgeon called Walpole Lewin agreed
to operate.

So on 13 July 1967 Giles Brindley's saucer-shaped,
eighty-channel, silicone rubber device, with its eighty
half-millimetre-square platinum electrodes and various
cables along which would travel small electrical charges,
was fitted between the woman's skull and her scalp and
attached to the occipital cortex of her brain. Where the
glaucoma had permanently damaged the optic nerves
that provided her with the ability to see, the device was
meant to compensate for the deficiency by passing currents close to the relevant nervous tissues. The problem
was that with only eighty electrodes trying to link up to
millions of optic nerve fibres, the results could only be
crude at best.

The operation was lengthy, unpleasant and not without risk. The surgeon had to literally screw the rubber
device to the patient's skull, then stretch her scalp back
over it. She suffered from severe headaches for some
time afterwards. But her co-operation was rewarded, if
only partially. Once the device was switched on, and she
was fitted with a special hat in which were mounted a

number of oscillators sending radio signals to the prosthesis, she could make out small spots of light where she had previously been completely unable to see. Later she was able to see arrays of dots similar to images of letters in Braille, although she could not identify them as quickly as her fingers could read the same letters.

It was an ambitious and successful project which impressed the world of science when its details were published in the *Journal of Physiology*, and the MRC immediately offered Giles Brindley the time and the money to develop his ideas further. In 1968 it established the neurological prostheses unit with him as its director, at first based in Cambridge but later in a cramped laboratory in south London when he was offered the chair of physiology at the Institute of Psychiatry in De Crespigny Park, Denmark Hill. Packing his books, his bags and his large collection of extraordinary contraptions, the man who was now Professor Brindley invited Peter Donaldson, a brilliant technician and a friend of fifteen years, to go with him. Their basic equipment amounted to not much more than a soldering iron and a bench magnifier.

Peter Donaldson was a technical officer in the physiology department of Trinity College, Cambridge, and a long-time colleague of Professor Brindley; he was to become a key figure in the long-term evolution of the unit, and its secondary driving force. A year younger than Professor Brindley, Peter had first become fascinated with engineering at the age of four, when someone gave him a Meccano set. From then on, his life's path was set, particularly when Meccano introduced an electrical circuitry device – a new addition which from that moment consigned his train sets, games and sports kit to the toy cupboard. In 1941, during the Second World War, Peter's father, a former submariner, sent him to Dartmouth Naval College at the age of thirteen. When the war ended and all the specially enlisted radar officers returned to civilian life, the Navy panicked and called for volunteers to train as naval electronics officers. Peter Donaldson was one of them.

He was sent to Cambridge University to read engineering, from which he emerged aged twenty-two stuffed full of knowledge and ready to resume his career in the armed forces. But a severe bout of tuberculosis changed all that, and he was considered physically unfit and given his papers. Eternally grateful to the medical scientists who invented the drug that cured him, Peter offered himself to the professor of physiology at Cambridge as a laboratory technician and general dogs body. 'If you can manage on £500 a year, the job is yours,' Professor Matthews told him. Although he was married with a young son, Peter accepted. He made a lot of the technical apparatus himself, and eventually taught students.

Giles Brindley first came into Peter's sphere in 1951 when Peter was a technician and he was a student. It was just after the student-turned-lecturer had secretly made his visual prosthesis in the privacy of his laboratory and it had been implanted in his patient that they began working together. Giles Brindley was adept with his hands and a very good all-rounder, but he knew his limitations, and after he had encountered a few problems he approached Peter to ask his advice on some aspects of the device. Peter, who had already become a bit disillusioned with the 'theory only' approach of the physiology department – after his high hopes of being at the forefront of medical science – jumped at the chance to work on something that would have direct value to a real, live patient. He helped perfect the external equipment for the next two visual prostheses. Operationally, the device was a brilliant success, and far more sophisticated than the world's previous implants – largely heart pacemakers – some experimental versions of which had been held together with something not unlike insulating tape. But the lessons Peter learned from the crafting of the visual prosthesis made him realize that much more thorough research needed to be done on the component parts and the manufacture of any future implants, to make them work and keep on working.

By nature a cautious man, Peter was the perfect complement to Giles Brindley. Over the next decade, he was to work almost exclusively on the materials side of the implants, trying to find a workable replacement for the rigid epoxy resin used to bind parts together, and investigating the effects of water and water vapour on the semiconductor components. The relatively new medium of silicone rubber was found to provide just the answer; it was flexible and porous enough to survive in a moist environment, especially when coated with medical-grade rubber. But when the team published several papers to that effect, some of them were regarded with the greatest scepticism by their engineering colleagues, who didn't believe that something porous could be used in a device that was largely electrical. What Peter Donaldson was able to prove was that what passed through the rubber was only water vapour, not water itself, and that the vapour didn't do any harm. As long as any gaps were plugged with a special glue using the silicone, plus an oxygen–metal chemical bond, the electrical components would not be affected. It was a major breakthrough, although it still wasn't widely accepted.

Frustrated by the response and keen to achieve results more quickly, Professor Brindley hoped for better progress. Peter's extensive research was invaluable, but it was extremely time-consuming, even if less so than most in the field. Turning his attention to what he described as 'the waterworks department', Professor Brindley realized that the implants they had already perfected could easily be adapted for use in bladder control. He decided to create something workable in his own workshop, then ask Peter to help him repeat the process in the laboratory.

Both men became quite obsessional about their work, and their devotion to each other was also evident. They were, by then, ably assisted by senior technicians John Cooper and Eric Sayer, who joined them from recently closed Medical Research Council units. Among other things, John Cooper devised 'Cooper cable' for connecting the various micro-electronic parts, and Eric Sayer worked on screen-making and -printing for the thick-film process needed. Another key player was Dr Mike Craggs, a research physiologist who joined the team in the early seventies to do his Ph.D. He proved that it would be possible to control an implant from signals recorded from the motor cortex – in the part of the brain connected with movement – literally taking thought to power a paralysed limb; and he devised surgically implanted plug-and-socket connectors that were vital to the success of later devices.

Having moved from De Crespigny Park into a comparatively palatial suite of offices in the new neurology building in Windsor Walk, Denmark Hill, in 1974, they began experimenting with the knowledge they had acquired when working on the visual prosthesis implant for developing other control devices. If a series of radio-controlled electrical currents could stimulate a series of nerves in the brain, the professor could see no reason why a similar current couldn't stimulate the nerves controlling a leg muscle, the bladder or the bowel. Apart from sparing the blushes of what he called 'leaky old ladies', there would be another huge target group who would benefit from such an implant – the paralysed, for whom bladder infection is a major cause of death and disease. The loss of bladder function is also the one aspect of their disability they resent the most. The team hoped to come up with something that could change all that. After a long period of research, they agreed that by going about bladder control in a slightly different way to previous implant attempts, they might get better results.

All previous implants had comprised devices which were attached to the bladder directly. This involved a complicated and risky procedure, riddled with pitfalls. Professor Brindley came up with the unique idea of bypassing the bladder and attaching the electrodes instead to the relevant spinal roots, where the motor nerves leave the spinal cord, then make their way to the related muscles. He believed it would be a comparatively simple operation to implant a radio-controlled micro-electronic device at the base of the spine and attach electrodes to the nerves that run from the sacrum – the bone in the lower back that is the keystone of the pelvis – to the nerves in the bladder which control the bodily function. The advantage of stimulating nerve rather than muscle is that it requires far less power to do it, allowing the implant to be smaller and to last longer before the batteries in the control unit run out or have to be recharged. He hoped that, as a result, patients would be able to empty their bladders or bowels literally at the push of a button by sending a radio-controlled stimulus to disconnected nerves which had previously operated automatically.

An operation of this sort would involve far less cable, it would eliminate the problems of surgery on the delicate bladder, and would be better physiologically because the bladder wouldn't know where the signals were coming from. It was an unfashionable and coura-geous move, but if the team could pull it off it would be a major breakthrough which would transform the lives of hundreds, if not thousands, of unhappy people. It was also leading-edge stuff right from the start. The team began making its own control units using microchips that were the best available at the time. As with all research projects, the testing and retesting took years of laborious work before they came up with anything usable.

Meanwhile, they still had the visual prosthesis trials to continue with. In 1972, they were ready for the second of these to be conducted. This time the patient was a middle-aged physiotherapist, blind from his teens, but the implant didn't work quite as well as the first one had, though it survived longer. Obviously, there was still a great deal of work to be done, not least on the electrical control device, which was so huge and unwieldy that it had to be transported on a post office trolley.

The team could see the limitations of this particular field, so they decided to attempt something slightly less ambitious, focusing their attention on the problems of the profoundly deaf. They began to develop an electronic device that would translate sound waves into electrical stimulation of the cochlea, the part of the ear where sound is received. Within a few years they had managed to invent a system which ran a hidden cable up through a patient's neck and was largely concealed under their clothes, reducing the size of the control box to something that could be fixed, although rather clumsily, to a belt. Unfortunately, the system had limited use and was also eventually abandoned, but the lessons learned from it were locked into the team's memory banks.

It was their next series of projects that were to have such impact and lead to areas of success they could never have envisaged. Working both individually and as a team, they began to concentrate on the problems of specific patients rather than kinds of patient, devising one unique implant after another to deal with individual problems.

Constantly looking at ways of expanding and diversifying their techniques, the team members bounced ideas off each other and came up with various ways of solving particular problems. Professor Brindley would present the case history of a particular patient who was suffering from a specific problem, and ask if there was anything they could put together at the workbench that might do the job. The individual problems ranged from paralysed facial nerves causing dribbling and speech impairment, to hand control for tetraplegics. His was the only unit of its type in Britain, so the team felt a huge responsibility to do the best they could for these patients. If *they* couldn't help them, there was no one else who could. In the course of the unit's first twenty years, it worked on projects as diverse as epilepsy control devices, pain control, and a device for extracting semen from paraplegics who wanted children.

The two key participants of every project were Professor Brindley and Peter Donaldson – Peter had relocated his family from Cambridge to Kent in order to continue working alongside the professor. His work was not only invaluable in its own right, it had an unexpected side-effect. As a teenager, his eldest son Nick, as well as his other three children, had been regaled with weird and wonderful tales of what their father and his colleagues were trying to achieve in their laboratory. Peter had his own workshop at home, and from an early age the four children watched, fascinated, as their father created strange apparatuses out of recycled pieces of 'rubbish' and took them to work. His stories of bringing useless parts of people's bodies to life with bursts of electricity held a Frankenstein-like appeal for an imaginative young boy, and from those earliest days Nick's career path was set. A natural engineer, at the age of nine he designed and built a canoe in his bedroom which protruded awkwardly out into the landing for several months. He and his father built and flew model aircraft in their spare time, and Nick became an able assistant in Peter's workshop years before he joined the Brindley unit.

A few years ahead of him was Tim Perkins, who had arrived in 1972. Tim was a flamboyant character with straggly beard and long hair. He joined the Brindley unit at the Denmark Hill site at a time when many electronics jobs were being advertised in the defence industry. Appalled by the idea of devoting his life to the art of destruction, Tim chose instead a career in construction, or rather reconstruction. He liked the idea of helping people rather than killing them, and he soon became a key member of the team. His chief skill was working with microprocessors and designing the software needed to operate the implants once they were in. Working largely alone, he created most of the external equipment as well as the software, while Nick and Peter continued working on the implant side and the materials.

The team were assisted by Nigel Chaffey, who worked on 'special' projects for Professor Brindley, and Judy Jackson, a paraplegic who had the remarkable experience of working on her own implants. Two neuro-surgeons from the neurosurgical unit at the Maudsley Hospital, Murray Falconer and Charles Polkey, both offered to help the team implant the devices into their various guinea-pigs, and countless medical staff assisted in the surgery and aftercare.

One vital member of the team who would come to play a major part in what was to become the Julie Hill project was Professor David Rushton, who became the unit's neurologist in the late 1970s. Professor Rushton was an amateur engineer and steam enthusiast and a brilliant clinician who had none of the pomposity of many of his colleagues. Fascinated by the unit's work, he was a willing participant and the perfect man for the job. With his help, the new implants were installed in scores of grateful patients, and the lessons learned from each trial improved and perfected the overall expertise.

Professor Brindley soon came to appreciate the ver-satility of his growing staff, and he set them to work making and testing the complicated electronic circuits required for the further development of the implants. By the time Nick Donaldson had joined the unit fresh from university, after delighting his father by asking to work alongside him, the team was ready to try out their first bladder implant. When, using baboons and guinea-pigs, they had ironed out many of the clinical, physical problems – for instance, by soaking implants in pots of salty water to see how much decay they could expect with something inserted under the skin – the bioengineers like Tim and Nick were put in charge of the electronic circuitry and computer programmes to make the implants work. But, sadly, their first bladder implant, in 1976, was a failure. The patient, a woman with multiple sclerosis, found it too painful to use – although it did empty her bladder several times – and the device had to be removed.

Professor Brindley was never willing to allow a setback like this to hinder his work. He urged his unit to keep on with their projects, and within a year they were ready to try something completely new. Taking the same sort of electronic implant as had been used in the bladder/bowel-control device and adapting it to stimulate leg and buttock muscles, using small electrodes implanted into the base of the spine, the team hoped to help paraplegics to exercise, stand and even walk.

They knew that they would have no shortage of volunteers. An average three people a day suffer a spinal-cord injury by breaking their backs or necks. There are currently an estimated forty thousand paraplegics and tetraplegics in the United Kingdom, ordinary people whose lives have been suddenly and dramatically altered by accident or injury and who are initially cared for at one of the eleven national spinal-injury units. Of the estimated thousand people injured every year, the majority are young and active – the very nature of their activities makes them more liable to this kind of injury –

and space at the units is constantly at a premium. To date there is no cure.

The highest proportion, 39 per cent, are involved in road traffic accidents, the vast majority involving motor-bikes and cars. The arrival of the motor age has been responsible for replacing falling off ladders as the most often recorded cause of injury. A further 24 per cent injure themselves through a domestic fall or industrial accident, 17 per cent through a sporting accident, 16 per cent through medical, surgical or neurological accidents, and 4 per cent through self-harm or physical assault such as stabbing or shooting. Most of these people end up in a wheelchair through no fault of their own. It could happen to anyone at any time, and yet there is not much understanding or sympathy for those who have been sentenced to a life of paralysis and disability.

For the Brindley unit, the sight of a wheelchair represented nothing less than the challenge they had spent most of their working lives trying to meet. Although at first their ambitions were very small-scale, they hoped eventually to be able to make something that would become attainable for most paraplegics, and even for people more severely disabled. And the dream didn't involve just making them stand or walk.

Through their contact with Professor Brindley's patients in previous years, the team had been made well aware that some of the worst dangers to the health of the paralysed are caused by poor circulation, and muscle wastage and deterioration. If the muscles are allowed to shrivel away through inactivity, sores can develop that can become infected and even cause death. This is why people confined to beds or chairs have to be turned so often. Bones previously protected by layers of flesh can puncture the thin layers of muscle and skin, and patients may not even know about it because they have no sensation. It was the team's chief wish to develop some sort of widely available electronic implant system that would allow the muscles to stay firm and support the bone structure, as well as providing a therapeutic cardio-vascular workout. In this way the long-term health of the patient would be ensured.

By 1977 the unit had two volunteers, both soldiers, one who had been paralysed in a car accident and one who had been shot in the back in Aden. The two men were fitted with the unit's first leg-control devices, crude implants which allowed them to stand and also to walk in a limited way, by using a frame and swinging their legs through it. Working on the same principle as the bladder and bowel devices, the implants were attached to six electrodes attached to the femoral (thigh) nerves and placed under the skin at the back of the thighs. By sending radio-controlled signals along two metres of cable, the electrodes sparked the nerves that controlled the leg muscles and straightened the knee, making those muscles expand and contract, so allowing them to take the weight of the torso balanced rather precariously above them on crutches.

These implants were a great success, and did not become infected. The hope was to replace them with more complex stimulators, as soon as the team had made them, which would be attached to the peripheral nerves in the legs. But this might take several years. A series of other implants were tried out in the early 1980s, in the buttocks, using the more complicated 'multiplexer' stimulators known as Mark 1 and Mark 2, but these failed because of crush injuries to the electrodes in the buttocks and because of a lack of follow-up physiotherapy.

Within a few years, the team was ready to implant its most extensive device. The operation involved putting up to twenty-eight electrodes on the peripheral nerves in the legs and six metres of cable inside the patient. But there was an unacceptably high risk of infection – which happened – and the infected implant had to be removed. The frustration was enormous, especially for the surgeon who had spent a working day putting all the wiring in and then a month later had to take the whole lot out.

The trials were some of the first of their kind in the world; similar tests had been undertaken in the United States, but the British ones had been among the most ambitious. In spite of the ungainliness of the device and the robotic-style movement it produced, the recipients were delighted with their implants and Professor Brindley felt vindicated after so many disappointments. Both of the soldier volunteers were so happy, in fact, that a year later they also received the first successful Brindley bladder stimulators, implanted into their spinal roots, making them less incontinent than they had been since they were paralysed.

With computer technology advancing and changing rapidly, the Brindley team hoped to be able to regularly update the leg-control implants in both men over the years to come, so as to gradually improve their performance. There were hopes that the electrodes could be eventually attached to the nerves at the base of the spine – as in the bladder implants – rather than just to the peripheral nerves in the legs. But although the leg implants worked successfully for over a decade, the trials were not the long-term success that had been hoped for. (Sadly, one of the soldiers died some years later after contracting a spinal infection, and the other was left with only limited function.)

Nearly four years were to pass before the team would attempt the operation again, and in the meantime they carried on developing and perfecting the other implants. The bladder device, particularly, took much of their time and attention, and in 1985, after being successfully implanted into a dozen patients, it was officially patented as the Finetech-Brindley Bladder/Bowel-Control Device, for which the team won several important scientific and engineering awards.

For Giles Brindley, Peter Donaldson, Nick, Tim and the rest of the unit, the successful development of the bladder device was a personal victory. When they had first become involved in neurological prosthesis work, they had each wanted to use the knowledge they had acquired to make themselves useful to their fellow human beings. The bladder device was the highlight of the unit's progress so far, and everyone involved felt enormously proud to have achieved something so fundamentally life-enhancing for so many people.

The work went on. For several years, a lot of effort was concentrated on enhancing the standing and walking implants, with more and more elaborate external equipment and multiplex systems being developed to try to stimulate even more peripheral nerves. The walking quality had never been very good, and the hope was to improve upon it by increasing the number of peripheral nerves stimulated, rather than going down the spinal nerve route, which appeared to be much more complicated.

Nick Donaldson led the way in this particular field, devising the complicated implant and cabling systems necessary for control. Four new patients volunteered for trials, but broken cables, electrodes and infection continued to cause a problem, even with the new state-of-the-art implants, and regularly led to failure. With each patient having to undergo lengthy surgery and multiple incisions, the risk of wound infection was high. By comparison, the bladder implants, which were attached to the anterior roots in the spine rather than the peripheral nerves in the bladder, were proving more and more successful, with much less infection and less electronic failure.

When Professor Rushton examined the differences in the success rates of the two types of implant, he began to question the reason for it. He decided to re-examine Professor Brindley's earliest experimental findings on baboons, work that dated back to the 1960s at the end of which the professor had rejected spinal-root stimulation for leg function. After coming up with the idea of a simple method of preventing post-operative infections by incorporating antibiotic into the silicone rubber of the cables, he also started looking at ways of reducing the extent of the leg-control implant, restricting it to the sacral anterior roots only – something that had never been tried before but that would give the implant the natural protection of the spine.

Within a few years, and at Rushton's prompting, the unit had come up with a much smaller implant that might just be able to do the job. Professor Brindley specified the system, Nick Donaldson designed the implant and Professor Rushton helped design the electrodes; the rest of the team put it all together. Years of testing and trials lay ahead of them, but there was growing excitement within the unit that they were really on to something.

Giles Brindley, by then Emeritus Professor of Physiology at London University, a fellow of the Royal Society and an honorary fellow of the Royal College of Surgeons, continued to channel his considerable reserves of energy into other projects while the trials proceeded. A slight, avuncular man with pale eyes and a kindly smile, he also enjoyed being his own guinea-pig; early on he had had an implant surgically installed which he liked to use to demonstrate normally impossible contractions of the abdominal muscles at the push of a button.

With his boundless enthusiasm and wide-ranging abilities, he created a unique environment for his team to work in, as well as bringing relief to many patients. He helped develop a hand-control implant device for the partially paralysed, perfected pain-control implants, and assisted hundreds of impotent men by developing implants to relieve impotence. He also invented 'scrotal slit' underpants, which allowed the testicles to hang outside the underwear, keeping them cool and fertile. Not surprisingly, the professor caused a stir with some of his more eccentric antics. He inspired hundreds of students in his time as a lecturer, and brushed off his unit's successes with characteristic humility.

But in 1990, the year I had my accident, it seemed that the end of an era was approaching. Professor Brindley was nearly sixty-five and his automatic retirement from the unit was coming up. Peter Donaldson, too, was a year off retirement and seemed destined to hand over to his eldest son. With the departure of such a dynamic pair, it was feared that the neurological prostheses unit would close, although nobody believed for one minute that retirement would slow either of them down in any way personally, and they were fully expected to carry on as consultants to other units.

In the twenty-four years that Professor Brindley had been mentor and director to one of Britain's most remarkable reservoirs of scientific talent, his government-funded unit had pioneered research into artificial sight, and implants for the deaf, the disabled and the impotent. It had been assisted along the way by numerous research engineers, sales engineers, transistor companies and other manufacturers, many of whom had given their time and services free of charge. In return, researchers from around the world had begun to draw on the unit for information and inspiration. Its most successful devices, its bladder-control implants, were being used in twenty centres in Europe and had already benefited five hundred patients.

The future of a unit like this in any other field might well have been guaranteed after such high-profile and well-documented successes, but it was well known that the MRC had a policy of closing units when their directors retired – especially such dynamic individuals as Professor Brindley. After all, who was there who could possibly fill his shoes?

His sixty-fifth birthday was coming up just as I was struggling to come to terms with the earliest implications of my disability in the spinal unit of the Salisbury District Hospital. At that stage I was unaware of the neurological prostheses unit's existence, or the future importance to me of the work of Professor Brindley, Peter Donaldson and their colleagues. My only concern then was how on earth I was going to be able to cope with my life in a wheelchair. I hadn't begun to think any further than that.

Eighty miles away in London, Nick Donaldson and Tim Perkins – married men with seven children between them – along with the rest of the unit, were fighting their own personal battles and facing up to the possibility of a very different future. It seemed ludicrous to them that the unit might be disbanded, wasting all the special knowledge it had accumulated over the years. But at that stage they could see no way of getting around the problem. The two main participants in this story – the neurological prostheses unit and myself – had no inkling yet of each other's dilemma.

FOUR

Shadows

L ESS THAN a month after my accident Kevin began work at his new job in what must have been one of the most difficult times of his life. Quite apart from the problems he was having in coming to terms with the reality of my disability, his first impression of his new company made him feel that he had made a horrible mistake, and he wanted to go back to his old firm where at least everything and everyone were familiar.

In normal circumstances I would have been around for him to bounce his fears off; we would have been able to discuss his concerns together and I might have been able to ease some of his anxieties. But there was nothing normal about our lives any more. I was helpless – emotionally and physically – in a hospital bed fifty miles from home, with far too many problems of my own to have the time or the inclination to talk about Kev's. Having just been told that I would never walk again, I found that his gripes about whether or not he would be able to get on with his new colleagues paled into insignificance.

It was only when I discovered, a few days after he

started working at Julius Meller, that Kevin hadn't even told them about me and the accident that I realized what a personal hell he must have been going through. He had been getting up every morning, feeding and dressing the kids and getting them off to my mum's, before driving ten miles to his new office in Portsmouth, where he was putting in a full day, eager to show his commitment, but without saying a word to anyone about me. Then, having arranged for my mum or someone else to collect the kids and put them to bed, he was doing a hundred-mile round trip to see me most nights in Salisbury. It was a punishing enough schedule for anyone, least of all for someone under incredible personal strain.

'Why don't you just tell them what's happened?' I asked him in exasperation one night, when he said he wouldn't be able to get away from work early enough to see me again before the weekend. 'I'm sure they'll make some special allowances.'

'I don't want them to make any special allowances,' Kevin snapped, his face pinched with tiredness and stress. 'I'm still in the probationary period and I can't take too much time off.' He stopped and looked up, his cheeks reddening.

I stared him straight in the eyes.

He lowered his head and, for a moment, I thought he might bawl. Obviously he wasn't coping and he needed to talk, but at that particular time he felt he couldn't. Then I'm afraid I lost my patience with him. Of course he didn't want to jeopardize his new position. Neither of us did. I wished to God I wasn't in the situation in the first place. But I was, and so was he, and if people making allowances meant that he could have a bit more time off, or if it gave him a bit of leeway with his punishing new deadlines when he was already close to physical and mental collapse, then he would just have to accept it.

'For God's sake, Kev, just tell them,' I blurted out. 'They'll find out sooner or later anyway, so you might as well come clean.' At my insistence, he plucked up the courage to tell his new boss, Jeremy Curtis, what had happened, and – as I suspected – his honesty was rewarded with kindness and sympathy. The following day, Jeremy, along with the directors David and Michael Meller, went to see him and talked it over. Nothing was too much trouble after that, and if Kevin needed any time off to help deal with me and the children, that was no problem, Jeremy said. If it had been left to Kevin, he'd never have said anything, and would have somehow tried to muddle through on his own.

I was so glad he'd told them. It took some of the pressure off, and as I was now out of danger and being well looked after in the constant care of the nursing staff at Salisbury, the new routines of our lives could start to take over. I wanted us to get back to some sort of normality, for our own sakes and the children's. I knew we couldn't both keep up the pretence indefinitely. As Kevin tried his hardest to focus on his new responsibilities at work, his visits to me began to tail off. It was a gruelling round trip each time, after all. He had a full-time job and the children to think of, and I was very busy being an invalid – something that seemed to fill every moment of the day. To be honest, I was glad of the respite from his misery.

It wasn't as if I didn't have company. My parents still came to see me almost every day, a remarkable daily vigil for them as they put their own lives on hold so as to deal with mine and my family's. From the moment I had mentioned to my mum that Kevin wasn't coping, she had all but taken over at home, fetching and carrying the children, cooking the meals, doing the housework and the washing, trying to make everything as simple as possible for Kevin and as routine as normal for the boys.

In a strange way, I think Mum sort of thrived on the challenges my accident threw at her. It wasn't that she wanted it to have happened – far from it – but she rose to the occasion brilliantly, almost relishing her chance to mother me again so late in life. She had always been good in a crisis. She had had to be. With my father away in the Royal Navy for a lot of their married life, on ten-month tours at a time, she effectively became a single parent to me and Neil, coping with everything from the household chores to home maintenance to paying the bills.

I arrived in this world, all ten pounds of bouncing baby, on 13 July 1961, in my nan's house because she was caring for Mum in the last stages of her pregnancy. Dad was away at sea and didn't come home until I was two months old. His first comment on seeing me asleep in the cot was: 'She looks just like a little Toby jug.'

He and my mum, Brenda, then aged sixteen, had met at the Court School of Dancing in Portsmouth in 1958 when Dad was nineteen and working as an apprentice coppersmith. Mum worked in a clothes factory. My father actually fancied my mother's best friend Margaret and went out with her first for a year, not courting Mum until 1959, by which time he was a dockyard apprentice. A few months later they got engaged, after he had joined the Navy. She had no intention of marrying a sailor to begin with – she knew all about the hardships faced by Navy wives – and in fact they broke off their engagement a few months later when he was sent to Hong Kong to join HMS *Centaur*. But after patching things up, they got married on 24 September 1960, and I was born nine months and three weeks later.

In 1963 we moved to Scotland with Dad, when he was with HMS *Maidstone*, then back to Portsmouth for two years while he was with HMS *Chichester*. In April 1964 my brother Neil arrived, by which time we had moved into married quarters in Portsmouth. Mum was determined to make sure Neil arrived when my dad, by then a chief engineer, was home on leave from the Far East. It worked, and Neil arrived just as Dad got back for the weekend. For the next few years, Dad continued to travel all over the world working on various projects, while we stayed put.

When I was six, we moved out of married quarters and into my parents' first proper home at Southbourne, which is also where I went to school. Dad may have been away for much of the time, but Mum never allowed us to lose touch with him. 'This is where your father is this week,' she would say, pointing to some remote spot in Africa, the Middle East, Australia, the Mediterranean or the Far East on a well-fingered world map pinned to the back of the dining-room door. I learned geography through my father's travels; I felt as if I had followed him all over the world. Having told us where he was, Mum would settle down to read us one of his many letters home, written on flimsy blue airmail paper. There was always a page for each of us children and it was wonderful to read his words, to know how much he loved and missed us. Mum always used to say: 'I know it's hard when Dad's away, but think of this. If he wasn't in the Navy and away for so much of the time, only able to keep in touch in his letters, we might never have known just how much he cares.'

I couldn't wait for him to come home. We would count off the days until he was due back. It was such a treat when we went to see his ship come in, or his plane arrive at the airport. We always went to meet him, never to see him off. On his return, he would run towards us, looking and smelling completely different to how I remembered him, scooping us up into his arms and kissing and cuddling us. He was devastatingly handsome, with twinkling eyes and an unassuming manner. He adored us and never failed to bring a present – I was very proud of my collection of stamps from all over the globe – and Neil and I were both given guitars once, even though they only ended up gathering dust in the corners of our rooms. Dad's nickname for me was 'Pudding' or 'Plum' and no one else was allowed to call me that; it was a special name I still love to hear him use.

My mother and I were incredibly close from an early age and got on very well, apart from the usual turbulent teenage years. An only daughter and her eldest child, I idolized her and loved spending time with her, especially as I grew older. We were each other's best friends and confidantes and often talked late into the night over mugs of cocoa. She was also very protective and loving. She has always been a great homemaker and a wonderful cook, and the sort of woman who needs to feel needed. And I really needed her – so much so that by the time I was fourteen or fifteen I actually began to resent my father coming home and spoiling our fun. When he was away, Mum used to be the life and soul, playing all her old Jack Jones records – she would have them really blaring out. Neil and I had her all to ourselves, and she would take us on fun weekends to Kent to see Auntie Joan and Uncle Bob, her sister and brother-in-law, or on holidays to Cornwall to see my nan.

None of my schoolfriends were from service families or had fathers who worked away, and it always felt strange to go to their houses and see a man there. Most of the time I longed for our home to be like that, for Dad to be around all the time, but when he did come back it felt to me as if Mum switched allegiance and we suddenly took second place. It was clear that my parents were very fond of each other, and I was jealous.

Neil and I had never got on. In fact, we hated each other for much of our childhood. I thought he was the little brother from hell and the feeling was entirely mutual. I think it must have had a lot to do with me being the eldest and Dad being away. When Mum went out, she would leave me in charge and that was it, we'd be fighting within minutes – wrestling, kicking and biting. We were like a pair of Gladiators – we fought to kill. Even when Mum was home, we were constantly at each other's throats and she had to separate us countless times. I don't know what it was that first set us against each other, but it went way back. Perhaps we were simply too alike. I used to regard friends who got on with their brothers with a mixture of awe and envy. It wasn't until years later that Neil and I became friends and began to enjoy the sort of relationship we should always have had.

School was a welcome distraction. I thoroughly enjoyed it. I had a good social life, especially at my secondary school, Bourne Comprehensive in Southbourne. English was my best subject, then history and biology. I was never very good at sport, although I could slog a ball a good distance in rounders. I belonged to a large group of girlfriends who all hung out together and had a good time. There was me and my best friend Angie, then Mandy, Gugi and Stephanie. Boyfriends did the rounds of the circuit, and then we all compared notes. It was tremendous fun, especially for me and Angie, whose house I virtually lived in.

I was always a tomboy, and incredibly accident-prone – especially on two wheels. I had been a mobile disaster area since I was a kid, breaking limbs and scuffing knees. My mother used to get exasperated. Fortunately, as I grew up and started going to the pictures or to discotheques organized by the youth wing at school, I became more feminine and interested in boys and my accident-prone days seemed over. The music we listened to back then was all seventies glam-rock, Slade, Sweet, the Bay City Rollers, although I also developed an early interest in heavy metal music.

I underachieved at school, mainly because I was never pushed hard enough. I gave up cookery for woodwork – becoming the only girl in the class – but I didn't achieve much academically, acquiring just four GCSEs with not particularly good grades. I was unsure of what I wanted to be when I grew up; I had looked at journalism and the possibility of becoming an air hostess, but neither career appealed especially. What I really wanted was to travel to all the places my father had been to, to wear a uniform and experience a life on the ocean waves as he had, so I set my heart on following him into the Navy and becoming a Wren, a member of the Women's Royal Naval Service.

With my mother's blessing, I applied to the WRNS and made it all the way through the selection process, right up to the final medical, when I came across an unexpected spanner in the works. 'No daughter of mine is going to be a *matelot*'s mattress,' my father announced with uncharacteristic gruffness when he was next home on leave, and that was that. There was no arguing with Dad when his mind was set. His word was law.

His decision upset me and made me really angry. I was fifteen and had thought he would be flattered by my wanting to copy him. 'Why won't you let me go?' I complained, but he wasn't having it. My chief consolation was that Angie had always thought it was a bad idea, and was delighted that I wouldn't be abandoning her for a life at sea after all. There was one other, surprise, consolation. It was April 1977 and I had just met a really nice bloke at a friend's party. His name was Kevin Hill.

I was fifteen and three-quarters and Kevin was twenty, which seemed like a huge age difference at the time, but there was something about him that instantly appealed. Not only was he tall, dark and handsome, with a mop of curly brown hair, a handlebar moustache and nice brown eyes, but he seemed so different from all the other boys I'd known. That was it, I think. They were boys and he was a man. All six foot of him. I was smitten.

'Do you want to dance?' I asked him, unashamedly, after admiring him from across the room. They were the first words I ever spoke to him. He nodded his agreement rather shyly and I pulled him on to the dance floor, slipping my hands underneath his blazer and pulling him closer. God knows what he thought of me. At that time I was very much into scruffy jeans and kaftans and Led Zeppelin. By contrast, Kevin was 'Mr Straight', smooth and slick, and his favourite group was Abba. Fortunately, we did have something in common – our sense of humour – and before long we were laughing and chatting together like the oldest of friends.

When the party was over, Kevin offered to walk me home, and as I took his hand in mine and headed for my door I allowed myself a little smile. 'I'm not letting this one get away,' I told myself happily. He was a junior accountant at a firm in Liphook, Hampshire, he lived in Chidham, West Sussex, and he had his own car – a Vauxhall Viva. When we got to my house, I handed him a piece of paper with my phone number scribbled on it and asked him to call. He said he would, and then walked away without giving me so much as a peck on the cheek. I felt cheated.

For the next seven days, I virtually camped by the phone, waiting for him to call and praying that he would. I was infatuated by the man and we hadn't even kissed yet. Angie couldn't believe it. 'What's so special about this guy, anyway?' she asked complainingly, after I refused to go round to her house for the third night running in case he called and I was out.

'I don't know, really,' I admitted. 'He makes me laugh and I just think we'd make a great team.' It sounded so corny, but it was exactly how I felt. There was a special spark between us, a bond that I hadn't felt before, and something inside me told me that Kevin Hill was *the* guy.

It was a whole week before he phoned. I discovered much later that it had taken him that long to pluck up the courage. Far from being the tough macho male I had assumed him to be, he was actually painfully shy. 'Hello, Julie, it's Kevin Hill,' he said, timidly. 'Do you remember me from Karen's party last week?'

Cupping my hand over the receiver, I beamed an excited smile at my mum and hissed: 'It's *him*!' Putting my mouth back to the phone, I cleared my throat and said as coolly as I could: 'Oh, yes . . . Kevin . . . Weren't you the one who walked me home?'

That threw him. There was a long pause and I wondered if I had blown it by being too casual. Then he found his voice at last. 'I was wondering if you were free and fancied coming out for a drink sometime?' he asked.

Not wanting to put him off his stroke again, I jumped in with both feet. 'Yes, Kevin, I'd love to. In fact, I'm free tonight – if you are.' Faced with such an offer, he could do nothing but accept, and so it was that we went out that night on our first date.

Over a few drinks in a little country pub just north of Chichester, I found out more about this man of my dreams. Kevin was the only son of a Ministry of Defence draughtsman. He still lived at home with his parents and had just split up with a girl in my school year called Sally. I don't think they'd done much more than kiss and he didn't seem too upset. We got on extremely well again, hitting it off brilliantly from the start and laughing till our sides ached. When he'd driven me home, he leaned over and kissed me. That touch of his lips against mine marked the start of a couple of years of us virtually living in one another's pockets, seeing each other every night.

Needless to say, my mother adored Kev, especially compared with some of the scrag-ends I had previously brought home. Kev was the perfect prospective son-in-law; he wore a suit and tie, he had a good job as an upstanding member of the community, he was as straight as a die and totally charming with it. I had the most enormous crush on him. He seemed so grown up, so much more mature than anyone else I'd met – I think that was the novelty. For him, I think the attraction was purely physical. I was his bit of rough – the feisty, hard-drinking, chain-smoking sailor's daughter. From his parents' point of view I was not at all suitable daughter-in-law material.

Not surprisingly, I soon had Kevin twisted round my little finger. I sorted out his wardrobe, bought him jeans and T-shirts and made him get 'with it'. I introduced him to my friends and to the sort of music and parties I liked, and led him away from what I considered to be his boring, square lifestyle. I even managed to persuade him to part with some of his hard-earned cash and buy himself a sporty Triumph Spitfire, in aubergine, with a hard top. The Viva had to go.

Poor Kev, he accepted it all uncomplainingly, although he did persuade me to take a steady job as a cashier with Barclays Bank in Emsworth, and to start saving 'for our future'. But by the end of our first year together, I realized that he was more committed to that future than I was, and the prospect scared me. To my very great shame, once I had transformed him into just the sort of bloke I wanted him to be, I chucked him. I think I just got bored with Mr Nice Guy and craved someone with a freer spirit. 'I'm sorry, Kev, but this just isn't going to work,' I told him coolly one night as he dropped me home after the pub. His jaw dropped and he looked physically winded when I added: 'I think we should have a break from each other for a while.'

Trying to explain my reasons for ditching him to my distraught mother, I remember saying: 'I've just got the feeling that there is perhaps someone else out there, just waiting for me.' I was panicking really. I was only sixteen and I felt I hadn't seen enough of life yet and was already on the marriage path. Mum shook her head and said, not for the first time, that she didn't understand me.

Kevin was broken-hearted. He saw quite a bit of my best friend Angie and her boyfriend Andy – the couple we had regularly gone out together with as a foursome before – and they reported his unhappiness back to me. Meanwhile, I launched myself into a rebellious and completely unsuitable relationship with a rough-and-ready sailor called Martin, bought myself a moped, and for the next eight months was hell-bent on enjoying myself.

Martin was into motorbikes and leather and couldn't have been more different to Kevin. He had a huge Kawasaki and represented danger, excitement and thrills. He was 'Mr Not So Steady Eddie' and – for the brief time that we were together – he was just what I needed. Mum was very worried about me and thought we were getting too involved too soon. She thought I was on the rebound, and was very grateful when Martin went off to sea and our passion was confined to letters. But a funny thing happened when Martin went away. I didn't miss him at all, and after a while I didn't even bother to reply to his steady stream of love notes.

Shortly afterwards, in October 1978, I went to a friend's wedding on my own. It was held at West

Ashling village hall and the bride was Mandy, from my close circle of girlfriends at school. I was shocked to see Kevin there, with a girl called Andrea, a teacher-training student he'd met at a night club. Try as I might, I couldn't stop looking at the pair of them – the way she was hanging off his arm, that look of infatuation in her eyes. I felt devastated. It was that day more than anything else that made me realize that I loved Kev and missed him more than I wanted to admit. The next day I rode my moped all the way to Chidham to see him at his parents' house, and hammered on the door.

'I've been thinking,' I said falteringly, my crash helmet in my hand, when he finally opened the door. 'I was wondering what you thought about the possibility of us getting back together again.'

Kevin looked deeply suspicious and shrugged his shoulders casually, as if he didn't care either way. His brush-off cut me to the quick. 'Maybe,' he replied.

'Well, how about meeting up for a drink next week?' I asked, hopefully, trying to avoid eye contact with his mother, who was hovering in the hallway behind him.

'Perhaps,' he replied, stuffing his hands deep into his jeans pockets and leaning against the door frame.

'Well, I – I'll call you,' I added, hesitantly.

'OK,' he said, and, seeing that I had nothing to add, he closed the door.

The following night, I went to a party with Angie and drowned my sorrows. 'I love Kev, I really do,' I wailed drunkenly, my mascara running down my cheeks. 'I want him back.'

Angie looked at me and considered the matter gravely. After a while, she said: 'Then get him back.' It was a simple enough comment, but one that galvanized me into action. She was right. All of a sudden, I felt as if my life had a new and focused direction. I was going to get Kevin back into my life if it was the last thing I did.

Within twenty-four hours I had called Kev, and we'd agreed to meet secretly at a car park at a local beauty spot to discuss our future. Us getting back together was not going to be popular with everybody, least of all his parents and Andrea. Sitting in his car, facing him, ready to plead my case, I tried to look as contrite as I could. 'Kev, I've made a terrible mistake,' I started. 'I realize that now. I love you and I miss you and I want another chance. Please, can't we give it another go?'

His face was deadly serious and he stared at me in quiet disbelief for a while. I had hurt him badly, I knew that. I had broken his trust and I would have to earn it again. Finally, after a long pause, he said: 'There would have to be some basic ground rules.'

My heart soared. Beaming at him, I replied: 'Anything. You name it.'

We got back together again in October 1978, and four weeks later we announced our engagement, much to everyone's surprise. I was just seventeen and Kevin was twenty-two. My mum was delighted. The break had been good for Kevin and me. The bond between us felt stronger than ever, and as I stood at his side, ready to become his bride, I felt utterly invincible.

I soon discovered how foolish it was to believe in your own invincibility. As I was returning home from work on my moped, my scratched visor hindered my vision and I was momentarily dazzled by the headlights of an oncoming car. Swerving to avoid a collision, I rode the moped into a ditch and flipped myself over the handlebars. After blacking out, I woke to find myself lying in a hole with a group of strangers staring down at me, talking about me as if I wasn't there. 'I'm not dead!' I shouted, taking them all aback. For a moment, I'd thought I was lying in an open grave. An ambulance came and took me to St Richard's Hospital in Chichester, where I was treated for a broken arm and a bad gash to my leg.

Kevin was extremely concerned about me, and came rushing to the hospital with my mum to see if I was all right – Dad was away in some foreign clime – I was delighted to see Kev's worried face and knew in that instant that I had made the right decision. How lovely it was to have a fiancé so obviously devoted to me. Having established that I was going to live, and once he'd gleaned the full, stupid details of my accident, Kev's expression changed from anxiety to amusement. 'You silly sod!' he said, and disappeared to fetch himself and Mum a coffee.

A week later Dad returned home from sea, unaware of me and Kevin having got back together, or of our engagement or my accident. Almost as soon as he arrived and saw me at home with my arm in plaster and Kevin at my side, he announced that he was going down the pub for a drink. Kev went with him, eager to officially ask for my hand in marriage. He didn't know Dad very well and was so nervous, he was sick in the toilet. But when he did finally blurt his question out, Norman turned to him, patted him on the back and said: 'Absolutely.' After that, they both got drunk, and Mum and I joined them later to celebrate.

Kev and I went to Samuel's the jewellers in Portsmouth and chose a beautiful diamond solitaire engagement ring. My only sadness was that the plaster cast on my arm and the swollen fingers sticking out of it detracted a bit from the ring. We went round to Kevin's parents' and rather sheepishly broke the news to them. After an uncomfortable silence, Kevin's mum, Anne, said: 'That's nice', and rather stiffly gave me a hug. The reaction of his father, Ken, was much the same.

We had planned a long engagement of about eighteen months, so that we could save for the £2,000 deposit we needed for our first house. We had chosen an as yet unbuilt two-bedroom terraced Wimpey home on an estate in Waterlooville. Kev had already taught me the importance of saving, something I had never done before and found quite hard to start with, but I soon learned the value of squirrelling money away – which was just as well, because three months after we got engaged I was sacked from my job at the bank for failing to meet the exacting standards of the probationary period. Thankfully, I managed to find a new job almost straight away, in the sales office of a petrol pump manufacturers, Avery Hardoll in Havant, where I was to remain for the next five years.

Having lost my moped, at first I had to travel everywhere by bus, until Kev agreed to help me pay for driving lessons. I applied for my test after a couple of lessons and when the letter came through it was for ten months' time, which seemed an age away. We were getting married in July 1980, and I had hoped to be fully qualified by then. To my horror, a cancellation test suddenly came through, on a Friday, for the following Monday. I decided to go hell for leather and spent the entire weekend practising with Dad. I passed my test with flying colours, even though I had officially only had six lessons.

Kev had set his heart on a brand-new S-registered Ford Capri just before we got engaged. He had even put a deposit on it and was going to trade in the old Triumph Spitfire against it. But we both knew that a new car wasn't feasible, so the order was cancelled and the deposit returned. We got a second-hand blue Cortina instead. Not long afterwards, Kev graduated from junior to senior accountant, and with his new responsibility came a company car. The Cortina was mine. For the first time in my life, I had wheels of my own.

Everything was finally coming together. In April 1980, three months before our wedding, our house was finished and ready for us to move into. We spent many happy evenings there, planning and plotting, but I refused to allow either one of us to move in until we were actually married. With the wedding all set, the dress bought, the cake made and the house ready, we both went down with a big dose of the jitters. Kev was worse than me. He became a total sod with premarital nerves and he and Mum fell out big time, with him refusing to take part in the arrangements and yet arguing every point. She had gone into full organizational mode, and he didn't want to know. I felt like the jam in the sandwich, all the while nursing my own fears and reservations.

The night before the wedding, Mum came to my bedroom. She knocked gingerly on the door, then, sitting down beside me on the bed, she put an arm around my shoulders. 'Julie, are you really sure about going through with this?' she asked. 'It's not too late to change your mind, you know.' I looked at her and tried to quell my own feelings of anxiety. It was the biggest decision of my life, I knew that. I was eighteen years old and hadn't really seen much of life at all. The next day I was going to walk down the aisle on my father's arm to marry someone I'd had a crush on since I was fifteen, someone I had once thought unsuitable, someone who could be a right pain in the arse when he wanted to be. But inspite of everything, deep down inside I knew I was doing the right thing. It was a gut feeling that told me to go for it. I smiled and told her not to worry.

The day loomed cold and windy. In July. As I looked out of the window at the grey clouds, I wondered if it was a bad omen. But, regardless of the weather, we had the most glorious day. I wore a full-length white satin gown and carried a posy of pink roses, a copy of my Mum's bouquet. I was driven to church in a beautiful black vintage Rolls-Royce. Angie was my chief brides-maid and three of my cousins were pageboys and brides-maid. Kev wore a beige three-piece suit and brown leather cowboy boots and looked like a seventies pop star.

The ceremony was at the beautiful Thomas à Becket Church in Warblington, with a lovely vicar who made Kev and me feel instantly at ease. Standing at the altar, saying our wedding vows to each other, staring into each other's eyes while we promised to love and honour each other 'in sickness and health, till death do us part' was one of the most poignant moments of my life.

We signed the register to the song 'Whiter Shade of Pale' by Procul Harum and the congregation sang 'Morning Has Broken' by Cat Stevens. The reception was at a hotel in Emsworth called the Brookfield, then we all went back to my parents' for a buffet and disco in their garden and double garage. We left at 10.30 p.m., running laughing under an arch made by the outstretched arms of all our guests. Kev booked us into a gorgeous hotel, the Millstream at Bosham, five miles down the road, where we woke up blissfully happy the next day, my nineteenth birthday.

Returning home to my parents' we discovered that the party had gone on riotously all night, and that there had even been complaints made in the village. The police had arrived in the early hours, and had stayed. There were bodies all over the floor and mess everywhere. We spent the day helping them clear up and then set off for our week-long honeymoon – my first ever trip abroad – to Poros in the Greek islands. It was bliss. Absolutely wonderful. The worst part was coming home.

Moving into our new little house, actually living together, was very strange. I realized then how young and naive I was. Here I was, suddenly thrown into the role of housewife and cook. At first we couldn't afford a washing machine and I had to wash all Kev's snotty hankies by hand. It was hard work, adjusting to married life, but we muddled along. Kev had been given a big pay rise once he had married, so we never really had to struggle financially. With Andy and Angie married later that year, everything seemed perfect. We were all happily settled down; we had lovely homes and perfect husbands and life was sweet.

It was the time of the property boom and we were Thatcher's children, ambitious go-getters who wanted to make as much money as possible while we were still young. Eighteen months after we had moved into our new house, we sold it for a huge profit and moved to a bigger and better property, a three-bedroom semi-detached in Southbourne, just across the road from where I used to live. We also became involved with a company called Amway for a while, selling household products. I gave up my job to work at it full time. It was perfect for me, chiefly because I found that I was good at selling, but also because I was pregnant by then and thrilled at the prospect.

If Kevin had had his way, he'd have had a vasectomy at fifteen. An only child who as an adult had rarely come into contact with other people's children, he had never really wanted any of his own – the idea just didn't appeal. But as soon as we found out I was pregnant, that changed and he was as delighted as I was. Angie fell pregnant at the same time – both babies conceived on a canal boat holiday in the Cotswolds – and we were due within a day of each other.

There were, though, a couple of unwelcome events in the week or two before the births. A close friend, Christopher Goddard, was killed in a car accident, aged nineteen. His parents, Doris and Jim, had been lifelong friends of my parents – Jim was a shipmate of Dad's and Doris was Mum's best friend. The funeral was set for the day my baby was due, but fortunately he was late and I was still able to go and pay my respects to the young man I had known all my life. It was such a sad day. Then a few days before the birth, Kev had a car accident. A lorry pulled out in front of him on the A3 and he ended up under the tailgate. Fortunately, he only broke his hand, although he was very shaken by the experience.

Angie went into hospital first and gave birth to a healthy baby boy she named Aaron. I was induced a week later and little Nathan was born on 12 March 1983 after a marathon twenty-two-hour labour. I was only just out of my teens, and a mother. It was the most emotional moment of my life. Kev was there, right up to the end, and then ducked out just as Nathan arrived, for fear of passing out. He was back at my side within minutes, though, and we were both thrilled with our new son. Mum and Dad arrived shortly afterwards, and everyone was crying – they were as pleased as Punch.

It had always been my intention to stay home and care for our children, and I did so willingly. Nathan was a gorgeous baby and I found I could still work at the selling business part-time. But one day we realized there was more to life than Amway, and we gave it up. The experience had taught me one thing I hadn't known before – I was a natural in sales. Not that I was going to have much time to put it into practice. Within a year I was pregnant again, and baby Daniel was born on 11 May 1985. Daniel was just as sweet as Nathan, but a bit more demanding. He grew into a happy toddler and a wonderful mimic, shadowing his father's every move. When his father was home, that is.

Kev's new role in the company was becoming extremely demanding. He started to go abroad on business trips, he worked horrendous hours, sometimes all night, and travelled all over the country. On one trip he was away in Toronto for six weeks, leaving me alone, literally holding the babies. During this time Nathan became ill with a serious bout of gastro-enteritis and I ended up moving back in with my parents for emotional and moral support.

They were glad of the company now that they were on their own. Neil had joined the Navy not long after Kev and I got married, and his rebellious teenage days were over. He quickly settled down to a life at sea and we started writing to each other for the first time in our lives. With both of us mellowing a bit by now, we began to forge a friendly relationship. This was strengthened when he had a serious motorbike accident and was rushed to hospital with a shattered kidney. It was two weeks before he let any of us know he had been injured. Dad and I drove down to Somerset to visit him in hospital and found him cheeking the nurses and telling us everything was going to be all right. Hugging him with a mixture of relief and anger, I felt incredibly close to him for the first time and realized just how much I would have missed my infuriating little brother if he hadn't pulled through.

Back home, with Kev returned from Canada, our domestic situation became chaotic. We were trying to sell our house and rise up the property chain, and we moved into a mobile home in Angie and Andy's back garden, as a temporary measure between moves. But the people we were buying from backed out, leaving us in limbo during the winter of 1989/90. It was freezing cold and incredibly cramped and miserable in the mobile home. The children were five and three, and I was at my wits' end coping with it all.

The only saving grace was the small business Kev and I had set up with Andy and Angie – we called it AJK after our initials. We had a press with which we printed off business cards, invoices and letter heads. Angie and I were in charge of sales, which simply meant that we sat down with a telephone each and worked our way through all the names in the Yellow Pages, asking if they needed any printing done. The business went from strength to strength and we ended up renting a small unit to run it from. Andy even gave up his job as an electronics engineer to help run it. In the space of a few years we managed to build the company up to the point where it had an annual turnover of £180,000. When it was at its peak, we sold it for a profit.

The success of AJK and Kev's continuing advancement at work allowed us to get our dream house at last. It was modern but built of brick and flint in the old style, and it stood back from the neighbouring houses with its own tarmac driveway. It was all that I had ever wanted. Now I just had to find another job to satisfy my new need for self-fulfilment. Having worked so successfully for AJK, I was no longer content to be just a housewife and mother. I needed something more and, before long, a job offer came my way. In October 1989, Pink's, a local drinks wholesaler who had been one of our customers at AJK, asked me if I'd like to work for them in the Chichester and Petersfield areas as a sales representative. I was thrilled to have been given the chance to really prove my skills at last, and jumped at it. It was a huge ego boost.

Kevin wasn't quite so sure. He didn't mind me working from home with Angie, but going out on my own and socializing with pub landlords was another matter. I refused to let his doubts spoil it for me. As far as I was concerned, the job was superb and right up my street. I found confidence in myself that I didn't even know existed; I bought myself a whole new wardrobe and started to meet a lot of very interesting people. I was still in the little league compared to Kevin's earning power, but it did me a world of good after years of being home as a mum. My parents and Angie were extremely supportive and took over all my childcare needs while I worked, although the job was pretty flexible and I could generally get home in time to pick the boys up from school, even if it meant I had to go out again later.

It wasn't all easy running, though. Shortly after I joined the company there was a major reshuffle. In a messy bout of internal politics, two of the senior directors left and set up on their own and the firm was divided. The new company was called Harfield's of Chichester. As I was the most recent employee at the existing company, Pink's, I lost my job. I was bitterly disappointed. We had just moved into our new home, we had a massive mortgage and I felt as if I was only just getting into my stride. 'I'm not going to take this lying down,' I told Kev angrily the night it happened. 'I'm going to do something about it.' The following morning, I went to see one of the breakaway directors, John Swafield, and offered my services. To my delight, he took me on. Revenge felt sweet – although I had to go through another three-month probationary period. No problem, I told myself. I did it before and I can do it again. I'll show them.

My biggest headache was Kev and the continuing bad undercurrents between us. I didn't feel they were insurmountable, but they were beginning to niggle. One of his biggest bugbears was how much I was drinking – the job encouraged it – and occasionally I drove home over the limit, something that absolutely infuriated him but that was much more socially acceptable in the late 1980s than it is now. He also became very jealous, calling me a 'honey pot' to other men. He was paranoid about the company I was keeping and the sorts of places I was going to. He was convinced that I was getting untold sexual advances from the men I was doing business with. If I was being honest, I would say he was probably right. If I'd been in the mood, I probably could have jumped into bed with five or six blokes by then. The point was that I hadn't, but he didn't trust me.

Whenever he confronted me about it, his face was like thunder and the stance he took was uncompromising. 'I suppose all these landlords are chatting you up, are they?' he asked, frostily. 'Is that why you like this job so much?' I told him he was being stupid and that none of the advances had been serious, but he wouldn't listen. In the end, I lost my temper completely and told him he had nothing to be jealous of. 'You've got to trust me, Kevin,' I shouted at him. 'If you don't, then we haven't got much of a marriage.'

The moodiness and the unspoken tensions continued for several weeks. I couldn't do a thing right. It was a worrying time, made worse by the fact that Kev suddenly announced that he was going to start looking for a new job. As he did the rounds of interviews and re-interviews, I wondered where we were heading as a couple. He clearly felt the need for greater financial security and personal challenges in his life. I was finding my own and resenting him for not sharing in my happiness, and the two of us seemed to be drifting further and further apart. My mum knew things weren't right. She had noticed the atmosphere between us and was naturally worried. Her obvious concern only made things worse, and by the time Kev had found a new job and handed in his notice at the end of March 1990, with four weeks to serve, we were hardly talking.

My stubbornness as far as my job was concerned made his blood boil. By April 1990 he had just about had enough, especially when, on the night the accident was to happen, I failed to come home at the time I'd said I would. It had been a long day for me, with the Ladies' Licensed Victuallers' Association, and I would much rather have been home with the family, but I couldn't just abandon my clients. It was an important opportunity for me to prove myself to them – my most valued customers. Kev just didn't seem to understand this, and in the series of phone conversations we had during the course of that evening, as I explained that I was going to be later still, he became more and more angry.

Our final words to each other that night were not very pleasant. After snapping that he would be in bed by the time I got home, he hung up. It's something he will regret for the rest of his life, because he still believes that his unreasonable moodiness made me hurry home unnecessarily fast.

The rest, as they say, is history.

There was no turning back the clocks for either of us. The accident had happened, the damage had been done and I was going to spend the rest of my life in a wheelchair. With Kev back at work in his new job, withdrawing further and further into himself as he dealt with his guilt, his anger and his fears, I was left pretty much on my own in hospital to deal with my own tumult of feelings. He clammed shut emotionally for fear of losing control and I felt much the same. We deliberately skirted around the major issues of what would happen next, how we would cope, where we would live and if we really could manage without my income.

Our marriage was stretched to breaking point as we each struggled with the emotional conflicts caused by our trauma. We spoke only about the children or kept on the safe subjects of his work or the many cards and messages I'd received. Both of us secretly wanted to rage – at each other, at life, at the unfairness of it all – but somehow we managed to keep our emotions in check, to just under simmering point, in those first few months as we circled each other suspiciously, each knowing that sooner or later something was going to have to give.

FIVE

Searchlight

LIFE FOR me became a constant stream of daily challenges and rituals. From the moment I was woken up at eight o'clock to be given a bed bath and breakfast, to the moment lights went out at ten o'clock at night, I had things to do and people to meet. There were three meals a day to get through, all disgusting – I lost a stone in four weeks – and a constant stream of medical staff at my bedside to pull, push and prod me. I had to be turned every three hours to prevent pressure sores. One of the physiotherapists would try to encourage me to use free weights and to teach me how to cough again – something people who are paralysed from below the waist have to relearn – and I was inundated with books and magazines to read, as if I could concentrate.

Each bed had its own television, so there were eight sets in the ward, switched to various channels and all blaring out in competition with each other, along with what seemed like a constant buzzing noise, as patient after patient pressed their buzzers to call a nurse. The only time I got any respite was when the staff agreed to wheel my bed out into the quadrangle, in the middle of the ground-floor spinal unit, so that I could listen to the birds and feel the sun on my face. Lighting a cigarette and inhaling deeply, I would look up at the sky and pretend for a while that I was lying in the garden at home sunbathing, without a care in the world.

From quite early on, I was swamped with visitors. At first it was something I wanted, to touch base with the people that meant the most to me – Angie and Andy, Alan and Ann (dear friends from Bath), as well as other friends and relatives. For them, too, it was important to see me, to realize that in spite of everything I was still the same old Julie. That I wasn't a dribbling, gibbering wreck who smelled of stale urine and could no longer hold a conversation. Once they saw my smiling face, the relief on their own was evident, and after that we just did our best to carry on as normal, although it didn't always work.

One visitor I hadn't expected came wandering into the ward rather sheepishly one day, clutching some flowers. It was Helen, the woman who had been so kind to me at the scene of the accident. She had apparently written to St Richard's Hospital a few days after the crash, enquiring after me, and her letter was sent on to Salisbury. My parents had been handed it and had gone to visit her at her house in Emsworth, not far from my home, to thank her for her kindness. 'I'd very much like to go and see Julie, if that's at all possible,' she told them. So Mum, with her typical spontaneity, arranged to bring her in. It was lovely to see her, although rather emotional for us both.

'You must be Helen,' I said as she approached my bed nervously. She was much taller than I remembered, in her mid-thirties, with short dark hair and no make-up. I reached out a hand and she clasped it in hers, as she had done so comfortingly on the night of the accident. It felt good to have her at my side once more. She was as gentle as I remembered her, a mature student with a teenage son, softly spoken and very compassionate. She was able to fill in some of the gaps for me, to explain how she had watched in horror as my car left the road and launched itself up the bank. She said the other driver, a young woman, became quite hysterical at the scene and couldn't cope, so after they had fought their way through the hedge to reach me Helen had sent her to call for help. 'I can't thank you enough,' I told her. 'You saved my life.'

She brushed off my thanks and said how sorry she was that I had been so severely injured. After a few minutes of general chat, we realized we had nothing else to say to each other, and she left. Our paths were to cross occasionally in the following years – in Emsworth High Street or in the local supermarket – but never quite so meaningfully. It was a relationship that had sprung up in unnatural circumstances and that had to come to a natural conclusion. I owed her a great deal and would be eternally grateful, but we could never have become friends – just the sight of her face, the sound of her voice, would have reminded me of a night I would really much rather forget.

There was plenty to keep my mind occupied, anyway. The system at Salisbury is that all new patients start in the acute ward at one end of the spinal unit, progress to a four-bed ward, then to a single room, and finally a self-contained flat for a weekend. The layout means that you move further and further down the hall towards the main door until you can finally leave. My rehabilitation was expected to take several months, the first of which would be spent in the acute ward, with my bed being gradually tilted into an upright position and me being constantly monitored as I slowly began to mend, mentally as well as physically.

It was also an opportunity for me to get to know my fellow inmates. First, there was Becky, my next-door neighbour, the young woman whose cheery resilience in the face of adversity bolstered us all, and who never seemed to let her situation get her down. It was weeks before I set eyes on her – up until then, we were just voices to each other through a curtain. When I did first see her, strapped into her wheelchair, I was surprised at how pretty she was and jealous of her long blonde hair. She was, quite simply, gorgeous.

Becky was the only daughter of a loving family, with three brothers who all doted on her. She was also determined, courageous and hilariously funny. A straight A student, she was bright and breezy and had a marvellous sense of humour, especially for someone in her situation. We clicked into each other's wavelengths immediately, even though for the first few weeks of our friendship she had been forced to put up with my constant moaning and groaning. 'Beck', as she became known, was there for me in every sense of the word, and – in time – I think I was there for her too. She filled a hole in my life that was painfully empty. She became my confidante and my best friend. Becky was someone who would help me, and many others, to start to come to terms with what life had thrown at us and teach us how to stay cheerful.

There were other remarkable people in the ward too.

Vivien, a tiny, frail woman in her late thirties, was paralysed from the neck down after a horse-riding accident. She had great difficulty breathing and was very poorly when she first arrived on the ward. Several times she came close to death, something that we were alerted to by the endless ringing of alarm bells around her bed – this was known in the unit as 'going off'. Poor Vivien 'went off' many times, but somehow she always managed to fight back, if only to complain ever more bitterly about her predicament.

Jim was a nineteen-year-old paraplegic injured in a motorbike accident whose bed was immediately to my left. His spinal break was at T9 – thoracic vertebra number nine, exactly the same as me – and yet, in the inexplicable nature of spinal injuries, he had more movement in his upper body than I had. He was fiercely independent, and reminded me a lot of my brother. Alice, who was in her eighties and had broken her back in a fall at home, was paralysed and rather unwell the whole time she was with us. She was very frail, and her age conspired against her as far as recovery was concerned – none of us expected her to survive very long.

Then there was Steve, a seventeen-year-old rugby player who became tetraplegic after an overenthusiastic sporting tackle playing in the Bath under-eighteen team. He was a wonderful lad with a terrific personality, who bore his disability with great courage. He spent his eighteenth birthday in the ward, surrounded by his adoring family and mates, and we all gathered round to watch him blow out the candles on his cake.

Eamonn, in his early thirties, had become a paraplegic after slipping off a roof following a heavy lunch. A Guinness-loving Irishman and a big strong fellow, he was bright enough to do the *Independent* crossword each day, which amazed us all. He had suffered a low break in the spine and so he had the most movement of all of us, coupled with some sensation in his legs. I used to joke that it was 'only a flesh wound'. Single, but with a lovely girlfriend called Caroline, he later became the inspiration behind most of the parties in the ward, which usually involved some serious drinking. He and I taught Becky how to use what limited muscle movement she had in her upper arm to flick her wrist in such a way that her hand would hook and close itself around a bottle of beer. She never looked back after that.

The last in the ward was Laurie, a middle-aged father of three, who became paraplegic after falling out of a tree. We didn't talk that much, although he was in the bed opposite me. I think he found it very difficult to cope and closed in on himself. I do remember him trying to drink from a can of Guinness once, while he was still lying on his back, and he got into a terrible mess with the beer pouring into his ears.

We were a motley crew of broken-down humans, all coping with our recent dramatic change of circumstances any way we could – some much better than others – and we tried our best to bolster each other through the hard times as well as supporting each other through the good. We cried together and developed an emotional bond that went beyond all the usual social attachments. We were as diverse a group of people as you could find, and yet we all had one thing in common, our disability. Dad understood our unique relationship completely. He said it was exactly like the bond you get between shipmates after months at sea. In many ways, we were all at sea together – bobbing along as best we could and trying not to be engulfed by the crashing waves.

The friends and families also gained emotional support from each other – Steve's family and Becky's were especially wonderful to know, and there was a lot to be learned from each other's experiences, although the lessons weren't always easy. Poor Kevin found the sight of Alice's white-haired husband struggling to push her along in her wheelchair almost too much to bear – the idea of growing old like that, with me dependent on him into pensionable age and beyond, frightened the living daylights out of him. He decided to start on a new health and fitness regime that would keep him strong enough, long enough, to be able to look after me in our old age. When Alice died, of a heart attack in the night, we were all extremely upset. One of the 'team' had fallen by the wayside and it made us all appreciate our own mortality even more, especially when her grief-stricken husband came in the next morning to collect her few belongings.

But life, and the accident rate, went on. Alice was soon replaced in what was a never-ending conveyor belt of unlucky new candidates for the spinal injuries unit. The newest inmate was a fit young man in his twenties called Skip, a lovely bloke from Weston-super-Mare, married with a young daughter. He had the same level of break as me and we went through physiotherapy together. He was equipped with great long arms like an orang-utan, so he was much better than me at a lot of things, and he had a terrific sense of humour. Sadly, his marriage eventually crumbled under the strain of his disability. Watching him desperately trying to come to terms with the fact that things would never be the same again made me thankful that I was past that stage, and made me realize how far I had already progressed.

Others who were in the ward when I was there, as people came and went, included Rowella, a fifteen-year-old. A chimney had fallen on her during the storms of 1990 and she was what is known as an incomplete paraplegic, paralysed from the waist down. The product of a split marriage, she had two televisions because each parent had paid for one, and her attitude was, not surprisingly in the circumstances, to milk the situation for all it was worth.

Another inmate was Mark, your typical wide-boy with a tough-guy exterior, from Paulsgrove, a suburb of Portsmouth. He had a lovely partner, Maz, who was the salt of the earth. Mark was the sort of person I probably wouldn't have cared for at all in ordinary social circumstances before the accident, but thrown together in our unique situation, we were able to scratch beneath the surface, and underneath his I discovered a wicked sense of humour and a heart of gold.

Day by day, the eight of us lay side by side in our beds, in various stages of progress and development. We were brilliantly looked after by the nursing team – people like David Grundy, my consultant and a senior member of the spinal unit. A very quiet, unassuming character, he inspired total confidence and we all felt safe and respected in his care. There was Katrina, the team nurse, whose job it was to make sure we got through all the stages and made it to the exit. She was very efficient, caring and professional. There were the ward sisters, Win and Elizabeth, and the SENs – Elaine, Avril, Amanda, Maggie, Helen, Anne, Jo and Paula, all dedicated professionals too. To my mind, Paula was perhaps the most dedicated spinal nurse of all, someone who had the ability to make me feel like an individual rather than a patient. She knew exactly how far to stretch the boundaries to get the best out of me, and helped to breath 'normality' back into all our lives. It was Paula who eventually took us out to show us life again. A great hugger, she was the same age as me, but had the insight and intuition of someone a good deal older. She was to become a friend to us all.

Some of the best everyday carers were the auxiliary nurses, the ones who have to do the 'nitty gritty' and are there for all the nasty bits – people like Jane, Val, Sonia, Tim, Pearl and Nikki. They were the ones who gave us bed baths or showers, who poured the tea and made us toast. They were real stalwarts, with broad shoulders to cry on and the right sort of empathy for dealing with the likes of us.

If the patients on the ward had one thing in common, it was that we were all completely helpless and dependent on our carers. Surrounded by small tokens of our former lives – treasured photographs of loved ones, cuddly toys, books and games – each one of us lived inside our own private bubble; our range of vision depended on our position or how far we could move or lift our heads. Like babies, we had to be fed and watered, washed and wiped, as well as given drugs and emotional first-aid.

One of the most difficult aspects of being paralysed is to do with the normal bodily functions previously taken for granted and which were always taboo subjects. Everyone has to go to the toilet – we would die if we didn't – but when you can't any longer feel if you need to go, or if you have already been, the whole process becomes a nightmare of indignity after indignity.

The 'bowel round' used to start at five in the morning. To spare our blushes, the nurses tried to do it while we were asleep, and with no sensation in the relevant area it was something that could in fact be achieved while we were sleeping. But, like most on the ward, I was awake the minute I heard the first curtain being pulled around a fellow inmate, and the scrape of the plastic bowl on the trolley.

Lying defenceless on a bed day after day while a stoic nurse in rubber gloves quietly fiddles around down your rear end, manually evacuating your bowels, has to be one of the lowest points in the recovery of the recently disabled. You can feel nothing, the curtains are drawn around you, but you can hear and smell what is happening, and the sadness of being unable even to wipe your own bottom is overwhelming. Every disabled person I have spoken to feels the same way, and all agree that it is only made just bearable by the cheerfulness of the very special people whose unhappy task it is to deal with it.

Most of my darkest moments in those early stages were to do with my depression at losing control over my bodily functions and my menstrual cycle. I didn't even know when I had started my period; the nurses had to tell me, and the shock at the loss of control sent me plummeting again. The nights were always the worst. I would lie in the dark, unable to sleep, wracked with guilt and sadness, wondering what I had done to deserve such a fate. Switching on my little bedside lamp to provide a welcome pool of light, I would read and reread the hundreds of cards and letters I had received from people, most of which said simply how very sorry they were. Their inadequate sentiments echoed my own. Some of the messages were truly heart-warming; it was amazing how some people seemed to know just the right thing to say or do. Others could barely put pen to paper.

People who had previously been just casual acquaintances became stalwarts of cheerful support and dear friends, while a lot of my oldest friends – people I had always expected would be marvellous in a situation like this – completely collapsed and backed off as fast as their legs could carry them. This is how Angie was. She and I had been best friends from the age of eleven and were often mistaken for sisters. Short, dark-haired and pretty, she had always been there for me. We had married at the same time, fallen pregnant at the same time, and even gone into business together, which can be a very dangerous way of stretching a relationship.

Of all the people I considered close, I would have expected her to be the most supportive, to help Kev and the kids, to be a regular visitor to me. But within a few weeks it became clear that she simply couldn't cope with me. Six months pregnant, she devoted herself instead to helping my mum and dad and doing what she could for the people around me. She was grieving so much for the loss of the old Julie that she couldn't see that I was still there, underneath all that unpalatable disability. And the more unable she was to deal with my problems, the more I withdrew from her. It took years for us to rebuild our friendship, and the loss of it at that crucial time pained me greatly.

But there were other, more pressing problems on my mind, chiefly that I still had to come to terms with the fact that I had been handed down a life sentence of permanent disability, with hard labour. The injustice of that, especially when I felt I had committed no crime, cut me to the quick. With the benefit of hindsight, I now appreciate that those sad, lonely nights needed to be borne and that struggling through them helped me enormously. They allowed me the time and the space in a cocooned environment far from the real world to gradually accept what had happened and what was likely to happen in the future. I couldn't change the situation or spend the rest of my life being bitter about it, so I was just going to have to make the most of it.

For Kevin, though, there was no safe haven where he could quietly come to a similar conclusion. He was having to deal with everything on his own – his distress, mine, how it would affect the children, not to mention life in the real world. Having sat the boys down that first day and told them that Mummy wouldn't be home for a little while, he had thought he had covered the basics. It was the best possible time for it to happen, he reasoned – the children were too young to fully understand all the implications and yet too old to need to have me around all the time. He knew he had to become mother and father to them for a while, comforting them when only I would do, organizing their days, coping with the humdrum things of life as well as the much bigger issues crowding into his head. His response was to go into automatic pilot and get on with everything that had to be done, and clamp down on his innermost feelings in case they exploded.

For me, seeing the children for the first time after the accident was very tough. Kevin had discovered by chance, from overhearing the boys whispering, that they secretly believed I was dead and that he had lied to them about my condition. As soon as I found out that they thought I was six feet under, I knew that they had to be brought in to see me, whatever state I might be in. With the nursing staff's agreement, all visible tubes were removed from my head and face. I was half lying, half propped up on a pillow, and I spent the hour before they arrived that Tuesday morning trying to compose my tired features into a welcoming smile until I could almost manage a beam.

I had felt very anxious when they came into the ward; my eyes followed them up the aisle towards my bed. Kevin had told them that I would have to stay in hospital for a long time, and I wondered how they would cope when they saw me. Mum had obviously primed them a bit – they were beautifully washed and groomed, flowers in hand, my two little babies all grown up at six and four and having to face something so hard for them to understand.

'Hello, darlings!' I said, as they came close, stretching out my arms in welcome.

'Hello, Mummy,' they each repeated politely, and stood staring at me as if I was a stranger.

Denied the simple right to reach down and hug them, I tried to show all my joy in my eyes and expression, so that they would be in no doubt that Mummy was fine and happy. It was awkward at first – they were on their best behaviour and so was I – but they soon livened up and it was a joy to be reminded of their boundless energy and vivaciousness. We chatted for a while about the little things, about home and Daddy and school, and they relaxed a bit towards the end. I think the visit probably reassured them – Mummy was fine, she was sick and in bed, but she was alive.

As they turned to leave, each of them gave me a little wave and I bit my lip to stop the tears. The moment the double doors swung shut and the children were out of sight, the dam burst and I started to cry, howling inside for the Mummy they had lost for ever.

But the worst was yet to come. The following Friday Daniel came in to show me his new school uniform. He was starting school on the Monday, a huge event in any child's calendar and in his mother's, and a day it had never occurred to me I might not be there for. Watching him showing off his new outfit, pleased as Punch, the reality of my situation hit me between the eyes like a sledgehammer. I was so helpless, so completely depend-ent on others that I was unable to take part in this major event in my young son's life, a moment that I would never be able to look back on, and my little boy was facing it without me. It was my mother who would see Daniel off on his first day at school; she had stepped into my role and was being a mum again, reading to them, feeding them, being with them, when it should have been me. The tears were pricking my eyes as she and Daniel left the ward, and that night I hit my lowest point yet.

There is one question that everyone in my situation gets to ask themselves at least once on the long road to recovery and rehabilitation. The question is 'Why me?' and the moment you ask it is generally the point where you hit rock bottom, just before you start to come up again. Some never make it back up – the suicide rate is very high among the recently paralysed. I know now that the answer to the question is 'Why *not* me?' when so many around me had better cause for despair than I had. But on that longest of long nights, the answer escaped me and I wept inconsolably, comforted by a wonderful auxiliary nurse known as 'Auntie Val', who was a kind friend to us all.

The only advantage to hitting rock bottom is that from that moment on, the only way to go is up. My crying days were over for a while, and I knew that I had to get on and go forward, for the boys' sake if nothing else. Not that it was always easy putting on a courageous face. As a wider circle of friends and relatives started to visit me, peeping apprehensively out from behind even more bouquets of flowers, they relaxed visibly at the sight of my scar-free, smiling face beaming back at them and welcoming them to my 'humble home'. They would arrive at the spinal injuries unit braced for doom and gloom, and leave positively upbeat. 'Julie's doing fine, Julie's a fighter, she's so brave,' they would tell each other and themselves, relieved that I wasn't suicidal.

We settled into a proper little routine, Kevin, my parents and I. They seemed to be coping brilliantly without me, something that hurt just a little, but it meant at least that I could concentrate on getting well. Kevin came to see me two or three times a week and I saw the children for an hour every Saturday and phoned them every day to see how they were. I wanted to know about every single thing they had done; it was a vital point of contact for me. They brought me pictures and presents, chattered animatedly about nothing in particular, as I sat there straining to appear well and cheerful. By the time a visit was over or a call had been made, I was always completely drained, flopping back on to my pillows and giving in to a tiredness the like of which I had never known before.

Back home, my mum and Kevin were trying to keep everything as normal as possible for the kids, but Kevin soon came to resent what he felt was her interference; both my parents seemed to be treating me like a child again, and they treated my husband much the same. Mum was only trying to help, but she probably did too much. Supported by her best friend Doris, who had been a tower of strength to her ever since my accident – even though it had brought back terrible memories of her son Christopher's fatal crash – Mum and Dad helped Kev with the washing, the cooking and the ironing, cleaning the house, and sorting out the boys' clothes for school.

Kevin was throwing himself into his new job, then when he got home after work he began decorating every room of the house we had only lived in for a few months before the accident, coming into the ward with wallpaper samples and paint colour charts for me to help him choose. It was his form of therapy – he was never one for opening up to other people and he couldn't begin to now. Friends who attempted to help him, who tried to persuade him to tell them what he was feeling, got the brush-off. Nobody could get close, especially not me. The shutters had come down and it was all he could do to keep himself going. During his visits to me he hardly said a word, and although I knew what he must be going through I took umbrage at his brooding silences at a time when I needed him to be there for me. From his point of view, I seemed to be moving further and further away from him as I formed closer relationships with the people around me. Inevitably, I was surrounded by people on whom I relied for everything from empty-ing my bladder to keeping me going emotionally, and as time went on I felt that I was getting more love from my new friends and acquaintances than from my own husband – and I told him so, which only served to button his lip tighter still.

Try as he might in those early stages, Kevin couldn't see beyond my disability. He couldn't see *me* any more – Julie, his wife, the woman to whom he had been married for ten years; who had first become infatuated with him as a naive fifteen-year-old. He had always seemed so sure of himself back then, the grown-up accountant with a car and a career path and a clear idea of what he wanted to achieve. A decade and two children later, after spending those years struggling to better ourselves, we had a lovely home, company cars and a golden future. It wasn't until the accident that I realized how much we had drifted apart.

Ever since the crash, Kevin had been on the brink. Unable to cope emotionally, hardly able to bear thinking about what had happened to me, what it meant for our life together as a family, he had battled on, pretending to be on top of things, dealing with his job, the house, the children, the shopping, my parents, sitting dutifully at my bedside – when all the time he was screaming inside. 'Why me?' is a question often asked by the people close to an injured person too.

He had become paranoid about wheelchairs, ever since that first night at Salisbury when he found himself surrounded by them. Having never even noticed any before, he started to see them wherever he went – in the supermarket, in the street, at the pub at lunchtime, as he was driving home. He began to think that there was a conspiracy, that they were out to get him, to punish him for making me have the accident. Seeing one in the middle of his working day would be enough to turn his blood cold. Wheelchairs swamped him by day and haunted him at night.

Although he was on a good wage, he was also desperately concerned about money and our financial future. My firm, Harfield's, had sacked me a week after the accident, claiming that as I was still on probation and had written off the company car they were not liable to give me either invalidity or redundancy pay. Kevin was sick with worry – our huge mortgage payments had been dependent on both our incomes, and now there were the added expenses of adapting the house to suit my needs for when I eventually came home. Selling up and moving to a bungalow became a real possibility, although I was dead against it, arguing that there was only one disabled person in the family, not four.

On one particularly bad night, when Kev had come home from a very trying day at the office, still not sure if the new job was right for him, he found the kids tucked up in bed, his supper cooked by my mum and ready waiting in the microwave, the lawn mowed, the ironing done, the house spotless, silent and still. Breaking down for the first time in weeks, he wept for the loss of his wife, of his old life, the former domestic routines that now seemed so perfect by comparison. 'Oh God,' he railed, unable to see beyond his despair.

Wiping his eyes, he went upstairs and stood silently by an open window looking out on to the garden. Feeling that life was too much to bear, he began soul-searching and looking for a way out of his predicament. 'I could do myself in, here,' he thought to himself, coolly assessing the twenty-foot drop to the patio below. 'I could fall from this window and jack it all in now.' It seems incredible to me now, and to him, that he seriously considered killing himself as an option. It would have been a course of action so completely alien to his calm and placid nature that it now seems almost laughable. But in that dark hour he saw it as a possible answer to his problems, an escape from the awful future that now stretched out ahead of him. He hated himself for being so negative and he wished he could be more positive, but he didn't have it in him. With him out of the way, he thought, our lives might be less complicated. I would be well looked after by the hospital and my parents, and he would be at peace from the torments of the life that was now his.

Forcing himself away from the window, he walked across the landing to the children's bedroom, where he stood in the doorway and watched our young sons sleeping, blissfully unaware, their thumbs in their mouths, and with their furry toys arranged all around them as usual. Although he had never expected to want children, their arrival had opened up a part of his heart he didn't know existed, and he loved them more than life itself. Silently, he began to cry again. Seeing them so peaceful and thinking of how they would feel when they found him dead in the morning was the only thing that stopped him ending it all there and then. He closed the door, then took himself off to bed so as to be ready to face another day.

Meanwhile, I was facing demons of my own. In the four weeks I had spent flat on my back in the ward, I had watched others all around me progress from their beds to wheelchairs with a mixture of horror and fascination. I had never quite been able to imagine a connection between me and such a device. My life had never been touched by disability before – no one I knew, friends or relatives, had ever been disabled – and the experience was new and more than a little frightening. When the day arrived for me to be moved out of the safe harbour of my bed and placed in a wheelchair for a fifteen-minute trial period, I was filled with dread. After a month of lying down with just a gradual increase in the tilt of my bed, the very idea of being fully upright and suddenly mobile was not one I relished at all.

My nursing team, Paula, Avril and Katrina, headed by Val, the physiotherapist who had been building up my body to prepare me for this moment, arrived. It all seemed so momentous. The steel and leather chair was wheeled forward and studied carefully by us all. As I lay there, helpless, they dressed me in a sweatshirt and put jogging bottoms (the uniform of the disabled) on my leaden legs, after a lot of undignified manipulating and contorting. They put my feet into hideous white trainers that were several sizes too big so as to avoid pressure sores. Then, to my great dismay, I was manhandled into a huge plastic body brace that would enable me to sit upright. The idea of the brace was that it would support my broken spine, so it had to be incredibly tight around my waist and chest. By the time it was all laced up, I looked like something out of the Jane Fonda film *Barbarella*, my boobs squeezed upwards and forwards in a very uncomfortable position. It was May 1990, baking hot, and I was just about ready to pass out with the heat and exertion before I had even got near the damned chair.

My ever cheerful nursing team now gathered around me for the big moment, and with a 'One, two, three' they swung me up and out of the bed and dumped me into the chair.

Looking up at them from my new position, feeling quite dizzy and sick at being suddenly upright, it was all I could do to stop myself screaming: 'Put me back!' I felt completely mortified sitting in this contraption – it was totally alien to me. A thousand thoughts raced through my head. 'What are people going to think? How will they view me now? This is horrible.' But there was the team all beaming down at me, seemingly delighted with my sudden transition from bedridden invalid to fully fledged paraplegic.

They obviously expected me to smile back or at least show some sort of sign that I was pleased with my progress, but I couldn't. Far from liking my supposed new-found freedom, I felt desperately unhappy at what seemed to me to be the brutal ending to all my secret hopes of ever being able to walk again. When you are sick, you are in bed in hospital. When you are better, you get up and go home. For me, I now realized, there was to be no getting up. This was it, my prison for the rest of my life. I was encased in plastic and metal and leather and I hated it.

Unbothered by my downcast expression, Val wheeled me out of the door and along the corridor for my first glimpse of life outside the acute ward, before pushing me through the double doors of the bustling physiotherapy room, a huge, light and airy place that had, all the same, an atmosphere of disappointed endeavour. I loathed the chair, I resented leaving the ward, and I felt extremely unwell experiencing motion for the first time in a month. Catching a glimpse of myself in the full-length mirror for the first time since the accident, I gasped inwardly at my own reflection. It wasn't the haggard face, the withered legs or the dishevelled hair that shocked me, but the broken body, slumped awkwardly in the ugly apparatus which was to be my outer skin for the rest of my life. In that instant my self-esteem hit the floor and stayed there for what seemed like a very long time. I didn't like what I saw one little bit, and with the combination of the shock and the exertion I vomited and passed out. I was immediately whisked back to the cosy haven of life between the sheets, but the empty wheelchair was left menacingly by my bed.

The next day I had to do it all over again, and it took several hours for the nursing staff to cajole me into trying the chair out again. The way the unit worked was that each one of us patients was in charge of our own team. If we wanted to sit and do nothing, we could, but we would be gently persuaded into action before too long. What I needed was a good talking to, and after a morning of sulky inactivity I got one from Paula. 'What are you going to do – stay in bed for the rest of your life?' she asked. 'There's a whole new life waiting for you out there and you can only get there by getting out of bed and into that chair.' She was right, I knew, and the second time it didn't feel quite so alien, although it was still very strange, sitting in my National Health Service 'tank' with its cumbersome, unwieldy ways.

The reactions of my family to the first sight of me in a chair were mixed. Kevin stayed stony-faced and silent, his jaw clenching and unclenching as he fought to control his emotions. As it had for me, the wheelchair represented his very worst fears; it marked a point of no return and he felt so negative about it, so angry at its intrusion into our lives, that he could hardly bear to open his mouth to speak. Mum burst into tears when she first saw me in it. I had wheeled myself to the day room we called 'the potting shed', where she was sitting having a cigarette, and popped my head round the corner at her. She quickly recovered herself, gave me a hug and the two of us went for a wander down the corridor.

But it was the boys' reaction that I dreaded the most. I was so worried that they would see me as some sort of monster in a machine, and be frightened by it. I needn't have worried, though. At their first sight of me upright for a change, they grinned from ear to ear, then leapt full pelt into my arms and demanded a ride. Life is so black and white for children; if I wasn't in bed any more then I must be getting better. The chair was just another way of getting me around. From that day to this, they have never once been fazed by it.

I had no choice but to get on with my life and all that it had thrown at me. From then on, I was in training for how to be a paraplegic. It's something that has to be learned and slowly memorized, all the little routines and health and safety measures. It took many months before I was truly comfortable with my wheelchair, and it wasn't helped by having to wear the body brace for four months during the summer. I hated myself, I loathed my body, and I developed an unhealthy obsession with the way my feet looked on the foot-plate. If they weren't exactly together, neatly side by side, I believed I looked like a cripple.

I became very particular about how I looked. My clothes had to be just right – as far as that was possible, given that skirts and dresses were banned for ever on the basis that they rode up and snagged on the metal parts of the chair, plus they allowed my legs to be shown, two dead and useless items I no longer wanted to exhibit.

It was a long time before I came to realize that I was actually very lucky. Because my break was at T9, half an inch above my belly button, I had full use of my arms and upper body. Also, I learned later, spinal patients are regarded as the elite among the disabled. So I was 'in with the in crowd' and slowly, gradually, it made me feel a whole lot better about my situation, even if I knew that all this would change the minute I went back to living in the real world.

Pushing me ever closer to that world in preparation for my re-entry into it, the staff at the hospital informed me I was ready to go on my first official outing – a day trip to the New Forest, with Kev and the boys. There would be no staff, no one else to help me – just the Hill family, on their own for the day. Although the boys were clearly excited by the prospect, I was absolutely terrified. Kev was less than enthusiastic and did little to prepare for the big day. Paula explained that he would have to be trained to perform what is known as a 'standing transfer', to move me from my wheelchair to the car or any other surface by way of a tight, face-to-face bear hug. On her instruction, Kev had reluctantly come into the ward one afternoon and been trained to do it by one of the physiotherapists – a mortifying experience for me, when I caught sight of myself in the mirror and realized that my track-suit bottoms had slid down during the transfer, showing off a 'builder's bum'. Once he had mastered the technique, Kev left without a word, and I wondered if he was finding the process as difficult to cope with as me.

By the time the big event approached, I was on

tenterhooks. I so much wanted it to be a day that we could all enjoy and remember. It would be the first stage in what I hoped would be a recovery phase for us all. But a few days beforehand, Kev left me in no doubt that he wasn't going to be able to cope. 'I'm not going to be able to make it,' he told me unexpectedly, giving me some unconvincing excuse. I felt shattered and deeply hurt. But my dear little brother Neil stepped in, and offered to take me out instead.

On the morning of the outing, I woke early to prepare myself for the ordeal ahead. I was so frightened of making a fool of myself, of wetting my knickers, falling from the car or slipping from Neil's grip. I didn't want to do anything that would embarrass him or his girlfriend Bridget in public. My hands felt clammy with nerves and I was smoking eighteen to the dozen. When Neil arrived he could sense my nervousness, and he sat down on the bed next to my chair and took my hand. Tall, lean and fit, with short dark hair and big brown eyes, he was a quiet, reserved young man and extremely loving, something I hadn't appreciated earlier in my life. 'Don't worry, Jules,' he said. Seeing the look in my eyes, he added softly: 'It'll be fine.'

I looked apprehensively from his face to Bridget's. They clearly expected me to burst into tears. Neil, of all people, knew that I very well could. Beaming at them suddenly, I grabbed the wheels of my chair and started moving forward, scattering them in my path. 'Come on then,' I said, gleefully. 'I'm dying for a pint.'

Neil's face lit up with relief, and he patted his jacket pocket. 'No probs,' he said, 'I've got plenty of cash.' We laughed together companionably and prepared to set off on our pub crawl. What I had forgotten was that it was

Kev, not Neil, who had been trained to make standing transfers – and Kev wasn't here.

'No worries,' Neil piped up again. 'Give me a quick crash course and I'll do it.' And so my little brother, the person I had kicked and bitten and scrapped with throughout our childhood, was now quickly taught by Jane, one of the auxiliary nurses, how to perform this rather difficult technique. God bless him, he was a natural – and he even managed to avoid me getting the dreaded 'builder's bum'. He was brilliant.

In spite of Kev's absence, or maybe because of it, I can honestly say that I had the most terrific day. Neil was an absolute trooper, carrying me in and out of his little Triumph Spitfire as we toured almost every pub in the New Forest. The sun was shining, the pubs were friendly, and we downed one delicious glass of beer after another. The wheelchair completely ruined Neil's credibility, strapped to the boot of his Spitfire, but he never batted an eyelid. He must have transferred me a dozen times that day. He wanted me to go everywhere and do everything, even if I occasionally complained that it wasn't worth the hassle.

All the years of brother–sister rivalry lay behind us now, and more than Kev so far had, Neil had treated me as if I was me, not a disabled person. From that day on, we became the very best of friends. Bridget, too, was wonderful. A postal worker with a fine arts degree, incredibly bright but rather shy, she never once made me feel awkward, and wasn't at all fazed by my disability. By the time she and Neil delivered me back to the hospital, I was high on a heady combination of happiness and alcohol. It was almost enough to make me forget that Kev had let me down.

SIX

Glimmerings

I SPENT the next six months in Salisbury District Hospital, moving further and further towards the exit, a prospect which continued to fill me with dread. I was terrified of life on the outside; I only felt comfortable with my new status when I was surrounded by people who were in a similar position. What would it be like being Julie Hill again, back in my own home, having to interact with my friends and relatives and neighbours? Wouldn't I feel the odd one out in every conceivable way? A big part of me wanted to stay in the acute ward for the rest of my life.

My recovery wasn't textbook. There were several setbacks, including a life-threatening deep-vein thrombosis, or DVT, in my leg exactly seven days after I had first sat in the wheelchair. A DVT is a blood clot caused by long periods of muscle inactivity, and it's a fairly common problem for the recently paralysed. My legs were regularly measured to see if there was any new swelling which might have indicated the presence of a clot. The problem is that if one forms, then breaks away from its position in the vein and works its way to either the heart or the brain, it can be fatal, causing a massive heart attack or stroke.

Once a clot had been identified, I had to be kept flat on my back with blood-thinning medication to stop it travelling around my body, and monitored daily to see if there was any new swelling that would indicate that another was building. The condition put me back in bed for ten days, undoing all the progress I had made. It was a real stumbling block and deeply distressing for me. I had just reached the stage where all I wanted was to get up and on, to learn the wheelchair skills and keep progressing, but now I was back to square one and just as miserable.

The new daily obsession with my legs did nothing to help me come to terms with the loss of their use. Once the medical staff had pulled back the covers, measured and manipulated them and then left me alone again, I would sit staring at them, willing them to work, the sweat beading on my forehead with effort and concentration. Perhaps there had been a medical misdiagnosis, I would reason, perhaps through sheer will and bloody-minded determination I could make them move again. It was several days before I realized that it was a completely pointless exercise – I had irreversibly severed the connection between my thought processes and the muscles that would work my legs. I would just have to accept a life without them.

More humiliating than anything were my continuing bladder problems. I was constantly wet, unable to know when I had been to the toilet or needed to go again. I gave myself the nickname 'Old Slack Bladder' to try and make a tragic situation semi-comic, but it didn't help, especially when I left puddles of urine all over the floor or on the physiotherapy mats. It was so depressing. A big part of the rehabilitation for paraplegics is learning how to master the use of intermittent catheters and to measure your input so that you can know what the output will be and when. In the end, I became so frustrated by being constantly wet that I asked to go back to the first system I had used when I arrived at Salisbury, a normal catheter attached to an ungainly leg bag (a urine-collection device strapped to my leg).

'That's a move backwards rather than forwards, Julie,' my physio, Val, warned me ominously. The staff were not in the habit of permitting backward moves. In the language of the unit, we were meant to be moving together to a newer, brighter future. I sometimes felt like a member of a political party.

'I don't fucking care,' I snapped. 'I just don't want to leak all over the floor like an old lady any more.' My patience was wearing very thin and it showed in my uncharacteristically angry outburst.

Not surprisingly in the face of my obvious distress, the nursing staff eventually agreed to my demands and allowed me to go back to the more primitive system. As they had predicted, the leg bag did absolutely nothing for my self-esteem, and I sank very low psychologically again. It was because of this problem that later, at my insistence, I ended up having a number of operations on my bladder to try to improve my continence level, each one of which cost a great deal of time and patience.

The only thing that kept me going at this point was my new-found zeal for fitness. Intensive physiotherapy was building my upper body strength, something I desperately wanted to improve upon so that I could be more independent. If only I could transfer myself from my bed to my wheelchair without help, I could make my own way to the lavatory and deal with the leg bag and other toilet-training aspects myself. Until that time, I was still locked into my Barbarella body brace and completely dependent on others.

A highlight of my week was swimming in the hospital physio pool – a really odd experience when you have no sensation below the waist. I could see the water rising up my body, but could never feel it until it reached my ribcage. Unable to control my legs, although I could float on my back reasonably well, if I turned face down I sank or tilted dangerously sideways under the water. It was all very new and frightening, but quite exhilarating to be weightless.

One unexpected bonus to being more independent and mobile in the chair was my new-found social life on the ward. I had earned the right to enter the halfway world of those about to return to life on the outside. I had notched myself up a rank in the eyes of the nursing staff and was able to claw back a few grains of self-esteem. It felt good to sit chatting and having a beer with my new mates in the potting shed. I could even wheel myself along to the canteen and have a meal with my visitors if I wanted to. It was a very gradual transition towards the exit and, although I still feared it, I was gently building up my courage to face it.

By the eighth week I was just about ready for my second trip outside the ward, a Wednesday afternoon shopping trip into Salisbury, organized by Val, the physiotherapist. 'It'll be a good opportunity for you to see how easy it is to cope in the great outdoors,' she told the five of us who were going. There was me, Jim, Skip, Laurie and Mark.

What she failed to mention was that the bustling city of Salisbury, with its narrow medieval streets, high kerbs and uneven York stone pavements, was one of the most inaccessible places for someone in a wheelchair. Every shop was approached by steep steps. So many pavements seemed to peter out to accommodate the city gates. It was June and the streets were thronged with tourists. I felt as if every single person who passed me struggling along the cobbled walkways was staring at me, their eyes boring into my soul, pityingly. It was a nightmare.

Not long after disembarking from the minibus and attempting to negotiate the impossible street, we staged a mutiny. 'We want to go to a pub and have a beer,' Laurie announced, and we all thumped our hands on our wheels in unified protest. Val reluctantly agreed, and directed us to one of the only pubs in town with disabled access – which was round the back, past stinking barrels and food debris. Once we got inside, bolstered by Dutch courage, we became quite rowdy. After a while, when people came in and stared at the six of us in a circle round a low table, the lads I was with gave them what they expected – dribbling and drooling and looking for all the world like helpless imbeciles. We laughed so much and drank so much beer that I was never more grateful for the extra-large leg bag.

It was certainly an experience, a taster for life on the outside, but it was not one that I can say I really enjoyed. Before the accident, I was just like anyone else whose life has not been touched by disability; I knew all the social conventions, I had all the awful, preconceived ideas of what disabled people were like, and now – suddenly, unexpectedly – I *was* one. Being amongst the public, seeing the looks in their eyes, only served to remind me of that and how much my life had changed. It hurt more than I can say.

There were several more acclimatization trips, to get me used to the world outside the unit, but none of them really did the trick. On one, I went to see Angie after the birth of her third child, Rowan, and found myself unable to cradle her new baby properly in my arms because of my ongoing balance problems in the wheelchair. Sitting up when you can't feel your bottom or waist is an extraordinary sensation – it makes you wobble, until you get used to it. By gripping the wheels or the arms of the chair, I was able to centre myself and stay balanced; but when I took my arms off, I felt as precarious as if I was standing on a tightrope for the first time. Trying desperately to cradle Rowan without dropping him, close to tears at the realization that I couldn't even hold a baby without feeling awkward, I began to appreciate just how far I had yet to go.

The trips outside the hospital also served to remind me how much had to be sorted out at home before I would be able to move back in. Kev and I had never really talked about how it would be when that happened, how we would cope. But by coming to appreciate the importance of disabled access, the need for ramps and wide doors and large turning circles, I knew that our lovely new house, the dream house I had always wanted, was inaccessible to me in its present state.

'We need to work some things out,' I told a sullen Kev on one of his weekend visits to see me. 'I've been talking to some of the others and apparently we need to see if the social services will help us pay for the changes we need to make to the house when I come home.' Kev just blanked me at first. He couldn't bear to think about all that, to consider the life that was to come – the one where he and I and the kids would be in that house on our own and would actually have to get on with it. Eventually, with gentle cajoling and some pressure from my parents, enquiries were made, and the answer that came back shocked me.

'You'll have to move,' a representative from the social services said after a first inspection. 'You can't possibly stay in that house, it's completely unsuitable to Mrs Hill's needs.' Their next comment staggered us. They offered to pay the mortgage on a new, more suitable property, if Kevin left work and stayed home to care for me full-time. It would save them considerable time and money, they argued, if he was to become a full-time carer. The idea appalled both of us and we both said no immediately. From then on it felt as if the social services virtually washed their hands of us, telling us that we were on our own.

In response to the stance they were taking, our friends and relatives very kindly set up a trust fund which produced £6,000 for the alterations necessary to our home, raising the money by anything from sponsored runs to a sponsored sail the wrong way round the Isle of Wight. Among those involved were Neil and Paul Bridger, two friends who enlisted the help of the British judo champion Neil Adams. Others sent cheques as a way of expressing their solidarity. I was humbled by people's kindness. Even Charles Church, the company who had built our home, rose to the occasion. They agreed to erect the special ramps up to the front door for free. To our delight, having heard what others were doing, the social services eventually agreed to pay a contribution towards the overall cost. By the time all the money had been counted, we had enough to pay for a small wheelchair lift in the house to take me from floor to floor and to widen the doorways. The back garden path would have to be tarmacked so that my wheelchair wouldn't get bogged down, and we would have to have an automatic device fitted to the front door and garage doors for easy access.

There was even better news to come. As I had been working at the time of the accident, we had put in a claim for disability benefit for my 'industrial injuries', not really believing that we would get it. We were more than pleased when the authorities agreed. The money meant that our immediate financial worries were over and I would be given enough to cover my loss of income and to allow us to stay in our existing home. The down side was that it meant if I ever went back to work again, I would forfeit the benefit. There was some small part of me, even then, that resented that. Just as I had been getting my confidence back after motherhood and forging my career as a saleswoman, everything had been snatched away from me. Now, I was not only going to find it difficult to go back to work because of my disability, but the benefit system I was locked into would actively discourage it. I seemed destined to a life of domesticity and boredom.

There were, of course, many advantages to having the money, and I was truly grateful for it. At least it would allow me to be mobile – I now qualified for a specially adapted car under the Motability scheme, which allows disabled people to buy a new car every few years at a tremendous discount. It would be specially fitted with an automatic gearbox and hand controls, so that I would be able to drive to and from school, to the shops

and to see my parents. I wouldn't be housebound or dependent on others all the time. It was a tremendous boost to my long-term hopes for independence.

With my worsening relationship with Kevin becoming a real cause for concern, I needed all the help I could get. By now, he was a completely closed book and had turned down all offers of help. There was counselling available at the hospital if he wanted it, and unofficial counselling on hand from any number of friends, but the thought appalled him. We had become so distant that the few conversations we had became more and more strained, and I felt we had never been so close to splitting up. I even braced myself for it – I know I was including it subconsciously in the plans I was making for life outside the spinal unit. This is why the car meant so much to me. I knew that with my own transport, I could probably manage without him.

Things eventually came to a head one lovely warm evening in July, three months after the accident. Kevin and I were sitting in the quadrangle outside the entrance to the spinal unit, ostensibly to enjoy the night air. But there was no joy between us by this time. Talking to him was like pulling teeth. He had grown increasingly distant in the previous weeks, to the point that we had reached an all-time low. At this crucial stage in my recovery, I had to know what the future held for us before I started making plans to come home. However much the idea frightened me, I knew that I had to give him an ultimatum. It had been a long time coming, and on that particular night, the moment felt right.

'We've got a long and bumpy road ahead of us, Kev,' I told him slowly, willing him to take in the importance of what I was saying as he studied his hands. 'I need to know whether you will be staying with me because you want to,' I continued, 'or out of pity.' His eyes flickered as he registered what I meant. Drawing a deep breath, I concluded: 'If you're staying out of pity, I think it might be better if you left.'

I knew that I was strong enough by this stage to cope on my own physically; to take care of me and the kids and get around. What that would feel like emotionally, without Kev, I couldn't dare imagine. Just the thought of it made me feel sick to my stomach with fear and sadness, but I knew that this moment had to be faced and a decision made. As I watched and waited for his response, seeing him look away and hesitate, I just prayed he would make the one that meant he would stay.

Kevin rose fluidly to his feet. He looked down at me as my eyes filled with tears, willing him to stay. Without saying a word, he turned on his heel and left, a look of such concentration on his face that I knew he was going home to seriously consider his options. I stayed out in the quadrangle almost until nightfall, sobbing my heart out, agonizing over whether I had done the right thing, wishing that I had said more. Smoking one cigarette from the previous one and chewing on my nails, I put myself through mental torture. Had I made the biggest mistake of my life? What if he took me up on my offer and left? What would that mean for me, and the children? They needed their father. Divorce had never been on the cards for us before, but now, because of one stupid moment at the wheel, our life, our whole future, hung in the balance.

Paula, the English nurse to whom I had grown closest, came out some time later and gave me a hug.

She had watched from the window as Kevin left, and suspected the worst. The break-up rate of relationships between the recently disabled and their partners is understandably high, and I wondered how many other weeping wives or husbands she had comforted at times like this. We hardly spoke – there was nothing she could do or say to ease my pain. As with all the nurses in the spinal unit, her best skill was simply being there to help people pick up the pieces when they fell apart.

That night felt like the longest of my life. I hardly slept a wink, mentally tossing and turning, going through all the 'what ifs' and 'whys'. I couldn't bear the idea of moving. I wanted to stay in our lovely home, with the boys – all three of them, Nathan, Daniel and Kevin. I remembered back to when Kev and I first met, to our courtship and our glorious wedding day. I remembered the boys being born, seeing Kevin cry as he held each of them in his arms. We had worked and saved, scrimped and struggled to buy the home we longed for and achieve the lifestyle that we wanted for us and our children. It had all been going so well; even though Kevin and I had grown apart, it was nothing we couldn't handle and we'd fully expected to be celebrating our golden wedding anniversary together some day.

It was dawn before I finally drifted off to sleep, and I was out cold when someone suddenly shook me awake. It was six o'clock, and one of the night nurses was telling me that there was an urgent phone call. She brought the telephone to the bed and handed it to me, then left as I shakily picked up the receiver. 'Hello,' I said, my voice hoarse with tiredness.

Kevin sounded equally exhausted. 'Just to let you know,' he said, 'I've done nothing but think all night.'

There was a pause and I held my breath, waiting for his next sentence. When it came I could hardly believe my ears.

'I'm staying,' he said. 'And I'm staying because I want to.'

There was another pause. I couldn't speak.

'See ya,' he concluded, his voice catching. The receiver went dead.

Kevin's decision to stay with me was as much of a commitment to our future together as his marriage vows had been. Maybe more so. It was a watershed moment that allowed us to put the accident behind us and tentatively move on. From then on, we both knew there could be no secret recriminations. He wasn't to blame himself for being so unkind on the phone that night, and I wasn't to blame myself for driving badly. My tyre burst and could have done so at any time, with similar consequences. It was as simple as that, and to have dwelt any more on the guilt we shared would only have been destructive.

But his early-morning call to tell me he was staying wasn't an instant fix. It wasn't as if he could suddenly cope, any more than I could, after just one sleepless night of self-questioning. We still had a very long way to go, and when he came in to the hospital to see me the next day, anybody watching us together wouldn't have noticed much difference. There was still that awkwardness, that shy uncertainty, and we both felt very wary of anything the other said. But a point had been reached, and passed. We had decided to stay together, come what might, and that did ease the tension slightly.

A week or so later it was my twenty-ninth birthday,

and it had been decided that, as a treat, I should be allowed home for the day for a small party, attended by my family and friends and some of the staff from the hospital. Although it was I who had suggested several weeks earlier going home for my birthday as a 'goal' to be aimed for, now that the day loomed I was dreading it. I couldn't imagine what it would be like, having both the old and the new people in my life all together in the same place. I had seen Kev recoil from the sight of more than one of us in wheelchairs and I wondered how others would react.

I was right to be fearful. The party was absolutely awful. Although Kev and my parents had gone to a great deal of trouble, setting up a bar and a barbecue in Mum and Dad's garden, it quickly became a 'them' and 'us' situation, with me, Becky and the five nurses – Paula, Andrea, Elaine, Nikki and Claire – on one side, drinking too much, being too noisy and misbehaving as usual, while Kev and my parents, cousins, aunts and uncles watched stiffly from a distance, wishing it would all end soon and that they could go home. The only people who enjoyed themselves were Nathan and Daniel, delighted to see me out of hospital and spending a lot of the day clambering excitedly over my wheelchair.

By the time the minibus pulled up outside to take us back to the hospital, we were all eager to leave. Taking Kev's hand, I squeezed it and told him: 'Thanks, love, it was great,' but my eyes told him I was lying and his face told me all I needed to know. It had been a disaster. Staring sadly out of the minibus window on the way back to the hospital, I wondered if I would ever be able to feel comfortable in my home environment again or – perhaps more to the point – if Kev and the rest of the family would ever be able to completely accept me as the disabled person I now was.

A month later, in August of that year, while still an inmate at Salisbury, I went on a remarkable journey. Becky's friends and family had organized a sponsored swim on her behalf, between Guernsey and Herm, to raise money for her much-needed trust fund, and they had invited her to go and watch. 'Come with me, Julie?' she pleaded. 'It'll be so much easier to face if you're there too, for moral support.'

'But Guernsey is an island,' I said, rather pathetically. 'How on earth will we get there?' Becky just smiled and knew that I wouldn't let her down. Kev wasn't at all happy, and neither was the hospital at first. It was only when Paula and Elaine volunteered to go with us as carers that the powers-that-be gave their permission. Then, when Elaine couldn't make it at the last minute, we thought our trip was doomed – that was, until the amazing Paula assured everyone that she could look after the two of us on her own, an act of such selflessness and caring that we were both incredibly moved by it.

Beck's family arranged the whole thing and organized the sponsorship we needed. We were taken to Poole and wheeled on to a ferry, where we had our own berths. Peter, one of Becky's brothers, and Anton, her boyfriend, accompanied us. Anton had been around since before the accident and had stayed with Becky inspite of her disability. Sadly, their relationship failed in the end when Becky felt too stifled by Anton's protectiveness and called the whole thing off. But, for that weekend, everything was sweetness and light. We had a brilliant time; we stayed in a hotel called La Villette, and

Paula was a star, shifting and lifting us from chair to bed and into cars.

The plan was that, on the day of the sponsored swim, we were to follow the swimmers in a small boat, shouting our encouragement. The distance was a couple of miles and the swim was to be undertaken in relays. We were driven to the quay to get into our boat, then Paula wheeled Becky along the jetty, with me following on behind under my own steam. 'Where's the boat?' Paula asked innocently, unable to see one waiting. Peter pointed to the tip of a mast, at wheelchair level, belonging to a boat ten feet below us – and was instantly aware how foolish it had been to imagine that we would easily be able to climb aboard.

'No worries,' Paula said, dismissively waving the problem away. 'We'll manage.' And manage we did. With a lot of manhandling and lifting between them, we were gently lowered into the boat and set off to sea. It was an incredible weekend. To feel the wind in our hair and the spray on our faces as the boat bobbed along behind the swimmers, and to hear the gulls circling overhead, gave Becky and me the most enormous psychological boost. Anything felt possible. The swim was a great success, raising thousands of pounds for Becky, and the two of us returned to Salisbury, changed women.

During the next few months, I was moved further and further towards the main door in preparation for going home. In the last four weeks of my time there, I was placed in a single room on my own, right next to the exit. Although a big part of me wanted to escape the confines of the acute ward and be a mother again to the boys, an even bigger part wanted to stay, and I often viewed the 'Exit' sign with nothing short of horror. In spite of the freedom the Guernsey trip had given me, and the joys of going out with Neil and Bridget, I was well aware that life wasn't all high days and holidays. It was about the ordinary, day-to-day existence of living again with my family, of sleeping next to my husband and dealing with my own bodily functions in my own bathroom. A lot of my concerns were to do with how I would cope with that.

My fears weren't helped by an acclimatization trip home, accompanied by an occupational therapist and a social worker, who wheeled me from room to room to see how I could get along in the chair. The lift hadn't been installed yet, so it was agreed that the dining-room would become our bedroom for the time being, Kev's and mine. Apart from that problem, I was expected to be able to cope with everything else on the ground floor. It felt so strange, being back in the house that I had only really known for a few months before the accident. Since then, Kev had completely redecorated it. It felt like somebody else's home. I didn't even know where the basic household items were now kept.

In the countdown to my departure, two months before it was to happen, Kev and the boys and I were all despatched to the adaptive-living flat, a self-contained apartment in the spinal unit just beyond the physiotherapy department, in which patients and their families are expected to spend a weekend getting to know one another again. It was late August and one of the hottest weekends of the year, which would have been bad enough, but in an airless flat, the four of us crammed in together – Kev and I sleeping in the same bed together for the first time since the accident – it felt absolutely stifling.

I have never felt more awkward in my life than I did that weekend. I had to get myself in and out of bed, in and out of the toilet and attend to all my catheters and bags. I was incredibly self-conscious, which only added to the strain. Sex was, fortunately, completely out of the question anyway. It was thirty degrees, and although the bed was a huge double one we couldn't bear to be within a foot of each other because of the heat. Making love was absolutely the last thing on either of our minds. It was an unbearably uncomfortable time for me – although Kev and the boys claimed to be enjoying themselves – and all I wanted was to wheel myself back down the corridor to the familiar, comfortable world I knew.

Having survived that, though, I was then sent home every weekend for the next four weeks, something which continued to fill me with dread. The 'home' I was going to, it seemed to me, was Kev's, not ours. It was an alien place, a house in which Kev and the boys had lived alone for several months and set up their own little routines, none of which I knew anything about. Between them, Kev, Mum and Dad had kept the place spotless while I was in hospital, mowing the grass, vacuuming, cleaning, washing and ironing. They had created a comfort zone, a haven of calm in which they could be buffered from the tragedy of our new situation.

When I was home, that safe haven was shattered; within minutes of me coming in the door, everything seemed to be in a mess. The wheelchair left muddy tracks on the carpet and spread mud just about everywhere else.

I couldn't keep on top of the chores, the place looked like a pigsty; the room arrangements were all changed to accommodate me and we seemed to have far less space than I remembered.

I felt little more than an intruder in my own home. Surrounded by all the medical paraphernalia I needed, I seemed to create chaos and confusion wherever I went. As talk continued of walls being knocked down, doorways being widened and a lift installed, I could sense Kev bristling at this interference with his home. He is a perfectionist, a real stickler for the perfect paint job on the doors and walls, and as I crashed my way through the narrow doorways in the wheelchair, chipping his new paint or scuffing the woodwork, I could see his irritation.

When the time came for me to leave the spinal unit and go home for good, on 16 October 1990, I was incredibly apprehensive. I wished more than anything that I could stay in the cottonwool world of the ward, with its shiny flat floors and wide-open spaces, surrounded by people I had come to love. My friends held a farewell party for me, in the Grey Fisher pub, which had become our local. St John's Ambulance kindly provided a ferrying service for the many wheelchair users who wanted to attend. Neither Kev nor anyone else from my family was invited. It was my night and I knew it would be an emotionally charged one.

Needless to say, I wept buckets. I got plastered, along with everyone else, and cried and cried and cried. I had written a note to each of the key people in the ward who had meant so much to me – Becky and Paula particularly. I gave Paula hers on the night and left Beck's with Avril to give to her after I had gone. It was all a bit sentimental, but I told each of them how much they had come to mean to me and how I wished them well for the future. 'I value your friendship more than I can say,' I wrote to them both. 'Keep on keeping on.' To Becky I added: 'You'll be out soon too.'

Saying goodbye to her was the worst part. She was someone with whom I had formed a lifelong bond. Although we had arrived at the unit within days of each other, she, being tetraplegic, still had many more months ahead of her there, and to leave her behind when we had been through so much together felt like a kind of betrayal.

'I want you to promise me that you'll come back and visit,' Becky asked me, tears welling in her eyes. 'Don't forget me, Julie.'

Squeezing her hand, I replied between great gulps of emotion: 'Of course I won't forget you, you idiot. You're my heroine. And I'll be back really soon. Promise.'

It became a bit of a joke between us that just two weeks later I was back, lying alongside her once more. Making a cup of coffee at home for Angie and me, nervous and unsure of myself in the company of the woman who had been my best friend for so long but with whom I now felt very awkward, I had accidentally tipped the scalding liquid into my lap. Although I felt no pain, it blistered my thighs quite badly, and once the district nurse had been called, I was rushed back to Salisbury in an ambulance for treatment. Taking up my old bed in the place I had come to call home, it felt great to be back, even if Avril's first words to me were: 'Silly cow!'

During the next six months I was in and out of the

place like a cuckoo in a clock. My poor long-suffering kids would ask Kev glumly: 'How long is Mum going to be in for this time?' knowing full well an estimate of four weeks could easily turn into six or even longer. In the end, they just got used to it and so did I. I had no choice. I returned to Salisbury for five separate bladder operations and for surgery to shorten the rods in my back.

In those early days, my whole life seemed to revolve around my bladder and I desperately wanted some respite. My bowel function was fine: like all paraplegics, I had had to be taught how to manually evacuate my own bowels once a day as part of my normal routine, using rubber gloves and KY jelly. It wasn't something that I enjoyed, and to begin with I was completely repulsed by it, but it's amazing what you can get used to after a while. Now it is as normal to me as going to the lavatory is for anyone else, and it allows me a level of independence that I didn't have when someone else was doing it for me. After several weeks of submitting to the dreaded 'bowel round' in hospital, it actually felt good to do it myself. As long as the routine is rigorously maintained there are no problems, leaks or seepages, and it's a part of my life I can forget about for a lot of the day.

My bladder, though, was a different story. The first two operations I had were to try to tighten the muscles and hitch the bladder up somehow before inserting intermittent catheters. The third attempted to expand it, using part of my bowel. Afterwards, it still didn't work. The fourth and final operation was radical and a first for someone like me – it's called the Metrofanoff procedure,

and it was performed by surgeon John Cummings. The operation had only ever previously been used on children, and had never been tried on a paraplegic before. It involves sewing up the bladder at the urethra, and creating a small hole in the stomach, on the bikini line, into which is placed a non-return valve. By inserting a catheter tube in the hole in my stomach, I can empty my bladder at will, without ever being wet below. It means no encumbrances, no incontinence pads, no problems. The surgery completely changed my life, and since it was performed so successfully on me it has been tried on many more paraplegics with equal success. I have even been invited to bladder conferences to discuss it.

Before that happy outcome, though, each bladder operation was lengthy and complicated. It involved a general anaesthetic and a full recovery period. I spent more time in hospital that first year than I did out of it – three months in, three months home and then three months in again. No sooner was the bladder problem sorted than I had to have another operation on my spine, to shorten the Harrington rods by two inches, because their excess length created an uncomfortable lump under my skin.

But, much as I might have wanted to, I couldn't stay away from home indefinitely. I had to get used to life on the outside, for better or worse. Most importantly, I had to re-establish my role as a wife and mother, however long that was going to take. And it did seem to take for ever. That first few months after Kev first collected me and brought me home was hell. I still felt like a stranger, vulnerable and afraid away from the security of the unit. The dining-room was now our bedroom, every surface in the lounge was covered with

Welcome Home cards – a sight I had found overwhelming at first – and everywhere I went, I seemed to cause upheaval.

I discovered that during the course of a normal day it was the little, everyday things I couldn't do that frustrated me the most – reaching the kitchen cupboards to feed my chocolate craving, getting money from the cashpoint machine, being able to nip down to the shops easily for something. The boys adapted brilliantly, but Kevin continued to bury himself in his work, a sort of escapism. I suspect there were a hundred times when he just wanted to say: 'To hell with this!' and walk away from the situation, but he knew he couldn't. Work provided the answer. It kept him away from home and his mind on other things. He could justify his long hours by claiming that we now needed his job and the income it provided more than ever, and that he had to repay the company for all their previous kindnesses. I was just happy for him to be out of the way.

As I tried to get used to my disability in the real world, I soon learned that many others couldn't. Going shopping with my mother, I found that if I handed the money to the cashier she would almost inevitably hand the change back to my mum, as if I was no longer responsible enough to handle cash. Snatching it back with the words, 'Excuse me, that's mine,' I would get quite stroppy about the 'blind spot' that people seemed to develop when it came to me. Another common problem happened in social situations, when everyone else was standing around chatting and I was sitting in my chair, three feet below them, feeling quite ignored. Some people were clued up, and would come and kneel by me or sit in a nearby chair to make me feel more comfortable. For those who didn't, I found one sure-fire way of getting them down to my level. 'I can see right up your nose, you know,' I would suddenly pipe up, and they'd drop down to my level in a flash.

My parents were the worst. In the space of eight short months, I had completely lost all my momentum as an adult in their eyes and they tried to do everything for me. It wasn't really surprising, bearing in mind the difficulties I faced. I couldn't even have a bath at home, because the lift hadn't been fitted yet, so I had to go to my parents' house and use their downstairs bathroom each time I wanted a good clean. Dad was wonderful, lifting me in and out like a baby, but the consequence was that they treated me like a baby too. After just a couple of weeks, I lost my temper with them completely and told them to back off. 'Will you please stop!' I yelled at my mother one day, as she fiddled and fussed over me. 'Let's get something straight. I'm not a little girl any more. If I want help, I'll ask for it. I won't get better if you are doing everything for me all the time. It might be hard, but I've got to try.' I felt my face flush with anger and frustration.

Poor Mum. It must have been incredibly hard for her to see me in a wheelchair and resist the temptation to do everything for me. If I heard her say 'I'm only trying to help' once, I must have heard her say it a hundred times. I knew she was, and I'll always be grateful for her kindness and selflessness at my time of need, but at that point I just wanted to be left alone and I couldn't seem to make them see that. Because of the tension, Mum's relationship with Kevin hit an all-time low. He hated her interference, her fussing only made him feel more guilty, and he couldn't wait for her to leave.

In the end, I had to have a long chat with both my parents and ask them to give Kev and me some breathing space. 'We need to do this in our own time, and in our own way,' I told them. 'I'm a big girl now and you have to treat me like one. I've got to make my own mistakes.' Thankfully, they were fine about it. If anything, they went too far the other way, leaving me to struggle on my own for a while. I remember one day being stranded in the rain on the front doorstep howling for my mother's help, and she told me to stop whingeing and sort myself out. After that, we had to find a happy medium because it was obvious that I still sometimes needed her encouragement and support. Bless her, she gave me a most treasured present shortly after our little talk – a pair of beautiful gold earrings, each one bearing a tiny image of St Christopher, the patron saint of travellers. I have never taken them off.

It wasn't just my parents who were fussing – everyone was, especially my friends. They all wanted to know how I was, how things were going; everyone's attention was focused on me, and just as it made me feel uncomfortable and a burden, it made Kev feel more and more isolated. I now realize that my disability affected him just as much as me, if not more in some ways. I had no choices – the car accident had put paid to all of them. But Kev did have choices. He was still able-bodied, with all the pressures and needs that it brings with it. But all his hopes and desires were completely overlooked in the headlong rush to worry about me and what *I* needed. There were many times when he wanted to scream:

'What about me?' But, being Kev, he didn't. Instead, he threw himself even more into his work.

I thought that socializing together might help him relax a bit, but it didn't. In fact, it was extremely awkward to begin with. I found that I was often addressed in company through Kevin, as if I wasn't there or could no longer communicate. The 'Does she take sugar?' line had never before struck me as so true, and it drove me round the bend, watching people tripping over themselves in embarrassment when in my company. It was like a sort of bereavement they were going through, the difference being that the old Julie Hill everyone was grieving for was still around, still wanting to be seen; they just couldn't see me any more. The healing process for us all might by now have begun, slowly, but there was a lot more yet to mend than just broken bones.

It was so much easier in the company of my new friends, the ones I had made in the spinal unit. They only knew the new me, not the old one; they shared my frustration with the compassion of complete understanding. But if I invited them round they suffered the same problems I did, with the narrow doorways and restricted spaces. And if Kev came home from work and found a posse of wheelchair-users in the house, he was not at all happy, or even prepared to be polite. His attitude was: 'I haven't even got used to the idea of one wheelchair in the house, let alone four. Get them out of my sight,' and it only served to remind me that we were still poles apart.

But I gradually got into a routine, and plucked up the courage to take the initiative on a few issues, in areas of my life where I hoped to regain some independence and control. I took the car out for the first time since the accident – a wholly nerve-wracking experience – but it actually wasn't nearly as bad as I had imagined it would be. And I had to get used to driving again or I couldn't face my next hurdle, taking the children to school.

Something that had deeply troubled me from the day of the accident was whether or not the boys would be stigmatized for having a disabled mother. They had been through enough in the last year without being laughed at by their fellow pupils, and I quizzed them gently before I decided to take the plunge. 'How would you like it if I took you to school instead of Grandma?' I asked, as I tucked them into bed one night.

Their little faces lit up in unison. 'Oh, cool!' Nathan said, and Daniel agreed.

So it was, with a lump in my throat and my teeth gritted, that I pulled my car to a halt a few hundred yards down the road from the school gates the next morning. Heaving myself out and into my wheelchair, I wheeled myself slowly forward, the boys at my side, their eyes bright, and headed for the huddle of other mothers, women I hadn't seen in months.

Watching their eyes and gauging their differing reactions was educational. Most of them knew of my accident and that I was home from hospital, but they clearly hadn't expected to see me at the school gates yet. Some were gushingly dreadful, kissing me theatrically on each cheek and asking, gravely: 'How are you Julie, *really*?' Others couldn't even look me in the eye, and would simply cross to the other side of the road when they saw me approaching. But most of them were brilliant – they treated me just the same as they always had, as if they'd seen me only yesterday. 'Hi, Julie,' they called brightly. 'How're you doing?' They put me instantly at my ease and ruffled the boys' heads fondly, to make them feel more relaxed too.

It was their kindness that bolstered me to make the return journey that afternoon, to collect the boys and to see how their day had been. All my fears were unfounded. Nathan and Daniel came charging out across the playground, satchels flying, grins from ear to ear. 'Hi, Mum!' they each squealed, clearly delighted to see me after so many months' absence. 'Give us a ride!' After that they took turns to jump on to my lap and let me wheel them up and down the pavement outside the school gates, while their friends watched enviously, some even asking if they could have a ride too.

It was a major milestone to have reached, but it wasn't the biggest, by far. Kev and I hadn't had sex in nine months, ever since the accident. And now I was home again, I knew that the subject would come up. For the first few weeks, we managed to completely gloss over it. We enjoyed having the odd kiss and a cuddle in bed, but he was very sensitive to my embarrassment about my catheters and night bags. I couldn't honestly believe that he could ever fancy me again, the way I was. I didn't even feel like a woman any more, just a sort of living machine.

The first time we did have sex, it was awful. I made the first move and he wanted to please me, so he responded as best he could. He treated me as if I was a piece of Dresden china, not knowing where to touch me, or how much I could sense. It was a huge hurdle for him to get over, and my self-esteem in this area was so low I couldn't imagine why he even wanted to try.

Unable to feel anything below the waist, mortified by my condition, I lay back, holding my breath, blinking back the tears and waiting for him to finish. I felt like little more than a lump of meat, a piece of worthless nothing, and I hated myself. But I could sense that it had been a great release for Kev; that he had triumphed over a personal demon, and that at last he felt that it was one area of his life that hadn't been altered irrevocably by the accident.

After that, we attempted it more and more often, in a spirit of good humour and adventure. Having a good laugh about it definitely helped, and for the first time in years I was reminded of how much Kev and I had in common when it came to what made us laugh. Before too long we had become quite adventurous, and our sex life actually became quite good again – something I wouldn't have believed possible in a million years during the previous nine months. I came to understand that passion is not dependent on a spinal cord. It is a body and soul, heart and mind thing; all of which have to be in tune. Instead of sex being something we felt we ought to do at regular intervals, as so many couples do after several years of marriage, it became something we wanted to do. It needed preparation and building up to, but the sense of love and fulfilment surpassed anything we had known before, because it was a meeting of minds, not just bodies. It was wonderful to feel wanted again.

There were other hurdles to get over. I knew that I would have to go back to the scene of the accident and bury some ghosts. In all our journeys out towards Chichester, Kev had carefully avoided using the B2178, taking a roundabout route rather than pass the spot where my life had so suddenly changed. But I knew I had to go back, to make my peace. So I drove out there by myself. My heart was racing as I approached, then pulled the car to a stop on the opposite side of the road and turned off the ignition. Forcing myself to look across the road to the spot where my vehicle had gone off the road, I almost gasped when I saw the yawning gap in the hawthorn hedge, still there, that had been made by my car and then by the emergency service personnel arriving.

For the next ten minutes I sat there, tears streaming down my face, as I relived every moment of that terrible night. I made myself remember the sensations, the sights and the smells. I could almost hear Chris De Burgh singing, and the screaming and groaning of fracturing metal. Then came flashbacks of spinning headlights and of flying through the air, and the crump when I hit the ground – I almost jumped physically with the memory.

Once the flashbacks had passed, I opened my eyes and stared again at the funny little place where my independence had been lost. There was really nothing special or terrifying about it. Just a wide stretch of road, edged by a steep grassy verge in front of a line of tall poplar trees, and a cornfield beyond. If I had gone off the road ten feet earlier, there would have been no bank to launch me up into the air and I might just have suffered a minor whiplash injury. Ten feet further on and I would have hit a tree and almost certainly have been killed.

A sense of calm descended on me suddenly. My tears stopped and my heart rate went back to normal. I had done it. I had come back and survived the experience. The ghosts were laid to rest and I would never have to avoid this road again. With an overwhelming sense of relief, I started the engine and pulled slowly off.

My next big challenge was Christmas, something I had been dreading for months. We had always spent Christmas Day with my parents, but because their house was not adapted to my needs it was decided that it would be easier to spend it at our new home. The trouble was that I still felt like a visitor, and at such a traditionally happy family event I would be made only too painfully aware of how different this Christmas would be.

It was a nightmare from start to finish. Like most women, I had always decorated the tree myself, allowing the boys to help me where they could. But this year, I was forced to sit several feet away in my infernal chair, helplessly giving directions while they hooked all the pretty baubles and balls over the branches. 'Not there, Nathan, over here,' I would call as my eldest did his best with a tinsel garland. In the end, I wheeled myself closer and did what I could within my reach, but the loss of that most traditional of tasks was painful.

Mum and Dad were great, as usual, with Mum preparing all the food while I – once again helplessly – looked on. The lift had been installed by then, allowing me to sleep upstairs again, and the dining-room had returned to its original function. Our set of dining-chairs had mysteriously reappeared with one missing, so that I could wheel my chair straight up to the table. It was all I could do to swallow my turkey that day. Try as we did to be happy for the sake of the children, it was impossible not to make mental comparisons with the riotous Christmases we had enjoyed together before. Far from enjoying it, I only wanted it to end, so that we could move on and face the New Year, 1991, and the first anniversary of my accident.

SEVEN

Illuminations

T HERE WERE to be many more lows before the highs began. The hospital staff had done their best to prepare me for what life would be like 'on the outside', but until you get there and have to live it you can't begin to comprehend the difference. I was still the same person inside, I still thought the same and felt the same; the only change was that I now had wheels instead of legs. But almost everyone else seemed to regard me as a completely different person. I was an invalid, a stranger. It was as if my accident had somehow erased their memories of me and I had to teach them who I was all over again, remind them of the old Julie Hill. It made me very cross sometimes – I just wanted things to be back to normal. But they couldn't be, so I had to adjust, as everybody else had to, and hopefully we would meet somewhere in the middle.

One night, at one of my lowest moments since coming home, I knew I was at the end of my tether and that I needed outside help. Kev was in bed, so were the kids, and I was sitting alone, drinking wine and feeling very low. We'd had some friends over for the evening,

Andy and Angie and another couple, and I'd thought everything was going well. In response to a question about how Kev and I were getting along, I had even told the other couple brightly: 'Everything's great now. I think we're on an even keel, aren't we, Kev?' When I looked across the dinner table at Kev, my heart sank at his downcast expression. Then when he compounded my misery by saying, 'That's a matter of personal opinion,' I felt cut to the quick. It really hurt to hear him being so sarcastic in public, and it showed me that we were a very long way from fine. After our guests had left and he had stalked off to bed in silence (going back to his cave, I used to call it), I sat in the kitchen, smoking and finishing off the last bottle of wine. It was well past midnight and I really felt the need to talk to someone, anyone, preferably a stranger. I didn't know who else to turn to, so I picked up the phone directory and found the number for the Samaritans, a number I'd never had cause to dial in my life before.

'Hi, my name's Julie, I've recently become a paraplegic and I just need to talk about it, if that's all right,' I began, my voice trembling with emotion. A kind man on the end of the line told me his name was Phil and that was exactly what he was there for, and for the next twenty minutes he listened as I poured my heart out. It really helped, talking to someone I didn't know, who I would never meet and who wouldn't judge me. It was a moment not of despair, but of reaching out. Like Helen at the scene of the accident, Phil became, for a few vital minutes, my angel of mercy who saved me from the darkness.

I maintained my self-control; I was close to tears all through the conversation, but I never actually cried. I told him how hard it had all been, coming to terms with my disability, and trying to pick up my life where I had left off. 'The trouble is, I'm not sure if I can do it any more,' I said. 'And I'm so tired of having to try all the time.'

There was a long silence as Phil waited to see if I was going to say anything more. Sensing my rising emotion, he said quietly: 'And tell me, Julie, are you contemplating suicide?'

His gentle probing made me laugh out loud. I was so surprised, I nearly spluttered my wine across the table. Regaining my composure and trying not to giggle at the ludicrousness of his suggestion, I told him: 'No, of course not!' There was more silence. 'Look, honestly, Phil, I'm not. I never have and I never would. Truly. Not just for my sake, but for Kev and the boys. I am not planning on topping myself.'

Reassured, and with the tone of the conversation considerably lighter now, Phil was able to give me some very sound advice about how I had to keep going for the children and for myself. 'You seem like a very positive lady,' he said. 'You've got two sons who rely on you and a husband who probably needs you much more than you realize. You've just got to keep fighting until it gets better. And it will get better, I promise. In a few years' time, you'll hardly believe we ever had this conversation.'

Replacing the receiver at the end of our little chat, I felt as if a great weight had been lifted off my shoulders. Phil was right. There was nothing for it but to keep on keeping on, and as I drained my glass and turned out the light, ready to take myself off to bed, I felt instinctively that I would never feel the need to call him again.

Not all those around me were coping as well as I was, though. My mum, having been completely brilliant in the immediate aftermath of the accident, dealing with the kids, Kev, my dad and me, running herself ragged with all the chores she had to do, suddenly found that she was no longer needed. I was back home with my family, I had turned down most of her offers of further help and I was doing my level best to put the accident and all its pain behind me. And so now that she had effectively been made redundant after a year of stress and intense activity, my poor mother suffered a mini nervous breakdown, which took the form of panic attacks, anxiety and depression. She became agoraphobic, unable to leave her house or do her job as a part-time hairdresser. She needed antidepressants to try and bolster her spirits, and spent a great deal of the time in tears.

'I don't know what she's gone to pieces for,' Kevin sniped when he first heard. 'The accident didn't happen to *her*.' But he was wrong. As I was already beginning to understand, my accident happened not just to me, but to all my family. It affected each and every one of us in our own way. It had certainly affected Kev, and my mum was just another casualty of my burst tyre that April night. Now, with time on her hands for the first time since the accident, she was hit full in the face by the impact of what had happened. She was allowing herself to grieve – something she had been too busy to think about before. And her grief was real, as if she really had lost her child – which, in a way, she had. She had the classic symptoms of bereavement and sank into a terrible despair. The doctors put it down to a combination of the menopause and delayed shock about the accident. Whatever the cause, it was awful for everybody, not least me because I felt largely responsible for it.

My father and I did all we could for her, but it was a very long time before she was able to hold her head up high again and face the day. She was tremendously supported by her dear friend Doris Goddard, who had been so good to us all when it happend and who knew a great deal about grief, having lost her son Chris. Doris ran a shop in Chichester, but she dropped everything – both at the time of the accident and again when Mum was ill – to be there for her. It must have been hard for Doris. She would have had Christopher back in any state, paraplegic or otherwise, and here was her dearest friend in tatters even though I was still alive. She never once questioned Mum's distress; she only wanted to help. Their friendship had spanned thirty years and without Doris, I think, Mum would never have made it through.

It sometimes felt as if my own difficulties at home and now with my mother would overwhelm me. I felt so incredibly guilty for causing everyone so much pain and, left to my own devices, I think I might well have started to fester. But, fortunately, I wasn't allowed to because there was a moment of breakthrough around that time, through my first contact with the spinal injuries charity, Back-Up. It was, without any doubt, the first most significant stage in my recovery.

The Back-Up Trust was first set up in the late 1980s by Mike Nemesvary, a former British and European freestyle skiing champion, who broke his neck in a trampoline accident and was confined to a wheelchair, with just a little arm movement. Back-Up is the only charity focusing on sport for the spinally injured, and its aim is to encourage individuals with spinal-cord injuries to regain motivation, inspiration and independence through sporting activities. Meeting the challenge of returning to work or living on your own no longer seems quite so daunting once you've sailed across a lake single-handed, paraglided from the top of a mountain or skied down an icy slope.

The enthusiasm of everyone involved with the organization was infectious. Becky was already a devotee, and before I knew it I had been persuaded into a four-day water-skiing weekend run by the British Disabled Waterskiing Association with some fellow paraplegics and a bunch of amputees at Heron Lake near Staines in Surrey. My first reaction was: 'How on earth can *I* do that?'

The response came back, in unison: 'Well, go along and find out.' And so it was that I went, on my own, with a group of strangers, spinally injured people I had never met before, each one of us with a 'buddy' – and we had a ball. We camped out under the stars, ate sausages and beans, drank loads of beer and sang songs round the fire. It was June 1991, fourteen months after the accident, and I loved every minute of it. If you're a paraplegic, once you've got up on a sitz ski (an elongated knee board) and gone once round a lake, however bad you are at it, frankly, all your preconceived ideas of what disability is about go flying out of the window. I was terrified to start with and then totally exhilarated. The feel-good factor was ten out of ten. It made me realize that so much was still possible – it changed my attitude to my disability almost overnight.

I can date my psychological recovery from that weekend. From then on, I began to take a bit more care of myself – how I looked, what I wore, keeping up with my fitness training. If Kevin had ever expected me to go back to being completely dependent on him and others, he had another think coming. I was rocking and rolling. Seeing how much I enjoyed my Back-Up activities, a family friend, a woman called Rita Brazier who was an ex-Royal Navy sailing coach, decided to teach me how to sail. It was she who had organized the sponsored sail for my trust fund. Under her expert and cheerful tuition, I became the first paraplegic in the country to complete a Level Two sailing course in the Solent, in spite of the many misgivings of the Royal Yachting Association.

We even managed the capsize drill, a terrifying process where you have to pull yourself out from under a capsized dinghy using only your arms. There was also the very real danger that I might accidentally break a leg and not even realize it, as the boat scooped me up and turned me over with it. Fortunately I didn't, and it was brilliant. Rita was a wonderful woman, truly inspirational. After her success with me she went on to teach other paraplegics to sail, taking small groups from Salisbury and establishing a close link with the spinal unit, along with her husband Colin. Tragically, she died a few years later of cancer. She was forty-eight. The world is a much duller place without her.

Kev was still not happy about me doing all these activity sports. In some ways, I think he regressed right back to how he was at the time of the accident, and yet we were now over a year on. Our relationship was still very much hit and miss, and as I began to grow away from him and my parents as far as dependence was concerned, a lot of the earlier strain returned. 'Go off and do what you want,' he would say crossly when I asked if he minded if I went on yet another Back-Up trip. It was clear that he hated my involvement with other disabled people, who only served to remind him that I was one of them. My wheelchair still frightened the life out of him, but try as hard as he could to ignore it, it was never going to go away. Slowly, we began leading separate lives again, while still living under the same roof. It was a return to the bad old days. He couldn't see why I wanted to spend so much time with aggressively positive people, when he would have preferred it if I'd stayed at home.

But there was nothing much I could have done at home if I'd wanted to. By then I had a home help who came in to look after the house as well as someone to do the washing and the ironing. Kev was always working and the children were both at school. Just like in the months leading up to the accident, I wasn't prepared to sit at home and rot. I had new-found independence and I intended to use it. On one memorable weekend when Kev went to the Le Mans twenty-four-hour race with a group of mates from work, I went on a pub crawl with two friends I'd met through Back-Up and an old family friend, Laura. At the climax of our late-night celebrations, 'Wheelie Wendy' and I raced down the Emsworth underpass, with Laura on my lap and Debbie, an amputee, on Wendy's. At the end of it Debbie fell off and her false leg came off too, and Wendy's wheelchair sped across the roundabout under its own steam, leaving us in hysterics by the roadside.

Kev's response to this kind of escapade, as always, was to sulk, and if he wasn't sulking he was making some cutting comment about my disabled friends or about my inability to do something. Friends noticed his brusqueness, and my mum and dad became so concerned that they enquired privately about planning permission to convert their garage into a separate living unit for me and the boys, in case Kev and I split up. I began to wonder if he was ever going to accept me as I was. There were so many good times to be shared, so many daily personal triumphs over my disability, and yet he was never there to share them with me. He simply couldn't handle it, and I thought that he probably never would.

Not only was he being controlling and unreasonable, I felt, but even more frustratingly, he refused to talk to me about it or argue the point. I could hardly stamp my foot and flounce off. The bottom line was that he didn't want me to have any contact with anyone else disabled. He wanted me to sit at home, looking after the kids and him, hiding myself away from life, quietly accepting my fate. Faced with such an unthinkable prospect, I was placed in a very difficult position. As far as I could see, I had two choices. To do as he wished, and die a horrible mental death, or to ignore him and get on with my life the way I wanted to, in the hope that he would eventually come round to my way of thinking.

It was an uncomfortable choice. I was desperately worried about the future. I knew in my heart of hearts that I still loved him, for all his faults. He was my husband, the only man I had ever really loved, and the father of our two gorgeous children. I knew that our marriage was worth saving, especially after we had managed to come this far. I decided to bide my time and be patient and hope that he would make an effort to understand my feelings better.

By then, Angie and I were getting closer again as friends and we talked about Kev endlessly. 'I can see both points of view,' she told me. 'The trouble is, Kev is still angry with the world, and you're not any more. He needs to work this out, in his own way, and you need to carry on doing all the things that make you feel good too. The problem is that the more you carry on with the Back-Up events, the more Kev feels resentful.' She was right and I knew it, but I couldn't just stop the momentum of everything I'd started.

In February 1992, I went skiing in Anzère in Switzerland with a group of twenty-two people, including eight paraplegics. I had been really looking forward to the trip, but Kev's reaction to it had worried me. He could only see hassle and problems in me travelling abroad, whereas I viewed it as an enormous challenge. To be honest, I was also a little bit worried about the logistics of it all. It was my first time on a plane since before the accident. But I was amazed how well organized it turned out to be – the airline was clearly well accustomed to handling large groups of disabled passengers, and any hitches were smoothly ironed out.

Needless to say, I had a wonderful time. It was so exhilarating to slide down the slopes in the special bucket seat on a single ski, screaming at the top of my voice, even if I wasn't very good at it. We were all in the same boat and we had dozens of 'wipe-outs' (crashes), but no damage was done. In the evenings, we ate cheese fondue in the chalets and partied severely. It was a damn good laugh and I loved being with like-minded, upbeat people. To my surprise, though, I missed Kev and the boys like nobody's business. It was the first time I had ever been abroad without them. I rang home every night and the children wanted to hear all the details. 'Can we come too next time, Mummy?' Nathan asked. I laughed and promised that he could. When it came to speaking to Kev, his tone was cold and he obviously didn't want to know. I couldn't tell him I was having fun. He wouldn't have liked it.

When I got back home, the first thing I said to Kev was: 'How about a holiday alone together, just you and me, like we used to in the old days?' We had always had one week on our own somewhere abroad without the kids. But the look of horror on his face was priceless as he walked away from me – something that really got my goat because he knew I couldn't do the same.

I badgered him for months. I told him how easy it had all been, getting on a plane, getting to and from the chalet, even in deep snow. 'It just requires a bit of planning and forethought,' I reasoned. But he wouldn't have it. I think, by then, he had decided that his lot in life was this miserable existence, chained to work, married to a paraplegic, with no more holidays or treats. He had resigned himself to a life of misery and he just wanted to be left alone to get on with it. Simple as that.

My unhappiness was compounded when, during a return trip to Guernsey with Becky that summer, I burned a hole in my leg when, without realizing it, I sat too close to a heated towel rail. Sitting on the lavatory for an hour or more, sorting myself out as usual, I hadn't noticed that in the cramped little space my leg had been pressed right up against the hot towel rail the whole time, burning the flesh away. It was a serious injury that set me back badly and caused untold inconvenience while I was recovering. Unexpectedly depressed by the episode, I became more aware than ever of my vulnerability.

Kev's attitude didn't help. He viewed the entire incident with the disdain of the self-satisfied. 'I knew something like this would happen,' he said smugly. The look I gave him prevented him from ending with: 'Don't say I didn't tell you so.'

I knew I had to hang on in there, but sometimes my frustration and anger got the better of me. 'If this marriage is going to work, Kev, it's got to work for the right reasons,' I snapped at him one night. 'And by the way, if you're thinking of leaving, then I think you should know, I'm staying in this house and the kids are staying with me.'

All marriages go through bad patches, and those where one partner has suffered a spinal injury are particularly vulnerable. A great many fail. The guilt and the blame and the pain are just too much for one or both parties to handle. Paula and Claire had told me how many relationships they had seen crack under the strain. I wondered now if Kev and I would simply become another statistic. There was certainly more than one aspect of my life that had been irreparably damaged on the night of the crash. The trouble was, I simply couldn't imagine life without Kev, no matter how much of a bastard he was being. When he was great – and those times were now rare – he was absolutely bloody marvellous. He gave me every support, he was wonderful with the kids, and he seemed to be adjusting to the new life we all had to lead. I just needed to work out how to keep him that way.

Elsewhere that year, events were also taking a momentous turn for the experts whose work would eventually come to mean so much to me. It was in 1991, a year after my accident, that Professor Giles Brindley announced that he would be retiring from his neurological prostheses unit, at the age of sixty-six. It was to be the end of a unique experiment involving the interaction of man and machines. In the more than twenty years that his unit had been running, he and his staff had made micro-electronic implants affordable and workable. Research engineers from all across Europe had come to admire the unit's work after failing to achieve the same results themselves. Where they had failed, the unit had succeeded, and it became the byword in implant technology.

Personally endorsing his team and the valuable work they were still doing, Professor Brindley publicly expressed the hope that the Medical Research Council would continue to fund it under the guidance of his second-in-command, the able neurologist Professor David Rushton. Having previously shielded his team from the complexities of medical research funding by presenting his applications alone, Professor Brindley didn't quite appreciate that without his vigorous and dynamic input, the unit's work would appear rather colourless to the people signing the cheques.

In the light of Professor Brindley's decision to go, Peter Donaldson, his friend and colleague, also decided to retire. He was sixty-five and could look back on his career with considerable satisfaction. From starting out in the Navy and then being offered £500 a year to be a laboratory dogsbody, he had managed to end up on one of the most innovative and exciting biomedical projects in the world, and had helped to perfect devices that would change the face of implant technology ever after.

A farewell dinner was held in Dulwich in south-east

London, at which Giles Brindley expressed the hope that the unit would be allowed to stay open and that his talented colleagues could continue their good work. But it was not to be. In spite of widespread exposure in the national press and open criticism at a Department of Health meeting from the directors of other units, in 1992 the MRC decided to withdraw funding from the team and wrote to its members offering them redundancy or transfer to other, similar, units. The council explained that it could only fund half of what it called 'priority projects' to avoid an overspend of £3.5 million that year, and said it had no choice but to shut the Brindley and three other units.

For Nick Donaldson and Tim Perkins, desperately trying to continue with their work with the threat of redundancy and unemployment looming over them, it was a very difficult time. Tim was married with four children and living in west London. Nick was married to a music teacher, had two children at that time and was living in Kent. The prospect of losing their jobs or being moved elsewhere was not a welcome one, with mortgages and the growing expenses of a family. In Britain, jobs in medical research are neither highly paid nor easy to find. Men and women who devote their working lives to the betterment of science do so mainly out of vocational dedication. They make do with limited funding, adopting and adapting equipment already in use, cannibalizing and enhancing the existing gadgetry and often holding their devices together with little more than sticky tape and a large dose of hope.

Professor Rushton, Brindley's deputy, had already applied for more money to carry on with the team's work, but there were no guarantees that he would get it. The MRC had a history of abandoning projects once the original director had retired or died, and it could have been argued that with the successful development of the bladder/bowel-control device the unit's goals had been achieved. In the expectation of that happening, Professor Rushton found himself another job, as Professor of Rehabilitation at the London Hospital.

Nick Donaldson was as concerned as the rest of them about the future, and he had managed to secure himself a job as an honorary senior lecturer at University College London. In the light of Professor Rushton's new job and with the college's agreement to house him if he could find funding, Nick made two further, separate applications to the MRC for new grants that would allow at least part of the team to carry on with their work under the wing of his new employers.

The MRC decided to be generous. It suggested that if Nick was successful in applying for a project grant, in open competition, they would pay him as a member of their external scientific staff. With David Rushton's endorsement and his promise to remain as a consultant, the MRC finally agreed to a three-year grant of £230,000 to allow the new Donaldson team to set themselves up under Nick's leadership and move their work into the clinical phase. It would mean a chance to develop some of their implants and allow a leaner, more efficient team to choose a patient for trials. (There was a second two-year grant, increasing it to £500,000 over five years.) The new three-man team was to comprise Nick and Tim, along with Nick's father Peter, who had soon grown bored with retirement and decided to go back to work as an unpaid technician. For Peter's long-suffering wife Jane, who raises sheep and cattle on her smallholding on the Kentish Downs, the news that her recently retired husband was returning to full-time work with their eldest son didn't come as much of a surprise. Having never really expected him to give up work or enjoy retirement, it was she who had first suggested it.

Of the remaining members of Professor Brindley's unit at that time, Nigel Chaffey and Mike Craggs found work elsewhere, and Eric Sayer and John Cooper both retired. Understandably saddened at the disbanding of their unique enterprise, in which they had each helped make tremendous progress in the field, they were at least bolstered by the fact that a handful of its key members would be allowed to continue their years of research. They wished them the very best of luck.

They needn't have worried. Having had its new offices specially prepared and sterilized for the safe manufacture of implants, the new unit left Denmark Hill in September 1992 and moved two months later to the Department of Medical Physics in Capper Street, Bloomsbury. Once settled, it rose to the challenge, with an ambitious new project inspired by Professor Brindley's work with the paralysed soldiers and implanted leg electrodes. Although they were unsuccessful in the end, the tests had taught the team a great deal. Nearly two decades on, and with technology and surgical techniques advancing almost daily, they now accepted Professor Rushton's original statement that to have any realistic chance of making a paraplegic stand properly and even take a few unaided steps, the electrodes would have to be attached not to the nerves in the leg but to those at the base of the spine.

The aim was to try to make something in the working lifetime of the new unit that would be usable.

What they wanted was to get patients standing up, using a relatively simple device, and perhaps enable them to step up a kerb so that they could get to a front door or to a bank cash machine that was too high to reach from a wheelchair, or turn round in a doorway so that they wouldn't need a special lavatory. It was all about improving the quality of life. The team had come to realize that there was no point in concentrating on something that might help paraplegics walk only if they were rich enough, or in a hundred years' time.

Although they had wide experience of attaching electrodes to spinal nerves in their work with the bladder-control implants, they were entering unknown territory when it came to the nerves that control the leg muscles. The responses to electronic stimulation in that area were largely unknown and the risks were much higher. Tests in the morgue had only limited use – the responses could be seen but not described by the patient, and the overall effect couldn't be charted. Unfazed, they perfected what they hoped would do the job, a state-of-the-art implanted device they called the lumbosacral anterior root stimulator implant, or LARSI for short. What its rather convoluted title meant was that they were hoping to try something that nobody had done before: to attach electrodes to the roots of the motor nerves that go to the leg muscles in such a way that the electrodes would be protected inside the spine and would stand a better chance of staying connected and be less liable to infection.

The nerves that control the muscles in the arms, legs and abdomen run down the hollow centre of the spine before branching off, fanning out like the roots of a tree, subdividing, then rejoining and fanning out again before arriving at their destination. Spinal injuries often leave the nerves below the point of injury disconnected from the brain but undamaged. The muscles fed by these nerves may also be undamaged, but they too are completely cut off from their chain of command. What the team hoped to achieve was a sort of jump-lead that could be plugged into their nerves below the damaged area of spine, to stimulate them and restore lost function.

Most earlier surface-electrode systems had simply fired pulses to muscles that straightened the knees, and once their legs were straight the patients had to haul themselves upright. The new system would be much smarter and attempt to mimic the brain's own control systems. The plan was to firmly fix twelve electrodes to the vertebrae, six on each side, to stimulate the nerves where they emerge from the spinal cord in a bundle called the *cauda equina* (meaning 'horse's tail'). Four cables fitted to the twelve electrodes would be held clear of the spine while it was sewn up, and would then be wound under the skin to an implanted receiver. The implant would be a five-centimetre-diameter circular device coated in silicone rubber, about half a centimetre thick and the size of a jam-jar lid, stuffed full of tiny computer chips and micro-electronic cables. It would be inserted under the natural dent at the bottom of the patient's ribcage, just beneath the skin.

A special radio-frequency transmitter would be strapped to the patient's waist directly above the implant in a sort of corset, holding it in place. By pressing the button on a tiny Walkman-size computer, held in the patient's hand or slipped into an easy-to-carry bag, a preprogrammed radio signal could be sent to the transmitter, and in turn to the receiver, which would relay

the 'firing sequence' or message down the wires to the
electrodes concerned. The mini-computer would act as
the go-between for all the component parts, mimicking
the signals that the brain could no longer communicate
to the nerves. By pressing a small red button (linked to
the computer) on a stick that the patient would use for
balance, 56 milliwatts of electrical impulses – enough to
power a small torch – would be transmitted from the
implant via the electrodes to the nerve roots.

The electrodes would in turn send between twelve
and twenty electrical pulses a second down the nerves
to the muscles they serve. The impulses to the nerves
would carry about 10 volts, a current of about 4 milli-
amps, and last between 200 and 900 microseconds. The
carefully worked out sequence, managed by a complicated computer software program devised by Tim,
would change the duration and frequency of pulses to
each electrode by precise amounts, depending on what
was required of the muscles. By adjusting twelve sliding
controls on the tiny computer for each channel, just like
you see in a music studio, Tim could instruct the muscles
to work. On these instructions, the muscles would then
contract by exactly the right amount and in sequence, so
as to raise the patient to their feet or allow them to kick
or eventually even take steps. It was the first time that a
system had been devised to activate all the muscles in
the leg simultaneously, which gave the possibility of
controlling balance. The patient would only have to
press a grey button to instruct their muscles to allow
them to sit down again.

What was so unique and so advanced about it was
that it was to be mainly inside the patient's body, with
no visible wires or machinery, and that it was to be

connected to twelve electrodes – twice as many as had ever been attempted before. All the patient had to do was wear a small bag and a discreet corset (identical to the ones worn by people suffering from a bad back), set the control panel or 'mixing desk', grab their stick and be off. It would be a journey that no other paraplegic had ever made before.

The implications for the technique, if successful and developed still further, were far-reaching. In theory, every paralysed person in the world could learn to stand or even take steps again. Whoever was selected to take part in this unique experiment would become a work in progress.

There were a lot of risks, not least of which was the danger that by interfering with the incredibly delicate natural process, an implant could adversely affect the patient's mobility rather than enhance it. A slip of the scalpel or a wrong connection could leave the patient even more disabled than they were before the operation. It would be something that would have to be very seriously considered by anyone willing to be operated on. Also, the team could offer no guarantees of precise control over the muscles essential for standing. The electrodes might work, but the patient could end up so unstable that the implant would be useless.

There was clearly still a great deal of work to do on the clinical side, even if the workbench trials had been going well. But it was not long before Tim had designed and made an electronic control system that could separate the various functions and allow standing. With his bushy beard and booming voice, he had become an acknowledged genius of the electronics world, able to design multihundred-component circuits and write thousand-line control programs. By the time the new MRC grant had been awarded, he had designed something quite radical in the implant field: an implant-control system that could be carried around with the patient or even taken home, which would mean that they didn't have to come to the laboratory or to hospital all the time.

Coupled with Nick's Mark 5 implant, it was a beautiful piece of engineering, infinitely more sophisticated than anything the old unit had ever made and the smallest of its kind in the world. Designed to stimulate up to twelve nerves individually or in combination, its tuning allowed a very accurate degree of control of the nerves and muscle movements, and there was a built-in compensator and alarm system for poor placing of the transmitter, power failure, or to warn of slippage while in use.

By 1993 it was ready to be tested, and the team now focused their attention on finding someone ideally suited to become their guinea-pig. If it worked with the first patient, then the plan was for seven more to quickly follow. For the moment, they didn't dare to think beyond that magical figure of eight potential recipients.

Among the many lessons they had learned working with Professor Brindley's patients was that if they were to develop the implant technique further in the future, the unit needed to become personally involved with each patient chosen, helping in the initial selection process and giving support and advice through every stage. They had previously found themselves in situations where patients who had been thought to be ideal had become disgruntled with the experimental nature of the projects and had abandoned them midway, or where insufficient follow-up or support services had led to infections and disconnections that they could later do nothing about.

It was obvious from their past experiences that they had to be much more careful about the way they chose their patients, and that they had to give them a better personal service. It was sometimes difficult for these men of science, untrained in the skills of the bedside manner, not to treat a patient like a sack of potatoes or a biological specimen. Although they were uncomfortable with the personal approach, this time they knew that they had to establish beforehand not only that the patient they chose was psychologically strong enough to stick with the project, but that they themselves were prepared to give them every support.

Starting afresh with this new approach, the unit decided that to achieve the best results they should liaise with spinal units at two key hospitals – the Royal National Orthopaedic Hospital at Stanmore, north-west London, and the Duke of Cornwall Spinal Treatment Centre at Salisbury District Hospital. They would set aside some of their precious grant money to employ a research physiotherapist at each unit to find and then monitor the right person for the implant.

While the search was under way, the team began to prepare for the day when the right candidate would be found. It included David Rushton, now working in east London but still helping with the neurological investigations, and Tony Tromans, a leading consultant in spinal injuries at Salisbury District Hospital, who was willing to perform the operation once the conditions were right. There was also Sean Hagan, a clinical engineer and technician, who would work with the new patient for the first few years. All those recruited to the project had quickly to acquaint themselves with the whole technique, so that when they were asked questions about it by potential candidates they could give an 'idiot's guide' to what was really a very complex procedure.

In the earliest days of the quest for the first volunteer, Viv Harper, a medical research physiotherapist at Salisbury, and Fiona Barr, her equivalent at Stanmore, were given the task of looking through ten years' worth of medical records of hundreds of spinal-injury patients at their respective hospitals to see if they could identify the ideal candidate.

There were specific physical conditions to be met. He or she – there was no preference as to which – had to be of a certain age, have a relatively stable break in the middle of the spine – between the key thoracic vertebrae numbered one to twelve or the seven cervical vertebrae – but needed to still be able to use their upper body for balance when upright. They wanted someone who had not been fitted with any electronic bladder/bowel-control device because the existing electrodes could interfere with the new ones being implanted, and, for the same reason, it had to be someone without any metalwork attached to their spine.

Any paraplegic with a tendency to have fits – to do with epilepsy or any other cause – or unfortunate enough to suffer from the violent muscle spasms and contractions that some develop after injury would also have to be discounted, and there had to be the right level of tendon tension in the knee and the right bone density in the leg to enable him or her to stand. Finally, he or she had to be fit enough to handle the rigorous physical tests and invasive surgery that would be necessary.

They knew exactly what they wanted – a patient who not only had incredible determination and physical stamina, but who was well balanced enough to be able to cope with the years of gruelling tests, further extensive surgery and the trauma of possible failure at the end of the project. In short, they needed a human being with exceptional personal qualities who was prepared to become superhuman. Was there such a person somewhere out there, they wondered?

EIGHT

Flickerings

IT WAS a short article in the *Daily Mail* in the summer of 1992 that made me embark on the first stages of the treatment that was to change my life. Mum had seen the piece, about the 'Walk Fund' charity set up in memory of PC Philip Olds, a Metropolitan Police officer who committed suicide when he was unable to regain the use of his legs after being shot and paralysed during a robbery. The article highlighted a new technique, a special type of callipers to help paraplegics stand.

Standing up for a few minutes every day is a vital part of maintaining general health after being paralysed. Muscles that are not stimulated rapidly waste away. Bones press against the weakened tissue and cut off the blood supply, causing pressure sores – and as I mentioned earlier, infected pressure sores are a major threat to the lives of the disabled. The act of putting weight on to under-used bones helps improve mobility and prevents osteoporosis in later years. Then there are the other benefits. When you are constantly sitting down all your internal organs are bunched together. As soon as you stand, they drop into their rightful places, which helps with breathing and circulation and also helps to prevent pressure sores.

I had been taught the value of exercise and of standing in hospital and had come home with something I called 'the pulpit', officially called the Oswestry standing frame – a National Health Service-issue wooden monstrosity with which I stood, strapped in, unable to move, for as long as I could bear it every day. But it really wasn't my kind of furniture.

The *Daily Mail* article mentioned new full-length leg callipers, with the catchy name 'reciprocating gait orthosis', which looked like a much better alternative – lightweight, less bulky and easier to transport. Each calliper had to be made to measure, from a plaster cast taken from my legs, so that it would fit only me and no one else. Because of the close fit, they also offered me the possibility of being able to move a few paces with them. I asked the nursing staff at Salisbury and they said they could probably get them for me if I was interested, but I would have to get in training to use them. So began a six-week intensive marathon to get my upper and lower body strong enough to support my legs. Using free weights and parallel bars under the expert tuition of my marvellous physiotherapist Sally, I spent almost every weekday in the physiotherapy department at the hospital, sweating bullets and toning my muscles up, only taking time off at weekends.

When the RGO finally arrived, kindly paid for by my wonderful GP, I was surprised at how ugly and bulky it was. It consisted of the two customized heavy-duty white plastic leg-shaped supports into which my legs and feet were laid, and an equally unattractive hip brace which clamped tightly around my middle. I was strapped in around my ankles, calves, thighs and waist with numerous buckles and straps – the bloke who invented it was obviously very fond of leather. With my legs now sticking straight out in front of me, I placed my feet on the bottom bar of a sort of inverted 'fork-lift', and when I lifted myself up on to the stainless-steel frame with my arms, the cantilever arrangement brought me reasonably neatly to a standing position.

Since the accident, it has always felt very strange to stand. I can't feel my legs, I don't know what position my feet are in, and the sensation is like floating on air. The only similar sensation I ever experienced when I was able-bodied was when a leg got cramp or went numb through inactivity and felt like a leaden weight underneath me. That is the sensation those of us who are paralysed have all the time.

Strange as it felt, though, it was good to stand even if I did get vertigo for a while at first, as the blood rushed to my head. It was nice to be at eye level again, a wonderful novelty for someone who had spent the past two years in a wheelchair. Once I was upright, the RGO then allowed me to take a few straight-legged paces around the room by swinging one leg forward at a time, together with the appropriate hip and arm move-ments. 'This is one giant step for mankind,' I joked as I took my first awkward pace, although it did feel horribly robotic.

I took the RGO home, and resolved to use it every day so as to stay fit and to be able to move around the house more easily. The manufacturers claimed that some-one like me could put it on in the morning and not take it off again until the end of the day, using it whenever I felt like standing to reach a book off a shelf or open a top cupboard. But the reality was quite different for me, and within a few months the novelty had completely worn off. With the straps tight around my lower body and the plastic close to my skin, it was extremely uncomfortable and made me sweat like a pig. It was cumbersome and ugly and far more trouble than it was worth. It also meant that my mum or someone else had to be there to help me into the masses of leather straps and buckles that held me in, to be on hand while I hauled myself up into the contraption and to catch me in case I toppled over when I swung my legs through a few paces. Then, after the exhausting experience of being upright, even only for a few minutes, I needed someone to help me back into my chair and to unstrap everything.

And you couldn't say the RGO was exactly pretty either; there was no hope of people not realizing I was using it, or disguising it under clothing, unless I was wearing voluminous, unflattering outfits. Perhaps not surprisingly, after a year I was probably only putting it on once or twice a week – an awful lapse on my part after everyone had been good enough to provide it for me.

But however little I was using it, the RGO had at least given me a small taste of what it might be like to be more mobile. It wasn't that I was living my life expecting that any day I might be miraculously 'cured', or even that I hadn't come to terms with my disability, but I still held on to the tiniest sliver of hope that one day something might come along that would enable me to feel less disabled and more like the woman I had been before the accident. On the rare days when I did get depressed about my situation, I would fantasize about being able to run again, go cycling or swimming with the kids or – dream of dreams – to once again leave footprints in the snow.

Kev couldn't have been less interested in my rather pathetic attempts to move around using the RGO. His expression showed undisguised distaste each time he saw me in it – to the extent that I only ever used it when he was out of the house. Our relationship was still very rocky, and he still had his phobia about wheelchairs and anything else to do with my disability. Three years on from the accident, I felt that we should really have got past that stage by now, and I was deeply worried about our future.

The watershed came in October 1993 when I finally persuaded him to go with me on our first holiday together since the accident. It had taken me over a year of bullying and cajoling. I had sent off for the various holiday brochures, rejecting the ones specially designed for the disabled on the grounds that Kev's worst nightmare would be to find himself in a foreign country, unable to escape and surrounded by even more wheelchairs. Having discovered that good old Thomson Holidays make good provision for the disabled, I left their brochures lying around for him to see, even though he had steadfastly refused to even consider the idea. In the end, he begrudgingly accepted that he was in desperate need of a break – his first in four hellish years – and that we could go.

What followed was a 'do or die' week on the Greek island of Rhodes, the first few days of which were a disaster. Kev was like a cat on a hot tin roof at the airport and then in the plane, feeling so self-conscious and thinking that everyone was staring at us. He even had me at it, feeling paranoid. Then, when we got to the hotel, we found that the door to the bathroom was too narrow for my wheelchair to go through. Kev would have to carry me in and out each time – not the way I had hoped to prove my independence to him.

To top it all, waiting for us at the hotel was an urgent fax from Kev's office, informing him that there had been some major crisis and he would have to work from his hotel room for a few days. I had no choice but to accept him working and find my own amusement. 'I'll be damned if your office is going to ruin *my* holiday as well,' I told him.

Left to my own devices, I set myself up at the hotel bar, befriended the barman and systematically worked my way through the extensive cocktail list. I was desperately hurt and upset and I truly believed that our marriage would not now survive. But then something incredible happened. Kev stopped working – the crisis seemed to be over – came down to the bar, sat next to me on a bar stool and started to talk. He obviously felt very guilty at having left me on my own for two days, and as the cocktails I ordered for him started to take effect, we did something quite extraordinary – we began to laugh.

During the last few days of our holiday, Kev and I took the first faltering steps towards rebuilding our shattered marriage. There was a lot of laughing, a lot of crying on my part and we talked from dawn to dusk. He gradually began to unwind, and being actually able to physically relax soothed him. We rediscovered our mutual sense of humour, we had incredibly good sex for the first time since the accident, and slowly, tentatively, we began to fall in love with each other again. From then on, I think, he started to see *me* first and the wheelchair second.

Not long after our return from Rhodes, in November 1993, an article in *Forward*, the monthly newsletter of the Spinal Injuries Association, caught my eye. I was at my parents' house, having a cup of coffee and catching up with my mail, when flicking through the magazine that was delivered every quarter to my door I came across an entry with the headline: 'HELP WANTED'.

It described in detail the principles behind something called FES (functional electronic stimulation), in which surface electrodes are attached to the legs of paraplegics so as to produce muscle contractions with the use of electrical impulses. It didn't gloss over the system's limitations, but the implanted device that it described inside the body seemed to suggest a new and radical approach. The research project was being funded by the Medical Research Council. The article went on:

'The clinical research is being carried out by the two spinal units [at Salisbury and Stanmore] and there is funding for eight implants. Volunteers interested in joining the project need to be assessed with the existing surface standing programme before being considered for an implant, and be:

T2 to T12 complete paraplegics who have been injured for more than a year

in good health with full passive range of movement in their legs and no excessive curvatures of the spine

prepared to visit one of the above spinal units for approximately half a day every fortnight (precise timing varies depending on the stage of the project), carry out up to two hours of stimulation at home each day, and be an in-patient for two to three weeks for the implant operation.

Anyone interested in volunteering should contact either Viv Harper, Research Physiotherapist, Duke of Cornwall Spinal Treatment Centre, Salisbury District Hospital . . . or Fiona Barr, Research Physiotherapist, Royal National Orthopaedic Hospital, Stanmore.'

Hmm, I thought. I'm a T9 (meaning that the break in my spine is at the ninth thoracic vertebra from the top). Perfect. 'Hey, Mum, look at this,' I said, circling the article in red pen and handing it across for her to read. 'What do you think?'

She read it through carefully before asking: 'What's FES when it's at home?'

Unusually for me, I was able to answer her. I knew quite a lot about FES from a fund-raising video I had seen in hospital organized by the charity Inspire, whose management board I was involved with for a time. It is very similar to the well-known slimming-aid idea: small electrodes are placed on the skin above the main leg muscles and when an electrical current is passed through the muscle groups, they are sparked into life. Using the technique on paraplegics, it had been possible to make some paralysed people stand. The trouble was that it involved dozens of wires and electrical devices, and the person could never be more than a few inches away from the control box. It had been around for a very long time, but with not altogether satisfactory results. Some of the people who had tried it at Salisbury had claimed that it actually left them worse off, because it gave them severe, uncontrollable muscle spasms. For these reasons I was put off and had never been tempted to try it before – it was far too reminiscent of Frankenstein's monster for my liking.

What caught my imagination now was the indication in the advert that the new device on offer was an implant, meaning no more wires and possibly even a system that could be completely hidden under clothing. As a woman, always concerned about my appearance, that really appealed to me. The basic aim of the project – to allow people like me to stand and maybe even take steps – also rekindled the feeling of hope that I had never really allowed to slip away. Could I dare to believe that this was something that I might actually be able to achieve?

Having had the technique explained to her, my mother said: 'It certainly looks interesting. Why don't you give them a ring, love?' It was a casual suggestion that was to have extraordinary consequences. Little did Mum or I know, but that advert had stirred the interest of someone who would turn the life's dream of the surviving members of the Brindley unit into a reality.

The next morning, back at my house, I picked up the phone and dialled the number. I was put straight through to Viv Harper. In answer to my many questions about the project, she told me that she had been employed to help find suitable candidates for this pioneering research programme, jointly organized by surgeons, engineers, scientists and physiotherapists at Salisbury District Hospital, University College London and the Royal National Orthopaedic Hospital at Stanmore. She said the team had recently received a grant from the Medical Research Council which would allow them to sign up eight possible candidates over the next few years for clinical trials.

'I've been employed since January and we've been looking at people ever since as part of a rigorous selection process,' she told me. 'Only ten per cent of paraplegics are suitable for the implant. We already have three who've agreed to try it, but we're looking for more. Of the final eight, only one or possibly two will actually receive the implant, which is still very much in the experimental phase. There are dozens of hurdles to overcome before you can even be accepted, the most important of which is ascertaining if the "disconnected" nerves controlling your leg muscles can be stimulated electrically.'

I realized that the operation had never been done before and that they were really looking for a guinea-pig, but I was still interested all the same, and said I would like to go and see her and the team at the unit. She asked for my name and details, but when I gave them to her, her tone changed. 'Oh, I'm sorry, Julie. I've already pulled your notes from the files and you were virtually discounted as a possible candidate because of the metal rods in your spine,' she said. 'The surgeon has said that metalwork like yours would almost certainly get in the way of any implant.'

I couldn't help feeling disappointed, and my silence must have shown it. 'Why not come in and have a chat anyway?' she asked, sensing my reluctance to give up so easily. 'There still might be a chance, depending on where your rods are.' I agreed to go and see her the following week.

Six days later, with Dad at my side for moral support,

I went to meet Viv. She was slim and dark, with long hair tied back in a ponytail. She had a warm personality and was very laid back and chatty. Within minutes of arriving and introducing myself, I was stripped down to shorts and transferred to a padded bench in the medical physics laboratory, with my pale and wasted legs stretched out in front of me. Three years of inactivity had left them puffy, blotchy and unattractive.

How I hated those legs, I thought, as I stared down at them again. How many times had I sat like this, staring at them, willing them to work again, and feeling the bitter frustration of those who know they never will? It's difficult to describe the sensation to an able-bodied person, who can automatically operate whatever muscle they choose in less than the blink of an eye. It didn't matter how hard I tried – I could do nothing to close the gap between the workings of my brain and the nerves in my legs, so they lay dead and useless in front of me, heavy lumps of meat that only served to remind me, every day, of my disability.

Viv was alone, operating a small electronic device on the bench beside me, attached to wires and electrodes similar to the ones I'd seen in the FES video. She smeared an electrode with special conducting gel and placed it on my thigh, then plugged the other end in to the little box and wound up the dial to increase the electrical impulse. 'Frying tonight!' I joked, as Dad and I watched and waited for a reaction.

Before my eyes, the leg that had lain heavy and useless for three years suddenly changed shape as the upper thigh muscle contracted beautifully, forming a tight mound under the skin. I was absolutely amazed. 'Wow!' was all I could manage, and glanced up at Dad to meet his cheesy grin and to see similar excitement in his eyes. 'That's my muscle working!' I exclaimed.

All of a sudden, the idea became crystal-clear to me. If that electrode could make that muscle work, and others could make the other leg muscles contract, then with time and a bit of jiggery-pokery they might allow me to stand on my own or even take a step. It was a huge leap of the imagination, but I could suddenly see the enormous potential this technique had. It made practical sense to me, and I was firing on all cylinders at the thought. 'This could really be something,' I said to myself. 'It's certainly worth a shot. And I have nothing but time to lose.'

Viv made the muscle expand and contract several times and then switched the electrode to the other leg. That worked too, and she said that the response was ideal. 'You're certainly over the first hurdle. Your muscles are working beautifully.' No one had referred to my legs as beautiful in any way for a very long time, and I was thrilled.

'Brill,' I said. 'Now what?' The next stage was to meet Tony Tromans, the consultant surgeon from the spinal unit, a man I knew from my time in hospital two years earlier. He had never been my consultant, having joined the unit in April 1991, a few months after I had reached the exit, but I knew that he had a reputation for being very relaxed and a good laugh – the sort of person who tells the most appalling jokes but somehow gets away with it. He originally trained in orthopaedics and had been a senior registrar at Pinderfields Hospital in Wakefield, then moved into the field of spinal injuries after seeing an advert in the *British Medical Journal*. It is something he has never once regretted, because it allows him to practise 'real medicine', to sit on the edge of a bed and actually talk to patients. He had first become involved with the LARSI team as far back as 1991 when Nick Donaldson invited him and Ian Swain, the head of the medical physics department, to help him prepare a joint grant application to the MRC.

Looking much younger than his forty-odd years, with dark hair, twinkling eyes and a boyish smile, Tony Tromans was always a joy to be with. That day he wandered across to meet me in his lunch break, munching a ham sandwich while he listened carefully to Viv's account of my success with the electrodes. She handed him my notes. Perched on the edge of the bench, his cheeks as full as a hamster's, he frowned. 'This could be a problem,' he said, holding up the X-ray which showed the two seven-inch Harrington rods holding my spine together. 'These could be slap bang in the way when we get to the implant stage.'

I gulped hard and tried not to appear too down-hearted. Grinning suddenly and looking more like a naughty schoolboy than a surgeon, Mr Tromans snapped my file shut. 'But there's no point worrying about that just yet, is there, my dear?' he said, kindly. 'Let's book you in for the next stage and see how far along the road you can get.'

The next stage was a bone densitometry test – a systematic X-ray to measure the density of the bones in my legs to see if they were strong enough to be weight-bearing. If the bones had become too thin or brittle after three years of inactivity, implanting a device to make me stand on them wouldn't be worthwhile anyway. Looking at my wasted legs, I hoped I had been using them enough to keep them strong.

If I passed the bone test, the next stage would involve tests to measure the thickness of fat to muscle content using an ultrasound scanner, and that would be followed by twelve weeks' FES training at home, so that well before they even considered inserting my implant I could build up my muscle strength using the exterior electrode system. My joint contractures would have to be measured, as well as my neurological status, limb blood flow, cardiac output and muscle strength. My urine would be tested and my skin checked for its susceptibility to pressure sores; and the space in the core of my spine, the lumbar canal, would be measured with yet another scan to assess its size for any potential surgery.

Finally, I would have to undertake a tough psychological assessment to see if I was up to what I was volunteering for. My personal circumstances would be taken into consideration – whether or not I could fit the programme in with bringing up two small children – and the amount of time that had passed since my accident. The team didn't want someone who was so recently paralysed that they hadn't accepted life in a wheelchair yet and might have viewed the implant as some sort of miracle cure.

What Mr Tromans was basically saying was that he would start me on the route to selection and see how many of the tests I could pass. Having told me with a smile that I had so far passed muster, he brushed the crumbs off his clothes and went back to the operating theatre, humming quietly to himself.

'Would you like to go home and think about all this first?' Viv asked me, when she saw me looking a bit overwhelmed. 'Maybe discuss it with your family? As I said from the outset, it's a big commitment on your part.' But my expression had nothing to do with hesitation, it was my surprise at being accepted by Mr Tromans. I was hooked.

Shaking my head vigorously, I said: 'No, my mind's made up. If you'll have me, then I'd like to give it a go.' To my father, standing anxiously to one side, I added: 'I want to do this, Dad, I really want to do this.' Understandably wary of my unqualified enthusiasm, Viv insisted that I go home and sleep on it and promised to call me the next morning for my decision.

By the time I got home I was positively bubbling with excitement. Kevin's attitude was typically noncom-mittal. We were getting on much better, but he still couldn't get excited by what he considered my rather feeble attempts to try to stand. 'If it's something you want to do, then go for it,' he said, watching the motor racing on the television while he ate his supper. Neither of us had any idea of what was going to be involved, but although I was a bit afraid of what it might entail I knew that somehow it was right.

Young Daniel put everything into perspective for me the following morning. 'Why do you want to stand up, Mummy?' he asked me unexpectedly as I drove him to school. He had overheard me and Kev discussing it during breakfast.

I considered my answer carefully before responding. How could I begin to explain to an eight-year-old all the benefits the implant could give me? Deciding to simplify my answer, I said: 'Because it'll make me live longer.' I watched his face for a reaction.

'Well,' he said, grinning broadly. 'You'll just have to do it then, won't you?' Put like that, I knew how right I had been not to dither. As we prepared to enjoy another Christmas together as a family, I felt for the first time in ages that this New Year, 1994, was going to hold some exciting and special hopes for us all.

Over the next nine months I was subjected to a barrage of tests, using the strangest Heath Robinson equipment featuring great big electrical machines with giant dials and wires coming out of everywhere. With Viv, the patient's friend, clucking around like a mother hen, and Sean Hagan, the bio-engineer and techno wizard, plugging all the right wires into the right places, I often felt like little more than a rat in a science lab.

My first big hurdle was the bone densitometry test. I was laid on a bed and an X-ray device then proceeded, a millimetre at a time, down each leg, taking pictures of the density of the bone. It was tedious in the extreme. I had to lie completely still and the machine took nearly an hour to complete each leg. Fortunately, I passed with flying colours. My youth and general health apparently counted in my favour. It seemed that in spite of my poor assessment of myself, I was actually in quite good fettle for a paraplegic – mainly because of all the running around I did as a mum, getting in and out of the car half a dozen times a day to take the children to school and do the shopping, and doing all the household chores. Then came the fat-to-muscle-content test using the ultrasound machine. Once again, I passed, although there was not all that much muscle left and I was warned that I had some serious work ahead of me.

Once past those first important hurdles, I had to spend the next twelve weeks on a demanding physical fitness training programme. I also had to do a great deal of something called force-testing, where I was laid on a sort of surf-board and my leg was stimulated so as to kick out while calibrated devices measured the amount of force used. As my muscle resistance built up and the kicks became stronger and stronger, ultrasound equipment was used to measure the increasing density of my muscles. The last time I had seen an ultrasound scanner so often was when Kevin and I had watched Daniel kicking about inside my womb in what seemed like a previous lifetime. Now I watched with equal fascination as my muscles grew from shadowy embryonic size to fully fledged adulthood.

Having been taught the theory of muscle stimulation and the placing of electrodes, I was allowed to take the FES equipment home with me, where I had to learn how to attach all the right brightly coloured wires to the right electrodes and then to my legs. You needed a degree in electronics to figure it all out, and the mass of wires draped across my legs were like piles of spaghetti. There were electrodes up and down my legs, four on my buttocks and several more around my knees.

Once hooked up, I would lie in bed next to Kevin at night while he read or watched television, with the assorted electrodes plastered up and down my legs sending little impulses that made them kick up and down under the covers. First one would shoot up, then – thump – it would drop back down. Then the other, and so on. Up – thump. Up – thump. Up – thump. It went on for hours on end. Kev was very patient. He put up with it for about a month before finally losing his rag. 'For Christ's sake! Can't you do that somewhere else, I'm trying to sleep!' he snapped at me one night after I had nodded off with the machine still plugged in and my legs kicking up and down like an automated cancan dancer. I had to admit, he had a point.

After his outburst, I realized I had to find somewhere else to do it. I decided the best time was during the day while he was at work and I was sitting at the computer. With my trousers round my ankles, my calf and thigh muscles stuck all over with the little electrodes and the whole thing connected via the wires to the control box, I would set it to 'kick' and sit there for up to two hours a day, my feet thumping alternately against the wall. As my muscles built up, I added one-kilo weights to my ankles to make my legs even stronger. Playing computer games while I did it was the only thing that kept me sane.

There were certainly low points in that first year when I wondered what on earth I was doing, wasting my time with all this when there were no guarantees at the end of it and as yet little feedback from the team. The worst moments were when the boffins – or 'pointy heads' as I sometimes called them – controlling all the machinery buzzing and humming around me seemed to completely forget that there was a human being attached to the pair of legs they were so fascinated by. That's when I would lose patience and start giving them not-so-subtle hints that I was bored rigid and needed a break.

Weeks turned into months, and there seemed to be no dramatic progress. I was soon learning that there are three speeds in life – fast, slow, and research speed.

All the same, I had promised to give it my best shot and I couldn't back down now. Kev and I went on our first trip to the Gambia that year – another milestone holiday that proved to Kev, if more proof was needed, that anything was possible – and when we came home I continued to attend Salisbury's medical physics laboratory at least once a week for several months until I was finally ready to attempt my first FES stand.

I was sitting in a special chair with a control box under the seat, and a Zimmer frame was waiting in front of me with buttons attached to it, all wired up. Then the power was switched on under my seat and everything was live. Grabbing hold of the handle of the frame, I shuffled forward on my bottom ready to make the big move, while Viv pressed the appropriate button. It emitted a beep to indicate that it was ready.

'One, two, three, up you go!' Viv counted, as the surface electrodes attached to the muscles in my legs and the gluteal muscles in my buttocks made them contract and I hauled myself to my feet with my arms. Swaying gently as I stood, hanging on to the Zimmer frame, it felt very peculiar to be upright. I felt light-headed and dizzy, as the blood drained from my brain; but I also felt strangely euphoric. The stand wasn't great, but it was good enough to be able to take one hand off the Zimmer frame and drink from a glass of water that Sean the technician handed me to celebrate. It was a wonderful feeling. The next time I did it, I invited Kev and the boys along to watch and they were all well impressed. 'Blimey, Mum!' Nathan cried. He and Daniel stood alongside me, grinning, and I was thrilled that they could see me away from the wheelchair. I couldn't get over how small they looked, once I was at my full five-feet-five-inch height again.

I practised standing time and again in the next few weeks, to try and improve on the technique. More often than not, my attempts were recorded on to video tape so that the nameless engineers I had yet to meet who were working at University College in London could examine my posture. Unfortunately, my stands were often pretty shaky and I was never able to stay standing for more than ten minutes at a time because of muscle fatigue and cramp, which made me gradually sink lower and lower. I soon found that after the first excitement, the process had become a bit of an anticlimax.

But by the late autumn of 1994 I had improved my posture quite a lot, and was desperate to get on with the implant programme. By this stage, I had found out that there were four patients in line and that so far we had all come through with flying colours. In spite of my obvious problems, I was actually standing better than the rest of them, and felt I had a very good chance of being selected. As we neared the time when the doctors and biomedical engineers would have to make their choice, I became aware that I was facing some pretty stiff competition. There was only enough money at that stage for one person to have the implant operation – the rest would have to wait maybe several years – so I wanted to do everything possible to improve my chances.

For practical reasons if nothing else, the team had kept their human guinea-pigs separate from each other – there was only one set of machines at each hospital, so only one person could be dealt with at a time. There was also the psychological aspect of seeing someone else maybe doing better than you; the frustrations were real enough without adding to them. But as the discussion heated up about who would be most suited to the implant, and names were being dropped into the conversation, I started to hear the name Jenny more and more, and realized that she and I were neck and neck in pole position. The other two, both men, one called Chris, were less advanced along the conveyor belt than we were, and one, then the other, fell by the wayside.

It was at this time that I really became aware of how much the programme meant to me, and how important it was for me to win. It wasn't that I was desperate to be the world's first recipient of this remarkable treatment – I just wanted it for me, now, so as to make sense of all the time and effort I had put into it in the last year. What was extraordinary was that now Kev wanted it, too. He had seen all the hard work and effort I had put into it, and he had suddenly become very supportive of what I was aiming for. Never once did he say: 'Why don't you just forget the whole thing? It's far too much hassle,' and I really appreciated his support, especially after the previous few years of non-communication. Kev is a bit of an amateur science enthusiast, and he had become quite gripped by the idea of what I was aiming for; he had told all our friends and relatives about it, and I was hugely relieved that he was taking such an active interest. We both knew that even if I wasn't chosen, it would still have been worthwhile. I had the FES system to continue with at home – at least I could use that to maintain my stamina and make me a healthier, fitter paraplegic. But I wanted the implant badly – it was no use kidding myself. And I was really afraid that I might be rejected, especially when the question of the rods in my spine was raised again and the team began to openly doubt whether I really was the best candidate after all.

Jenny had no rods, as far as I was aware, and I dreaded her being chosen over me for that reason alone. She and I were both given CT (computerized tomography) scans to examine microscopically the exact area of the lumbar canal where the electrodes would be placed, to see if there was enough room and to exclude the possibility of something called 'arachnoiditis' – not a fear of spiders (which I have), but an inflammation of the transparent arachnoid membrane of the spinal cord.

Once that was done, we had to endure the awful 'pain and dysreflexia test', which basically involves something called an electro-ejaculatory probe being inserted into your rectum, then the voltage being whacked up to see what muscle spasms are induced and what they do to your blood pressure. I called it the 'cattle prod', and was not surprised to learn that it had been invented by Professor Brindley – someone I knew only by reputation – as a way of inducing ejaculations in paralysed men. There was no pain, just the indignity of it all and feeling like a jumping jack jerking around the table.

Dysreflexia is a common problem for the paralysed, although it affects tetraplegics more than paraplegics. When the parts of the body below the spinal break – the parts that have lost contact with the brain – are hurt or in pain (or would be, if they could feel pain), they may alert the brain the only way they know how, which is by pushing the blood pressure through the roof. It is a potentially fatal response, and most tetraplegics have to carry a special life-saving drug, nifedipine, to quickly lower the blood pressure if something happens that suddenly raises it. The pain and dysreflexia test was designed to see if Jenny or I were amongst the few paraplegics who might respond in the same way to pain, either during or after the operation. Thankfully, we both showed no response.

The day of that test was the one and only time I

met my rival – as she left and I arrived. Jenny was of a similar age to me, thin, dark-haired and slightly nervous-looking. We were friendly enough to each other, but we didn't linger for a chat. Tony Tromans had recently told us that we were almost identical with our scores, although I had won on standing and she had won on the internal mechanics. The competition between us was too much for us to allow ourselves the luxury of small-talk.

I had one final hurdle to get over, the magnetic resonance imaging (MRI) scans to see if the rods in my back would be in the way. Tony hadn't ruled out the possibility of shortening them further or even removing them altogether if they were, but it would be better if they were well clear of the key spinal root area. I was as nervous as a kitten having the scans, and thrilled when they told me that the rods wouldn't be a problem after all.

I felt that I had done my best, passed all the tests, and now it was out of my hands. The team would have to decide who would be best suited to handle the implant emotionally. Jenny and I had both undergone regular psychometric testing throughout the selection procedure to make sure that the psychological balance was right for dealing with the possible implications. If the team only had one shot at this, the last thing they wanted was the patient cracking up under the strain and all their many years of work being lost. We had both passed those tests well and our marks were entered on our score sheets. Tony Tromans joked that the competition was so close, he might as well just flip a coin. I felt like I was on a knife edge.

Now it was time for Nick Donaldson and Tim

Perkins to have their say. For some time they had only known me as the initials JH attached to Viv Harper's early reports. Then they had learned my full name and had seen me in action on video. After that, as I became better known to them through their group discussions on the various candidates' progress, I apparently became known as 'Julie', just as my chief rival was 'Jenny', and so on. But Nick and Tim had never personally met me or any of the other candidates in all the months we had been in pre-selection training, and the decision as to which one of us would be chosen was helped by their ability to be entirely impartial.

By the autumn of 1994, with just me and Jenny to choose from, they had an unenviable task. Each of us had points in our favour, and the team worked very strictly to the scoring system and according to the assessment of Viv, Sean, a senior biomedical engineer at Salisbury called Paul Taylor, and the head of the medical physics department, Ian Swain, who each tried to judge our individual personalities in terms of physical suitability, endurance and interest. Tony Tromans knew us both and his input was enormously helpful, but in the end it would be up to Nick and Tim to decide. Each test we went through had a point-scoring system of zero to five, and each individual score was added to our final score. We continued to be neck and neck.

I knew it would be a close call, but exactly how close I didn't know until very much later. There were several intensive group discussions about who was the best and why, and for a while the team was simply unable to choose between the two of us. Sadly, there was only enough money for one to go forward, and there was no telling how long it would be before the next trial. The responsibility of their decision weighed heavily on all of them – for the person who would be rejected as well as for the one they would take on. This had to be a long-term commitment on all their parts; it was for life, not simply for the duration of the research grant.

By the time the day came when the choice had to be made, Touch Productions, an independent television documentary team, had got wind of the pioneering project and were starting to film the early stages of the selection process. The team had willingly agreed to have its every move filmed for posterity, but it was horrified when the film-makers began to express a preference. They apparently thought that I was more photogenic and a better proposition in publicity terms as I had a husband and two small children. Jenny was single. Determined not to be influenced by that preference, the team now re-examined the facts and figures with even more care, sticking as strictly as ever to the points system.

At the end of October, a case conference was called in which all those concerned sat around a table in London looking at data graphs and statistical results to decide who it should be. I knew about the meeting and was on tenterhooks all day, wondering what was being said. What wouldn't I have given to be a fly on the wall! It surprised me how much I had come to want the implant; I couldn't face the idea of being rejected and told to come back in a few years.

When I heard nothing that night I feared the worst. I hardly slept a wink for worrying. The following morning, the phone rang. It was Viv with the words: 'What are you doing on December the fifteenth?' I had won – by one point – although bearing in mind the incredible ordeal I was about to allow my body to undergo, the word 'winner' was, to many minds, a bit of a misnomer. 'Do you want to think about it before you give us your final answer?' Viv asked me, once I had stopped squealing with delight into the phone.

'No. Absolutely not,' I told her. 'I'm not backing out now. As long as I'm home for Christmas, I'll go through with it.' Poor Jenny, she received the phone call I had dreaded, and she later withdrew from the programme altogether, not even allowing herself the benefit of the FES system. I only hope she found happiness elsewhere.

NINE

Spotlight

During the next two months, I virtually moved back into hospital. I now became the subject of a whole new range of complicated tests and measurements under Viv and Sean's careful guidance. There were a great many preliminary experiments to be done and I had to drive to Salisbury once a week for a full day's testing, the results of which were sent on to Nick and Tim at University College, as they continued to analyse, question and scrutinize every minute piece of data. Up until then their role had been that of 'sleeping partners', long-distance consultants, working on the software and advising on who might be the best candidate and why, based on each individual's personal data.

In the many years that they had been working together, devising their unique implant system amongst the clutter of their laboratories, they had dealt chiefly with animals, dead bodies, machines and statistics. Now that they had a real person to work with, someone who could talk back and tell them how it all felt, they seemed rather shy. Neither of them came to Salisbury to meet me in those early stages. I put this down to 'boffinism', having visions of mad-looking men in white coats surrounded by bubbling test-tubes and electric dials, unable to cope with life in the outside world, or – God forbid – meet a woman. The strange thing was, my fantasy turned out to be not that far removed from reality, especially when it came to Tim.

Regardless of their apparent reluctance to meet me, I plodded on religiously with all the tests, working towards our common goal. My progress at this stage was helped enormously by a most unlikely ally – Kevin. Realizing that the operation was now definitely going ahead, and beginning to believe that it might actually work, he had changed his attitude to it almost overnight. Not only did his interest increase enormously, but he began to accompany me to appointments, offering commonsense advice when technology failed. From being at least fifty per cent against me and my disability, he was now a hundred per cent behind me. His support meant a great deal to me after all the negativity he had shown. Being proactive really helped; it made us both genuinely interested in something that would affect us as a family and it felt good to be in tune with each other again. As Kev said to me on the way home from a day of testing, 'I feel like we've really got something in common again, don't you?'

Meanwhile, the television documentary crew headed by Malcolm Brinkworth and Benetta Adamson became more and more involved, filming my every move at home and in trials in the lead-up to the operation. My new 'celebrity status' put me in an entirely different light when it came to friends and acquaintances. Suddenly everybody wanted to meet me, to 'press the flesh' as Kev put it, and to talk about the implant programme.

Not that being the focus of so much attention was all that easy, to begin with. Having a film crew around all the time, sticking a camera in our faces and asking us how we were both feeling, was very strange. But we soon got used to it, and after a while we hardly even saw the camera, just the people behind it. Telling someone you barely know about your innermost fears and feelings can be surprisingly beneficial. Counselling was never an option for Kev; there wasn't much on offer then anyway, but even if there had been, he would have turned it down. This didn't feel like counselling, but it was. Sitting down and quietly talking to someone outside the family about intensely painful and private issues was incredibly cathartic, especially for Kev. He and the film crew developed a close bond, and they were able to make him open up for the first time about subjects that had been closed to the rest of us. I felt nothing but relief.

At Salisbury, the project was going full steam ahead. Professor Rushton had made a series of dummy electrodes and given them to Tony Tromans to practise on in the hospital mortuary. After working on one corpse, implanting the electrodes on to the corresponding spinal roots, Tony found that the design wasn't quite right and so he adapted the electrodes by dividing them and then modifying them. After two more rehearsals with Nick Donaldson at his side to see how it worked – his first time as a witness to an operation and his first sight of a corpse – and some late-night fiddling around on his kitchen table, systematically destroying then repairing the rubber cables that would be used in my operation, Tony felt he was as ready as he ever would be.

A nursing team had been built around me in preparation, and things were moving so fast that it was only when I was asked to sign a complicated two-page consent form to the operation, a few days before the big day, that the reality of it all hit me. The form pointed out all the possible pitfalls – the dangers of anaesthetic during such lengthy surgery and the chance that when I woke up I might actually be more paralysed than before. The various hard-hitting warnings of all the risks to my spine, my brain and my life made for salutary reading.

> I understand that this is a research project and that the outcome from the procedure is not known. The operation involves the opening of the spinal canal and there is a small risk of destabilizing the spine.

Seeing that in black and white really took my breath away – the thought that I could be much worse off after the operation than I was before. This was serious. The consent form went on:

> If this is recognized during the operation, a fusion will be undertaken, but there is a possibility of late instability and a further stabilizing operation may be required.
>
> The operation involves the opening of the dura (meninges) [the membrane protecting the spinal cord] and this will be closed at the end of the procedure, but there is a risk of leakage of CSF (spinal fluid) leading to extended bed rest or further surgery to repair the leak.
>
> There is a risk of infection of the implant which because of its intimate involvement with the spinal

cord and brain would be serious and would require the removal of the implant to achieve control.

I have been told that there is a risk of nerve damage at the time of the operation. This may affect the working of the implant and although there should be recovery over many months, there is some possibility of permanent damage preventing full function of the stimulator.

As a result of scarring within the dura (meninges), the possibility of further surgery such as for a bladder controller may not be possible. As a result of scarring within the dura, the free flow of spinal fluid might be impaired and this might give rise to damage higher up the spinal cord.

I have had the pain and dysreflexia test which was negative, but I understand that there is still a possibility of long-term post-operative pain and discomfort.

It was Tony Tromans's uncomfortable task to take me and Kev through the consent form point by point, adding a few of his own warnings along the way. 'The implants have been tested on the workbench and they do what they are supposed to do – on the workbench,' he said, his eyes twinkling. 'Are you happy with everything?'

My throat was suddenly dry. I nodded. 'Yeah,' I said finally, clutching Kevin's hand. 'I mean, I know everything now, don't I? I'm going in with my eyes wide open, basically.'

Tony carried on. He explained that in the worst-case scenario my spine could be so badly destabilized by the operation, or so badly infected by the implant, that I could suffer serious brain or nerve damage. My paralysis could move further up the spinal cord and I could end up far worse off than when I started. 'The greater risk is if the facet joints are damaged during the operation. They are the little bone spurs that link the bones in the spine and interconnect with the discs. There may be a risk, but if the facet joints are seen to be damaged, we'll take measures at the time of the operation to repair that damage, but part of that repair may involve wearing a spinal brace on the outside for a period for short-term stability, and then a bone graft for the long term.'

'What are the percentages of that happening?' I asked him nervously.

He tilted his head to one side and considered his response before answering. 'Can't say,' he finally said, adding: 'Well, you know, Julie, don't you, that we have to cover all the possibilities in the consent form?'

'Well, you'll just have to be careful then!' I said, my eyes glowing.

'It's something you can't say,' he added, still giving the matter consideration. 'There's a possibility that we won't recognize instability at the time of the operation and it will develop secondarily. If it does, we'll obviously have to take measures. That will involve an allayed spinal fusion.'

I gulped hard as Kevin asked a question: 'That would be another operation, to go in all over again?' I could see his mind racing ahead, thinking of all the possible problems that would cause. We had both heard horror stories of spinal fusion operations and of people left virtually rigid by the procedure.

Tony nodded. 'It's difficult for me to put an exact risk on it. For me to turn round and say it's a five per cent risk is meaningless. If you're in the five per cent, then it isn't good. It's almost impossible for me to say – it can't be quantified,' he concluded matter-of-factly, meeting my gaze.

I sighed and smiled for the first time. 'No problem then,' I said. 'Where do I sign?'

No matter how nervous I felt, I was driven once again by instinct; I knew I had to go through with it, I couldn't possibly back out now. I would never forgive myself if I didn't at least give it a serious try. It was no longer just about me and my needs; there were the boys to consider and Kev, who was giving me his full support. I had the film crew to think of – their hopes and expectations. Not to mention all the friends and relatives who had been so interested and supportive. No, tempting as it was to drive off alone into the sunset and forget the whole thing, I had a duty to everyone to carry on. Scary as it all seemed, I had gone past the point of no return.

My mother, a natural pessimist, was deeply concerned about me having yet another big operation. 'You're still my little girl and I can't help but be worried,' she told me tearfully the day before the operation. 'I won't be happy until it's all over.' We were still so close, Mum and I; we saw each other almost every day and spent ages on the phone to each other in between, a serious bone of contention with Kev and my dad when the phone bills came in.

She had been my rock for as long as I could remember, especially since the accident, making all the necessary arrangements with Kev to have the children collected from school, fed, watered and delivered home to their own beds each night. Now, she looked as frightened as she had the first day she came to St Richard's after the accident and stood weeping at my bedside. She couldn't really understand why I didn't just forget all this nonsense about implants and standing and get on with my life as it was. 'You can do everything you want to already,' she said. 'You've been on more adventure holidays since the accident than you ever did before, and you can stand if you want to with the FES. It just seems pointless risking your health for this.' I tried hard to explain it to her, but I still felt incredibly guilty at making her go through it all again.

'Don't worry, Mum,' I tried to reassure her. 'I've told them to be gentle with me and they said they would.' She promised she would be there for me after the operation, and I knew she would, but I could see her face was showing the stresses and strains of the past four years. Her friend Doris was taking her out shopping and for lunch while I was under the knife, but I knew she wouldn't be happy until she'd heard from the hospital that I had pulled through.

The children were wonderful about it all when I told them I was going back into hospital. 'As long as you're home for Christmas,' they chorused. They had become such well-balanced, independent boys, helping me out around the house uncomplainingly, fetching and carrying, even planting out the hanging baskets each year. I was so proud of them. I promised them I would be home, and after the third time of telling him that I had to be home by 24 December, Tony Tromans vowed that if he had to carry me home on a stretcher himself he wouldn't make me break my promise.

Try as I might to focus on Christmas, there was no escaping the fact that I had a lot to go through first. I was about to enter uncharted territory, and so were the team. Their own trepidation was evident in their eyes. Viv, I think, was especially terrified on my behalf and praying that nothing would go wrong. As a mother of young children herself and with the insight of her medical background, she was naturally concerned. Her biggest fear was that I might end up in continual pain from nerve root damage. If that happened, there was not much that could be done about it.

Much as I dreaded the idea of major surgery and returning in a body brace to the spinal unit where my dark days had first begun, I knew that I was doing it for a greater good – hopefully, mine. I have to say that there was little sense of the pioneer spirit in me then. I knew this was a world first, but all my reasons for doing it were, at the moment, entirely selfish. I wanted this for me, for Kevin and the children. It was as simple as that.

When it came to the science side of it, my under-standing of what was going to happen was as sketchy as it had always been. Frankly, most of what had been explained to me in the previous year had gone way over my head, but I think by this time I had come to an acceptance in my own way of what was about to take place. If there was anything I didn't understand, I asked Kev. His newly discovered fascination with biomedical science meant that by now he had absorbed a huge amount of information about the whole procedure.

But for now, it was just another scary moment in a series of scary moments that had started four years earlier that April night when my car left the road. If the accident had taught us one thing, it was that you should never be complacent about life. We were the couple who had it all, and we had lost it in a split second of destiny. Never in a million years back then would I have imagined that this was how my life would map out or that, in another series of fateful encounters, I would become famous as the world's first ever walking, talking, all-singing, all-dancing paraplegic.

The operation was planned for Wednesday 7 December 1994. In the weeks running up to it, I had been prodded and poked, tested, measured and interviewed. I had even had my first counselling session with a psychologist, an hour-long 'chat' to see if I really would cope mentally with all that I was about to go through. Two days before the op, I went in for blood and urine tests to make sure I was fighting fit. Fortunately, I was – one pressure sore or the slightest symptom of a cold would have led to the cancellation of the whole thing, and I would have had to wait until the New Year for another chance.

On the Tuesday evening, the night before the operation, I said my goodbyes to the kids and to Mum and Dad – fleeing from the house before the tears started – and Kev drove me to the hospital to settle me in. The place seemed deserted, apart from the film crew waiting to record my nervy arrival. With hardly anyone about, the temptation to turn round and go home again was enormous. Having dropped off my bags and checked me in, Kev said he might as well get on home. 'I've got a long day tomorrow,' he reminded me. He was going to go to work as usual and then drive to the hospital as soon as he heard the operation was over.

Asking the film crew to give me a few minutes' privacy with Kev, I wheeled myself down to the car with him, quite tearful and, frankly, terrified. More than anything, it was a fear of the unknown. I was about to make medical history, but there were no guarantees. Reminding myself that this was all a big adventure, and something that I had chosen to do because if I didn't I would spend the rest of my life wondering why I hadn't, I braced myself for what was to happen, whatever the outcome. In for a penny, in for a pound.

'I'll see you then,' Kev said, bending over to kiss me on the cheek and squeeze my hand as we reached his company car. His jaw was clenching with anxiety. He couldn't express his feelings any more than I could.

'Yup. I'll see you tomorrow,' I replied as brightly as I could, looking up at him, my words catching in my throat. We managed to make it sound as if tomorrow would be just another ordinary day.

'Good luck,' he said suddenly, pulling me into his arms for a final hug and kiss. He clung on to me for several seconds longer than usual, as if he never wanted to let me go.

I couldn't reply. For that instant, I felt like a gibbering wreck. Burying my face in his shoulder, I struggled to control my emotions before pushing him away. Without another word, he got into his car and drove off, giving me a sad little wave.

Back by my bed, my eyes dried, I looked again at the giant Get Well card Daniel had made for me, signed by all his friends at school, along with the teachers and the rest of the staff. It was full of action-packed images of me having fun. There were pictures of me in my wheelchair skiing down a mountain, sitting on a roller-coaster ride screaming, and water-skiing. But the one that caught my eye and that I stared and stared at now was a tiny one in the bottom left-hand corner of the card. It was a drawing of me standing, my arms in the air, smiling, with my wheelchair at my side.

Later that night, I met Nick Donaldson and the silver-haired Professor Rushton for the first time. They had both come to Salisbury in preparation for their vital contribution to the operation the following morning and thought it would be nice to finally say hello. It felt quite an honour, to meet them after all this time, and I told them so.

'I hope I don't let you down,' I told Nick, knowing that my responses to his implant could seriously affect his life's work.

He blushed shyly and bowed his head. 'On the contrary,' he said. 'It is I who don't want to let you down, after all your splendid efforts.'

David Rushton, ever the more serious one, sat on the edge of my bed and looked me in the eye. 'Now, Julie,' he said gravely. 'Are you really sure you want to go through with this? I mean, it's not too late to back down, you know.'

My mind flashed back to the night before my wedding and my mother's gentle words of advice. That had been the most important decision of my life, whether or not to marry Kevin. Despite all the trauma of our recent years together, I knew that I had made the right choice. Now, I was being given a similar chance on a similarly vital decision. And once again, I was determined to go through with it.

'Thanks, David, but no thanks,' I said quietly. 'I know exactly what I'm doing and I want to go ahead with it.'

He and Nick looked at each other almost nervously, and I realized that they were as anxious as I was about the operation. Bless them, they were such lovely, gentle people who had taken such an active role in improving the lives of the disabled ever since they had first teamed up with Giles Brindley. Meeting them helped focus my mind on the task ahead. I mentally added their names to the long list of people I was determined not to disappoint.

I had engineered it so that I was placed in Tamar Ward, not Avon where I had first been, but the ward that was now run by many familiar faces – Paula, Elaine and 'Big Jo'. It was Jo – a lovely bubbly person and a good friend – who organized it so that my new nursing team would be the ones who had known me from the outset, so that I would feel at home. To take my mind off the momentous events of the following morning, Jo even took me to the cinema in Salisbury that night to see *The Nightmare Before Christmas*, a frightening animated film featuring witches, wolves and warlocks. If my nerves weren't frazzled before we sat down, they were certainly shot to pieces by the time I came out. It was all I could do to get my post-film pizza down.

I was very glad Kev hadn't stayed – we would have been as jumpy as each other. He needed to get home and be with the boys, and I needed to be kept busy with someone who would completely understand if I lost control in the face of my fear. I was given a pill to help me sleep, and as my eyelids grew heavier and heavier I tried to think of anything but the next day.

One thought that kept me awake that night was how painful it might be. I had always been a big baby when it came to pain – as Becky and others would testify – and it bothered me that I wasn't going to be given the normal dose of anaesthetic for such major surgery. Although I had no feeling below my waist and couldn't have felt any surgery there anyway, I still had feeling by my ribcage, where they would be inserting the implant. My whole body needed to be numbed to a certain extent so as to remove the risk of spasm or dysreflexia, but the normal dose of anaesthetic would have desensitized my muscles and nerves to the point that the team working on me would be unable to test which electrodes were attached to which nerves. It was the anaesthetist's job to keep me on the fringes of consciousness without allowing me to suffer too much pain. I had met her already, a lovely lady called Penny Shaw, and when I woke in the morning after a fitful night's sleep it was she who was leaning over the bed.

'Good morning, are you ready for the off?' she asked cheerily. I told her I had changed my mind about the pre-med – I wanted to keep a clear head in case I changed my mind.

Lying back on my pillow, I felt I had the look of those condemned to death by beheading who can only hope the executioner has sharpened his axe. My last recollection before I went into theatre was of being frozen with fear and unable to see very much because my contact lenses had been removed. The film crew were at my side as usual, monitoring every expression, and I found myself wishing that my face wasn't scrubbed clean of all make-up.

As the theatre staff wheeled me through the double doors, they accidentally banged my bed against the wall. I urged them to be more careful. 'I hope you're better at driving the machinery than you are this thing,' I joked. It was the last feeble attempt at humour of a condemned woman.

Feeling tense and tearful as I arrived in theatre, I nearly jumped out of my skin when Tony Tromans leapt out at me in his blue gown and theatre cap, and started to sing *Morning Has Broken*, which seemed appropriate to him because of the early hour. What he didn't know was that it was the song that had been sung at my wedding. It was just the tension-breaker I needed, especially with a camera poked into my face.

'Bloody idiot!' I gasped, moments before an oxygen mask was placed over my nose and mouth. Closing my eyes, I took a deep breath.

I was on the operating slab for nearly nine hours, carefully monitored, watched and filmed. Tony Tromans had already done three trial runs on corpses in the hospital mortuary – this is what he referred to as the 'workbench'. There he learned to split the electrodes into four separate 'books', each one to contain three nerves, so that they would fit more easily inside my spinal canal. Each dry run had taken just over an hour, but I was to be under the knife for over eight times as long.

Tony started by making a ten-centimetre mid-line incision down my lower back, stripping the muscles off the spine and then performing a laminectomy, which meant removing four levels of bone, exposing the membrane protecting the spinal cord, the dura. Working inside a hole less than two centimetres wide, he was confronted with twenty different nerves, each two and a half millimetres wide, all bundled together, from which he had to identify the right ones. The first had to be a guess, and the only way to identify them was to run a current through each one and see which muscle groups it affected.

Picking up a nerve on a hook, Tony Tromans dropped it on to an L-shaped electrode and, with the help of Nick Donaldson standing at the mixer box a few feet away, passed a small electric current through it, so that he could see what and where the reaction was. It was all Nick could do to focus on the controls as Tony carefully attached each electrode to a nerve ending and asked him to test it, watching and waiting for the muscles in my leg to twitch or contract each time. Sitting either side of my legs were engineers who were watching to see which muscles twitched and on what stimulus. Having identified each nerve, if it wasn't one he wanted Tony placed it gently in vascular tape – flexible plasticized rubber tape in different colours which he used to identify the different nerves – before moving up to the next one.

Once he had identified the twelve nerves he needed, he had to split each one into two. Each nerve has a sensory and a motor part, one half for sensation, the other for movement, but the only way to tell the two apart is the very slight colour difference – one is white and the other is cream. It's unfortunate that they are not colour-coded brown, blue and yellow/green like an electric plug. The difference is very subtle and the slightest bruising can make it impossible to tell them apart.

A motor nerve is like an electric wire – impulses are transmitted to the muscles along a fibre, or axon, which is protected and insulated by a myelin sheath. It is extremely fragile and, if handled, can swell and die. But provided the cell body at the top of the nerve stays alive, the axon will grow again. If the myelin sheath is damaged, the axon will only grow back as far as the point of damage. In my case, two of the nerves were never to recover completely, but whether this was caused by permanent physical damage or a loose connection the team has no way of knowing.

Assisted by Professor Rushton, Tony Tromans had to make sure to fix the electrode only to the motor part. Although I didn't have any sensory function, he didn't want to damage that part in case it affected my sensory function elsewhere, or caused problems later on. Once identified and classified, the sensory nerve was laid gently beside the electrode, trying not to damage it. The motor nerve was then laid gently inside the U-shaped electrode, which had three gulleys inside it. There were four electrode mounts, allowing for twelve electrodes in all, and all of them were attached to just four cables, each with four wires.

After all twelve motor nerves were identified and positioned, a lid was put on to the bunch of nerves and, using a hypodermic syringe, sealed with a blob of silicone rubber glue so as to keep everything watertight. The glue only needed to hold it in place for three or four days until my own body scarring held it in place and it formed a tight seal. Tony Tromans described it as 'just like sealing up the bath'.

The whole process, combining the very latest in medical and electronic science, had only ever been carried out on a mortuary slab before, and yet here was I, the team's first *in vivo* (live subject), making medical history. It was the realization for all the team, of a twenty-year dream first inspired by Professor Brindley. To see what they had been working on for so long finally all come together in their lifetime was a very emotional moment.

But there was no time for sentimentality. There was a job of work to be done. The most testing part of the operation complete, Tony Tromans then had to carefully close up my spinal canal, using more of the special glue to prevent the spinal fluid from leaking, suture the dura and carefully pull the four protruding cables through a grommet and then a device known as a 'top hat' because of its shape, sealing it with more glue. The plan was to remove any twists or loops in the wire, so that they wouldn't knot, and to insulate the wires in silicone rubber sleeves and glue to stop them either short-circuiting or causing local stimulation of muscles. A short-circuit was a big worry: it could spark a muscle spasm in my chest or it could cause pain, and both were to be avoided. But the connectors Tony was using had been tried and tested in thousands of patients who were using the bladder stimulators and had a pretty reliable track record.

While waiting for the glue to dry, Tony and his team tested the implant again, stimulating it through the cables to confirm the different responses and to try the resistance of the electrodes. If there had been any major problems at that stage, and the electrodes hadn't worked the second time around, the surgical team would have had just enough time to go back into my lumbar canal and start again.

The main concern was the possible leak of CSF fluid from the spinal cord. Tony asked Penny, the anaesthetist, to do something called a Valsalva manoeuvre, which involved putting pressure on the lungs to see if there was any evidence of leaking down the stitch line. The manoeuvre was completed without any leakage, and Tony was confident that he had made a good seal and could proceed.

Taking the four untangled cables, each one coated in a special rubber solution impregnated with antibiotics which had a slow-release mechanism to ward off infection over several weeks, Tony now had to make a narrow tunnel through the layers of skin and muscle, routing it from the base of the spine, up my back ten centimetres and then round my middle towards my right ribcage to where the multiplexing receiver would be sited. He then had to feed each cable through the tunnel and out the other side, until all four were ready to be connected to the implanted receiver.

I was then turned on to my side while the receiver, the size of a large pocket watch, was sewn to a piece of muscle tissue into a natural indentation under my ribcage known as the lower anterior chest wall. The connections were made by a series of small plugs glued together and encased in an insulating sleeve. Fifteen centimetres of excess cabling, neatly looped up in two coils, was also left under my skin, causing a noticeable but unavoidable lump. Tony admitted afterwards that the extra cable was a bit of a mistake. He had asked Nick for it but when it came to the operation he found it wasn't needed, by which time it was too late to do anything about it. 'It was common sense taking one step, not two,' he said defensively. The only advantage would have been that if a repair had had to be done later, they could simply have cut away the affected part and reconnected it, using the spare cable.

Everything they had put inside me had been heavily coated to avoid infection, and as a further precaution I would also be given three doses of antibiotics once I had regained consciousness. Finally, Tony Tromans sewed up the various incisions he had made and gently turned me on to my back, the first time I had not been face down for several hours.

Now all they had to do was wait for me to wake up and recover my strength, before they could know whether the operation had been a success – or even whether they had inadvertently caused more damage than I had suffered already. I would be forced to lie flat on my back for several days because of the risk of spinal fluid leakage. It was a tense time for everyone, not least my family, whose knowledge of the whole process was limited – except for Kevin – to little more than the fact that they knew the team had, to some extent, been whistling in the dark.

At the end of the operation, the surgeons had no idea whether or not the surgery had been a success – which is unusual. They only knew they had done their best to attach the right parts to the right bits. The outcome wouldn't be known for several days, until I had fully recovered and they could 'switch on'. Until then, it was a case of a wing and a prayer.

I could take some reassurance, though, from the fact that it wasn't wholly experimental. The unit had many years of experience behind them in the field; there had been the two soldiers and all the other volunteers who, in their own way, had each contributed to the huge bank of knowledge that the team had built up. The problem was that there was still not enough of that knowledge about the workings of the human body to guide them; the team knew from the outset that they would be bound to make mistakes, which they would learn from, but they also knew that they would have to make those mistakes on me. Their motto has always been that 'persistence pays off', and they were painfully aware that my operation could become a very costly experiment in terms of money and time, as they felt their way through a so far untested process. It was a massive undertaking for everyone concerned – there wasn't one of them who wasn't well aware that they might have overlooked something or made a mistake. A huge responsibility rested on all their shoulders. Silence prevailed as I was wheeled out of the operating theatre and taken to the recovery room.

TEN

Switch-on

COMING TO my senses after the operation, my first
fuzzy glimpse of the world was Kevin's smiling
face. He had always been there for me at times like this,
after every operation, to squeeze my hand and say hello.
I was very glad to see him now. Just a foot or two
behind him, as ever, was Dad, my wonderful father
Norman, who, in his own way, had always been there
for me too. Even when he was away at sea when I was
a child, he had never stopped writing home, letting me
know where he was on the world map and how much
he loved me. Looking at the two of them now through
the fog that was my sight without contact lenses, I felt
very grateful even though I was still as high as a kite.

'How did it go?' I mumbled hoarsely, suddenly
feeling thirsty as hell and unable to swallow. Kev handed
me an ice cube to suck on, which was cool and refresh-
ing on my furred-up tongue. I felt ghastly, and I didn't
know it then but my face was puffed up like a pink
marshmallow after nine hours of lying on my stomach
during the surgery. Neither Kev nor Dad felt it was
worth mentioning or, if it comes to that, seemed to care.

They were just pleased to see me awake and apparently all right.

'Sounds great,' Kev replied, 'they're all very pleased.' He began to say more, but seeing that I was dropping off again, he whispered: 'We'll be back tomorrow.' A morphine-induced sleep took over then as I took a return flight to Cloud-cuckoo-land with my pixie chum. For the next few hours I stayed semi-conscious. I was reasonably comfortable in the acute ward of the spinal unit, surrounded by people I knew and loved, and all seemed well with the world.

But by the time the first dose of morphine had worn off, the discomfort had really set in. I felt very unwell and seemed to hurt all over. I was still very groggy, and although the only part of me that I could actually feel had been tampered with was the area around my ribcage where the receiver had been put, I somehow sensed that every inch of me had been battered and bruised. It felt as if I had done a few rounds with Mike Tyson, and lost.

The only thing really wrong was that I was completely exhausted. The operation really took it out of me. Tony had warned me that it would take at least seven weeks to recover, adding cheerily: 'At least you won't have the "ouch" factor – feeling pain each time you move the bits we interfered with.' For that I was truly grateful, but all the same I felt physically very depleted – which was not surprising, considering the kind of surgery I had just undergone. All I wanted to do was sleep, but uninterrupted rest was not an option. I was back to the four-man turns every three hours, in an attempt to avoid pressure sores, which could lead to a dangerous infection.

There was nothing to do but put up with the turning

and wait for my spine to stabilize, to see if it had been adversely affected by the lengthy operation. Morphine was available on tap now, with the wonderful self-dosing invention that allows people like me, with a very low pain threshold, not to have to beg for relief. Although I felt incredibly dopey, I was pretty much able to control my pain over the next five days.

People started to trickle in to see me, close family members and friends. Even though I was forced to receive them lying flat on my back, the atmosphere this time couldn't have been more different to the way it was after my first operation. Then, there had been tears and recriminations, sad, pale faces and long, awkward silences. Now my bedside was teeming with happy, chattering people, all delighted to see me, all excited about the implant and what it might mean. It was all so upbeat, and I couldn't wait to get upright again.

In spite of the lively atmosphere around me, though, and the apparent success of the operation so far, I was painfully aware of the feelings of the people around me in the ward – young men and women who had probably been spinally injured only recently and were now just beginning to face up to their own personal nightmare. The last thing they'd want, I thought, was the sight of someone who was years ahead of them as far as recovery was concerned and undergoing something that they might never even be offered. Not wanting to impose myself on them at a time like this, I had approached each of them in turn before the operation and gingerly asked if they minded me being there. 'I can always see if they can stick me in a room on my own,' I told them. But the response I got was fantastic. To a bed, they all urged me to carry on with what I was doing and thanked me for pushing ahead the research process that might one day help them. I felt truly humbled.

One person in particular who moved me with his courage was a remarkable young man called David Norman. David was a twenty-three-year-old diabetic who had overcome his medical problem to lead a full and active life. A talented student in his final year at university, he was also a keen sportsman and a naturally giving and warm person. His parents were called Bill and Elsbeth and he had a sister called Lizzie, and he was the apple of their eye. Two days before his twenty-second birthday at a party held at the local rugby club, he and his friends thought it would be fun to try 'bar diving' – literally diving head first off the bar and into the arms of their friends before being thrown up into the air and caught again. Unfortunately for David, something went badly wrong, his friends weren't quite ready to catch him and he fell head first to the ground. The consequence of those few seconds of youthful high spirits was that he snapped his neck and became a ventilator-dependent tetraplegic – the most paralysed anyone can be – unable to move anything but his head, unable to breathe for himself, feed or clean himself. His life was in ruins.

David had been on Tamar Ward for a year before I arrived for my big op, and it was instantly clear to me how much he was loved and respected by all the staff and fellow inmates. When he asked Jo if I would go and see him in the four-bed unit and tell him all about the implant, I was honoured. I had felt very awkward about being in the same ward as him but he soon put my mind at rest.

'It's a unique experiment,' I began, trying to share

some of the enthusiasm for the project with him. 'If it works for me, who knows where it could lead?' David listened carefully, taking in every word and asking questions. His clarity of mind was evident. 'It all sounds fantastic, Julie,' he said, speaking in that slow, deliberate way of all high-tetraplegics, as his breathing laboured under the strain. 'I'm delighted for you. I wish you and the team every success.'

I swallowed hard as my eyes filled with tears. I was deeply moved by his generosity of spirit. Here was I, with so much going for me in comparison to him, and yet I was daring to ask for even more. I wished there was something I could do to ease his pain. My guilt was compounded much later when I learned that David was in the process of doing something quite remarkable. He was planning to end his own life, and intended to do it as soon as the relevant authorities allowed. Being a diabetic, he couldn't exist without his insulin, and he had calmly and rationally decided that, rather than be a burden for the rest of his life, he would simply refuse his medication and drift quietly off into a coma. It was the most selfless decision I had ever known anybody make.

His parents were horrified at first, as any parents would be. They pleaded with him to change his mind, to see some positives in what had happened to him. But he couldn't. He wasn't feeling sorry for himself; it wasn't going to be an act of desperation or depression. It was the conscious decision of a well-adjusted young man that his life was over and he simply wanted to hasten the end. The hospital was incredibly supportive. They sent psychiatrists and doctors to give him what counselling and advice he needed, but agreed to comply with his wishes if his decision was the same after he had seen them.

A few months later, when all the talking was over, David said his goodbyes. In accordance with his wishes and with the support of all those who loved him, his insulin was stopped and within forty-eight hours he went into a coma and died. In his will he left his entire trust fund of £40,000 to Back-Up, to benefit other paralysed people. A memorial service for him was held in the spinal unit, and everyone who knew and loved him was there. David Norman touched my life only briefly, but I am a richer, better person for it. I have kept in touch with Bill and Elsbeth, who bore their son's death with great courage. His words of encouragement to me were never fresher in my mind than when I waited to find out if the implant was working.

By the end of my first week after the operation, I was allowed to sit up very slightly in bed, at an angle, although not really allowed to move very much, and was beginning to get fired up. Almost every member of the surgical team had been to see me individually to tell me excitedly that it would soon be time for the first switch-on, which would be the real moment of truth. I felt like the Christmas fairy-lights.

On the morning of D-Day, 12 December 1994, I overslept and was running late. But I needn't have worried because the M3 motorway was shut that morning and everyone was delayed anyway. Also I was told that there were some worrying hard- and software problems which Nick and Tim had stayed up all the previous night to try and sort out. Using dummy implants concealed under layers of foam, they had tried to solve the problem using logarithmic scales and playing with the computer. What they didn't want was to push a slider control too far or press a wrong switch and give me a surge of power that would send me leaping out of bed like a jack-in-the-box, destabilizing my spine and ripping open my stitches, or send me crashing to the floor.

The ten o'clock deadline came and went and by then I was so desperate for a cigarette that I asked Kev to wheel my bed along to the 'potting shed' for a quiet smoke with him and Dad. Mum was home looking after the kids, waiting for news. I was feeling very apprehensive, not least because I had developed a huge spot on my face and today was the day I was going to be in the spotlight – good word – once again. 'I hope this is all worthwhile,' I told Kev, puffing hard on my cigarette.

'It will be,' he promised me with a smile, but I knew that he was only guessing, as we all were.

Inhaling the smoke nervously, I suddenly saw what looked like a cast of thousands trooping down the corridor towards my ward from the electronics laboratory. There was Tony Tromans, David Rushton, Viv and Nick, Tim Perkins – to whom I was about to be introduced for the very first time – and about a dozen other people, including the film crew and assorted nursing staff, all bearing down on me with gleams in their eyes. After stubbing out my cigarette, I prepared myself mentally as Kev hurriedly wheeled me back to the ward. It was a big moment for everybody, and you could tell from the look of trepidation on Nick's and Tim's faces that there was a real chance that the bloody thing simply wouldn't work.

'Pleased to meet you,' Tim said, shaking my hand

warmly. He was just as Tony Tromans had described – a cross between Merlin and an Old Testament prophet, with his fuzz of grey hair and bushy beard. He had a wonderful smile and the slightly mad, staring eyes I'd expect from a boffin. 'I've seen you on video,' he added, referring to the footage of me using the surface electrodes. 'Very impressive – I admired the posture.' The thought crossed my mind briefly that if I'd seen *him* on a video before the op, I might never have agreed to go through with it! I thanked him nervously and wondered for a moment what on earth I had let myself in for, allowing my body to be used as a human guinea-pig for someone who seemed a little eccentric, to say the least.

As Nick, David Rushton and Tim busied themselves with the incredibly complicated home-made mixer box, which would hopefully send the signals to the transmitter, which would then make sense of them and use them to 'talk' to the receiver, like in a telephone exchange, everyone else sat or stood around waiting for something – anything – to happen.

With Kev and my dad at my side, I was laid flat on the bed. I was wearing shorts and a sweatshirt, which was lifted slightly so that Tim could place the transmitter close against my ribcage at the point where a large X had been written on my skin. 'That tickles,' I complained, as he touched an area of skin I could actually feel. Tim apologized, laughing, and placed the transmitter in the right position, on top of my clothes.

'I think we'll start with channels one, two and three,' David Rushton instructed Nick, 'because that tells us whether that's the tendon or not.' He positioned himself alongside my bare legs so as to see what response there would be. I felt like a tiny cog in a vast machine.

'Well, shall we see if anything happens?' Tim asked. Then he started to play with the controls: 'I'm setting the master slider on the right-hand side to about sixty per cent up, which should give us up to about a hundred microsecond pulses.' We all held our breath as the machine made a sort of wailing beep, which Nick told us had to stop before the transmitter was in the right position. Knowing this would be very much a trial-and-error process of programming the computer as we went along, I crossed my fingers and nodded that I was ready.

Switching on the computer box, Tim called out: 'You're fine on range there. Shall I wind up?' David Rushton looked at me, then nodded. 'And number one. Is anybody watching?' Tim added, as everyone stared at me. 'What do you expect to happen here?' he asked, staring at my static legs, adding memorably: 'It's either on the right or the left.' Bloody marvellous, I thought.

I have never had so many eyes boring into me as at that moment as Tim gradually moved the slider controls further up the mixing desk. All attention was focused on my legs, and I was willing them to move as hard as anyone. At first there was no response, and a few meaningfully anxious glances were exchanged. 'No, nothing,' David called out to Tim and Nick as they fussed and fiddled on the machines behind us. But just at that moment David saw something flicker in my left thigh and shouted: 'There it is!'

'Yes! Look!' I cried. 'That was a twitch.'

Tim beamed at me from the slider box. 'Yes, it's on the left. Do you want me to come up a bit more? Is there hip flexion there?'

David shook his head. 'No, it's quadriceps. Yes, you're still going up.'

Everyone continued to stare as the various muscles in my thigh (including the quadriceps) contracted into tight little bunches and miraculously lifted my leg an inch off the bed in front of our eyes. There it stayed, hanging in mid-air as we watched in amazement, everyone grinning from ear to ear, before it thumped back down on to the bed. 'Oh, yes, I like that!' Tim squealed with delight, and we all shared his enthusiasm. 'Is that as strong as it's going to get?'

David said excitedly, 'I don't know – go up a bit more', adding to me, 'Tell us if that's at all uncomfortable won't you?'

'No,' I said, still beaming. 'That's fine. Wow!' This was it, this was what we had all been working towards and it felt absolutely brilliant. There were no wires, no visible electrodes, nothing, just me and my skin and some pretty complicated and expensive gadgetry a few feet away. OK, the electrical input was coming from outside, but it was *my* nerves working *my* muscles lifting *my* leg for the first time in four years. *Mine*, and without any encumbrances. I was back in control and it felt wonderful. I caught my father's eye and he winked at me. It was all I could do to stop the tears from spilling – it was a very emotional moment for us all, a real high.

With my leg relaxed again and everyone congratulating each other on this first success, Tim piped up from the control box: 'Eleven more to go!' It was to be my first taste of how methodical and painstaking the tests would have to be.

Next, they tried it on the other leg, and that worked too, although mainly in my foot at first. My leg flexed and my toes curled. Just to feel it, to really make himself believe that it was working, David Rushton made his hand into a fist and put it under my knee so that he could feel my leg flex above it.

Tim was in his element as he watched it all happening. 'There, lovely!' he said. 'Just don't breathe, that's all. You're enjoying this, aren't you Julie?'

'Thoroughly!' I exclaimed, understating the case wildly.

We tried it again and again and again. The current was increased slightly each time, and each time felt better than the last. At one point my left leg was raising itself off the bed and bending rhythmically in a sort of cancan. It was absolutely brilliant, although by the time the switch-on test had been completed an hour later, I was physically shattered, I was still almost beside myself with delight, though.

The team couldn't have been more pleased, either, and it was written all over them. The tests had shown that there was no permanent nerve damage after the operation, which had been their biggest fear. The nerves that weren't working quite as well as the others were, they thought, still slightly bruised and swollen after the operation and would gradually improve as they healed.

All they needed now, they said, was the right computer program to make sense of it all. As they stood around talking gobbledegook – technical jargon that passed way over my head – I interrupted and asked Tony Tromans what it all meant to them. With typical understatement, he replied: 'It doesn't look to be anything too dramatic. The responses are not very fine at the moment, mainly because of the swelling from the operation. It may be several months before we really know what the true outcome is, but it's nice to see some response. It's working on all twelve channels, which is a great achievement.' I'll say.

Kev reached over and gave me a kiss and congratulated me. 'That was amazing to watch, love,' he said. 'Well done. It has really justified the operation.' I was so pleased that he felt that way. The implant had given us a chance to talk about something that we had avoided for four years, and now here he was, at my side, his eyes bright with happiness and pride.

The nurses I had known for years, the girls who had seen me first arrive in Avon Ward in April 1990 and had held my hand through all my trials and tribulations, were all there now, beaming. Viv, who had hurried back from maternity leave to be there, positively glowed. The few other patients in the ward were sitting up and grinning. Some of the more mobile ones had wheeled themselves in and were sitting in the background, awe-struck. Elation washed over me, and I flopped back on to the bed and closed my eyes against the flood of happiness. 'Merry Christmas,' Tony Tromans said, leaning over to give me a kiss. I opened my eyes and thanked him. It was the best Christmas present I could possibly have had.

With my spine stabilized and the danger period over, a few days later I was allowed home. Kev and the boys had been busy; the house was all beautifully decorated with holly and ivy, the tree was up and dressed, and all my Good Luck cards mingled with those for the festive season. My parents came over on Christmas Day and Mum cooked the turkey and all the trimmings. We had a very relaxed and happy day, toasting the success of the implant and each other's happiness. 'I'd just like to thank you all for being so brilliant,' I said, raising my glass. Looking around the table at the faces of the people I loved most in the world, I was overwhelmed with a sense of fulfilment and peace.

By the late afternoon, the boys were in their rooms playing with their latest computer games and Kev and Mum and Dad and I were still sitting round the dining-room table, drinking and looking back on recent events. 'I can't believe we've got this far and are still talking to each other,' I said, by now slightly drunk. 'God, this is lovely and *so* much better than the last few years.' It was a statement from the heart. I was genuinely impressed that we were all still here – and incredibly relieved that we were.

Kevin poured himself another glass from the second bottle of port. 'I'll drink to that,' he said. 'I don't know about you lot, but I feel as if I've been through hell and back and I'm just bloody grateful to still be alive.'

My mother frowned and looked across the table at her son-in-law, as if for the first time. 'What do you mean, Kev?' she said, lighting a cigarette and passing me the packet.

Looking up at her, his eyes shining, Kev began to open up for the first time about how he had felt at the time of my accident and afterwards, and to describe his despair. We had all got slightly maudlin with the drink, and it felt like a time for lamenting. We held our breath as Kev started to share some of his pain. He was, he said, thrown into an alien world by my accident, a situation that he found horrible and unnatural. But something inside had stopped him from walking away, although at times he wanted to, because he knew that at the end of the day I couldn't walk away, however much I'd wanted to. 'I couldn't be that evil. I would have been thought of by all our friends as "the sod who left her",' he said, tears in his eyes.

He told us about the night he had nearly ended it all; he wept as he recalled seeing the boys tucked up in bed and realizing that he couldn't go through with it. The release from his emotional shackles had only come recently, he said, from talking in depth to Malcolm and the film crew making the documentary about me. 'It was the first time anyone had really asked me how I felt,' he said, 'and to my surprise I found myself really opening up.' By the time he had finished we were all in floods of tears, all holding each other and apologizing for each other's pain. It was a conversation that had to be had; it was a long time coming, this baptism of fire, but we all felt better for it, especially Kev.

He had been scathingly honest and his outpourings represented an enormous release for him and for us all. I was hugely relieved that he had allowed his feelings to come out at last. He couldn't have kept them locked inside for ever. It also cleared the air at last between him and my mum. It was evident from her surprise that she had no idea how much he had been hurting – she had thought that he had been coping remarkably well. All the barriers came down that day, and as we faced the New Year with renewed hope I felt that another major milestone had been passed.

January brought me back down to earth when I suddenly started to suffer from severe spasms in my left leg, for no apparent reason. It would happen twice or more every day, sometimes lasting for hours on end and keeping me (and Kev) awake at night. Although my leg obviously couldn't feel it, it jolted my body so violently that the rest of me certainly did, and the only way to ease it slightly was to lie in the foetal position until it passed. I wasn't unduly worried at first – I had been told there might be the odd spasm as my wounds healed. But when it went on and on, I started to get a bit scared.

'You've got to sort this out,' I told Tony one day. 'I can't sleep and I'm worried about it happening when I'm driving.'

His expression only made me more concerned. He was obviously worried that he might have inadvertently caused me some permanent damage and that this could be the pattern of my life from now on. But when he was examining me one day, he found that if he pressed his fist deep into the area where the implant was it produced an unusual response. My leg went into an immediate spasm, jerking me around the bed.

'Ah ha!' he cried, grinning broadly. 'I think I know what the problem is.' And by putting me on a course of anti-inflammatory drugs and a new exercise programme he managed to eliminate the spasm completely. It had been caused by a pain in my sacroiliac joint resulting from the operation, and because my body was unable to let me know in any other way that there was a problem it had cleverly sent my leg into regular spasm to alert me to it. We were all hugely relieved.

Once that had been dealt with, I went back to a routine of tests, tests and more tests, to sort out thresholds and work out the best training patterns. After working at home with the implant and the slider box almost daily so as to keep up my muscle bulk, it was back to Salisbury for more training. Strapped into a 'force rig', which measured the forces generated by stimulating the nerve roots, I was able to provide the team with a series of physical responses with which they would plot a 'map' on the computer, so that a control program could be written for standing and possibly walking. The software was already developed to the point where both my legs came up at once rather rapidly, in what Tim called 'the Cantona swing', after the footballer who had famously kicked a heckling spectator.

Working in Salisbury and London, Viv, Tim, Nick, Tony and the rest of the team devised a whole series of test rigs and experiments to measure every little movement my legs made. It was all so raw, so experimental, it would have made me laugh if they hadn't been so serious about it. To start with, they used ordinary bathroom scales to measure the force each leg created when it pushed downwards. When my leg kept slipping off, Tim cut a piece of foam for me to rest it on and Viv attached two strips of stretchy bandage round my calf to act as a makeshift sling. Sticky tape featured a lot, along with all sorts of bits and pieces begged, borrowed or stolen from elsewhere in the hospital.

In another test to see how far my extended leg could be moved when splayed out, it was rested for a moment on a wooden stool in the spinal unit gym. When Duncan Wood, the electrical engineer who had replaced Sean Hagan (who had gone off to a new job in Bath), switched the implant on and the stool slid across the wooden floor, he was struck by a sudden idea. 'Hey! That would be a good way of measuring how far her leg moves!' he told Viv. So a mark was made on the floor in chalk, and the distance the stool slid each time was measured off in centimetres with a wooden ruler. Talk about improvisation.

The Velcro-lined corset which was eventually made for me as a means of keeping the transmitter in place around my waist was positively high-tech compared to the original idea – a specially adapted padded bra cup to be slung just below my normal bra. Until the corset was introduced as it is now, the transmitter was put in a plaster of Paris 'shell' which Tim made to fit against my skin. But it didn't work very well – it kept slipping down and confusing the receiver, so that every time it thought it wasn't getting enough power it sounded a wailing beep. This would give me a two-second warning to sit down quick, or else I would collapse to the floor as the system shut down and my legs gave way beneath me. The alarm worked in the same way when the battery got low, at which point I would have to sit down and recharge it.

The lab was cluttered with all sorts of gadgets, electronics, wires and machines – the flotsam and jetsam of the engineers' brilliant minds. As ever, it was all a question of trial and error. The mathematics couldn't be worked out until the computer had been fed the relevant information from my force-testing results. The team quickly discovered that depending on the sensitivity of the nerves and the power required, they needed different strengths of pulses. Some nerves controlled more than one muscle and some worked against each other, so there was a great deal of fine-tuning necessary to achieve a useful balance of muscles. I'm sure they made a lot of it up as they went along.

Everything had to be working at its best before I was able to return to the spinal unit to try my first stand with the new implant. When the day finally came – 9 February 1995 – I was incredibly nervous as I made my

way to the now all too familiar physiotherapy department at Salisbury. The film crew were going to be
recording every second, and Kev was with me to give
moral support. My wheelchair, with me in it, was
positioned between the parallel bars, with Viv sitting in
front of me, ready to catch me if I fell. Tim stood to my
side operating the twelve-channel mixing desk as everyone waited with bated breath.

Adjusting the slider controls to try and stimulate the
right muscles in the right sequence and to ensure that I
was within range of the radio signals, Tim announced
to those around me: 'Right, I'm going to have all the
right quad channels on together to get her up. Plus left
channels one and nine and a touch of channel eight
because that gave her a bit of hip extension.'

Warned to brace myself, I reached my hands up to
the parallel bars as Viv placed my feet in the correct
position for standing. Tim switched on, and threw the
master switch with the words: 'Don't be too disappointed if this doesn't work perfectly first time.'

Looking at him askance, I replied: 'I'll be really
surprised if it does, actually, Tim.'

Scratching his great hairy head with both hands, a
bemused expression on his face, Tim asked Viv: 'Are we
ready for this? In which case could we push her heels
back?' Viv did as she was told. Tim called out again:
'Are we co-ordinated? Is everybody ready?'

Viv, her face inches from mine as I prepared to haul
myself upright, looked me straight in the eye. 'Are you
happy, Julie?' she asked with her characteristic concern.
I nodded.

'OK, winding up, and up and up,' Tim said, pushing
the slider controls further each time. Looking across to

me, my head hanging down over my knees, watching and waiting for something to happen, he asked: 'Are you able to get up? No? . . . Yes!'

Right on cue, the muscles in my leg duly contracted and, after a few seconds, I was able to push myself into an upright position. But the result was a huge anticlimax – it was a real low, the exact opposite to the way I'd felt at the first switch-on. My hips were kinked awkwardly to one side, not at all correctly aligned, and I was extremely unstable. Tim frowned as I struggled to stay upright. 'Right, the hips aren't very strong,' he observed. 'I'm winding the hips back . . . are they still pulling? Yes.'

From the position I was in and the fact that I was being pulled backwards and to one side, I instantly knew that something wasn't right. Even with the greatest of effort I was unable to stand for more than a few moments, and then only in a strange Max Wall sort of position, with my bottom sticking out. Viv pointed out that my right knee was wobbling dangerously. She could see the perspiration pouring off me, with all the exertion, and I was delighted when she added: 'Can she sit down, please?'

Tim lowered the slide controls and I collapsed back into my chair with a heavy thump. 'Well done,' he said. 'Thank you.'

Catching my breath as I allowed my head to drop between my knees, all I could manage in response was: 'Cor blimey! That was different.' It was the first time I had stood for six weeks or more, and I felt incredibly swimmy with the rush of blood from my head. Viv fetched me a glass of water and I kept my head between my knees for a while to get my senses back. Once recovered, I was swamped by feelings of disappointment. I had hoped to be able to get right up off my chair as if the Queen had just walked in. But instead, my rickety movements were worse than they had been before the implant operation, when I had simply pulled myself into a standing position in the Oswestry frame. Something had clearly gone wrong. It made me realize more than I ever had before that there was a very long way to go yet. This implant business was no instant fix.

For Nick and Tim, too, my first stand was a tremendous low. It is a date still carved in their memories as a failure. We tried it again and again over the next hour, but each time it failed to come right. Everyone seemed to be buzzing around me, taking measurements and doing tests and all talking eighteen to the dozen. The sheer physical effort was exhausting for me, far more draining than any previous attempts, and my frustrations were increased by my inability to keep my balance. With the television crew filming my every drop of perspiration as I tried desperately to get it right, I could have done without that added pressure. I knew that the documentary-makers wanted a happy ending. They had been hoping to release their film later that year, but from their crestfallen faces as I struggled to stand, I knew that I was not only letting myself and the team down, I must have been a big disappointment to them as well.

The problems were multifold. There are forty-seven muscles in each leg, so ninety-four in all, controlled by twenty separate and very complex nerves – the result of millions of years of evolution – and I only had twelve small electrodes, the results of thirty years' work, trying to operate the lot. The team had to work out not only how to stimulate the correct arrangement of muscle groups, varying the level of stimulation in each leg and in the lumbar root to allow the knees to straighten, but also how to control my hip flexor muscles, the psoas, which were somehow adversely affected by the stimulation and causing my body to jack-knife. Should they give my hips and knees a burst of power first to get me standing, and then wind one channel down once I was up, to stop my knees and hips straining? Or should they try one-legged standing first, so as to get each individual leg right before trying them both? They simply couldn't know until they tried. It was a problem that would haunt me and the team for some years to come.

The medical conundrum I now posed marked the start of the incredibly tedious process of trying to get the technique right, which would involve month after month of bitter frustration and disappointment. Each weekly session lasted from ten o'clock in the morning to four in the afternoon. At times I felt like a pair of legs and nothing more. 'Just one more test?' Tim would plead, but the 'one more' would almost always turn into ten, and by the end of it I would be physically and emotionally shattered but still with the prospect of a fifty-mile drive home and of having to be a wife and mother to my family.

My only respite from the endless rounds of tests was a brilliant holiday in Kenya that year with Kev and my parents and the boys, in which I finally fulfilled my lifetime dream to go on safari. We had the most fantastic holiday – the most exotic the children had ever been on and the first two-week holiday Kev and I had ever enjoyed together – and, more than any other time, I felt as if my disability counted for nothing in terms of what

I wanted to do. If I could fly to Mombasa and drive out across the plains of the Tsavo National Park to watch lions and elephants in their own environment, so close that I could smell their scent, then anything was possible.

Coming home and having to face up to the prospect of how little appeared to be possible with the programme as it was gave me a bad case of post-holiday blues. I called the depression I sank into at this stage 'guinea-pigitis'. Although I was a fast learner, physically suitable for the programme and mentally strong, I had my limitations. The word 'patient' took on a whole new meaning, and although I tried hard to stay cheerful, I felt overwhelmed by the frustration of not being able to hurry things along. All the same, I was determined to keep coming back until we got the system working. The problem was, I just hadn't imagined it would take quite so long.

More and more tests were required, with bigger and better devices to measure my responses being developed all the time. Nick had the idea of creating an exoskeleton, a sort of outer skeleton into which I could be strapped and the movements I made measured. I imagined it would look something like a full-body version of the RGO. But the problem with a device like that would be the risk of causing me pressure sores, so something softer and more padded had to be thought up. After a while, he came up with an incredible device that a research assistant in north London called Alan Worley had spent two years perfecting on Nick's instructions, which might just be the answer to our prayers. 'It's called a multi-moment chair system, or MMCS,' Nick told me excitedly. 'It's a device fitted with transducers with bonded strain gauges, a bank of strain-gauge amplifiers and a PC-486. It measures the isometric moments in paraplegic lower limbs during electrical stimulation.' Ignoring my blank expression, he carried on. 'The human lower limb has seven degrees of freedom and the MMCS can measure all moments simultaneously: hip extension, -abduction and -rotation, knee extension and ankle-abduction and inversion, and dorsiflexion.'

Seeing that he was not getting through to me, Nick slowed down and simplified matters: 'It's a mechanical chair which measures every muscle and nerve and relates it to the amount of electricity being input and force being exuded. It could provide the most extraordinary data.'

'Well, will it make a difference if I use it?' I asked, cautiously, thinking that a multi-moment chair sounded suspiciously perverted.

'Oh, yes!' Nick and Tim cried in unison, adding more cautiously, 'Well, we certainly believe so.'

So it was that from 1995 onwards, once a month I made the two-hundred-mile round trip to the Royal Orthopaedic Hospital in Stanmore, for six-hour sessions in this supposedly wonderful machine. When I first set eyes on it, I couldn't believe what I was seeing. Far from being the state-of-the-art, high-tech device they had cracked it up to be, it looked like a huge and hideous collection of old junk held together with straps and clips and connected to a computer. Giles Brindley would have been proud of it. Ten feet long by three feet wide, made of wood and metal and weighing a quarter of a ton, it was a monstrous contraption I would describe as nothing less than a torture machine. And I came to hate it.

It was like a whole-body straitjacket. I was strapped tightly into it by means of a six-way harness against a back board, with my upper body secured by a series of fabric parachute straps across my chest and stomach, and my feet laced into shoes glued into rigid boxes. My hips were also strapped in, and my knees were clamped and restrained by rubber discs either side of my leg, against the skin. When my knees kept slipping out from between the discs, it was Kev, who joined me for many of these sessions, who was the first to spot that it was because the discs were the wrong shape. 'Why don't you make the little discs more like long, thin metal plates?' he asked Tim one day. 'Then Julie's legs wouldn't keep slipping out.'

It was a real Eureka! moment. Kev's commonsense idea was warmly received by the team. And he was so inspired by their response that he asked one of the toolmakers in the engineering department of his company to make something appropriate. The new polished-steel vertical plates, known as paddle knee supports, worked a treat, and Kev's long-term contribution to the project was sealed. After that, any suggestion he came up with was carefully considered and his consultancy value became vital. He also seemed to have a natural understanding of everything that was going on, and once he had fully understood it he could translate it into layman's terms for me. To this day, if Kev hadn't been around, I'm sure I still wouldn't really understand what my implant was all about.

Once Kev had helped sort out that particular problem

with the multi-moment chair, the complicated equipment could do its stuff. The idea was that during electrical stimulation, muscle activity at each of my joints would be monitored and recorded, so the engineers could map a mathematical model, a blueprint for me and all future implant patients. The results would then be programmed into the tiny computer in my control box and, hopefully, improve my standing technique.

The sessions were generally fairly good-humoured, fuelled by coffee and chocolate biscuits. 'Are you comfortable?' Tim would ask, tightening the final strap on the many harnesses, and when I told him I wasn't he would grin from ear to ear. 'Good,' he'd say. 'You're not meant to be. Now we can begin.' There would then follow hour upon hour of tests while I lay back watching them, or even reading a book sometimes, while Tim or Viv fanned me with folded-up pieces of computer paper to keep me cool.

The only respites were the intervals for lunch or tea or coffee, and the breaks I had to have every thirty-five minutes to lift me off the chair and prevent me from getting sores. The time between each break was calculated in an extremely high-tech way and became known as LBUs – 'ladybird units' – after the little kitchen timer in the shape of a ladybird that one of the team brought in for the job!

Aside from the odd amusing moment, it was totally boring, from ten in the morning to six o'clock at night, hours and hours of tests; and the theory behind it, as usual, was more than I could grasp. I developed a sort of mental haze as soon as it started. All I wanted was for it to end, especially when, as I often did, I felt like little more than an interesting rare specimen to those around me. On several occasions Tim became so engrossed in his mathematical calculations that he switched the current off without thinking, making me thump back down into my chair. 'Sorry,' he'd say, 'I forgot you were there.'

Not only was the implant programme much more complicated than I ever thought it would be, but I found the tests exhausting. It was a full body workout every time. My previously unflexed muscles would be contracted and expanded again and again, with force exerted against them, so that all this data could be fed into the computer and then printed out on endless rolls of paper. I would be so done in at the end of the session that I couldn't even drive home, so Kev had to accompany me each time. Sometimes I was so tired that I even fell asleep in the chair, in spite of all the whirrings and buzzings.

The engineers were beside themselves with excitement about the test results, which opened up vital new areas of knowledge about the workings of the human body. For the first time, they were able to say that this much power, going into that particular nerve root ending, gave so much power to that particular muscle, and so on. Previously they had only ever had dead bodies or animals to work on, using dye injected into the nerves to see which area stimulated which muscle. Now they discovered that in a live human being it wasn't so clear-cut. My muscle anatomy didn't match the textbooks. They came to believe that each individual's nerve patterns are like a fingerprint, unique to them, and not common to all human bodies. No one had ever attempted anything remotely like the systematic study they were carrying out on me. I had become the source of world expertise on muscle and nerve anatomy. I was suddenly invaluable to scientific research.

Because of me, apparently, great scientific discoveries were being made, but I began to detest the infernal machines that I was strapped into. I actually became chair-phobic. While they pored and cooed over incomprehensible page after incomprehensible page of mathematical data, all I wanted to know was what it was teaching them about me and how it could improve my standing technique.

I grew more and more disheartened, because I seemed to be taking one step forward and three steps back – if only I had been, in reality! While the important new findings were being written up as scientific papers and careers were being forged, I felt more and more like a tooth on a cog in a huge machine. It was hard not to be selfish. What did I really care if the tests led to medical textbooks on the workings of the human nerve system being rewritten? All I wanted was some sort of tangible result, a reward for all these endless months of tedium. I wanted to be the little figure in the corner of my Get Well card from Daniel, standing next to my wheelchair with my arms in the air. If Daniel could have seen me in the multi-moment chair, he'd have made the most nightmarish drawing of it.

There were times when I felt quite trapped by the situation I had put myself into. It seemed to me that the team had me over a barrel, and I often felt like the victim of some cruel form of emotional and physical abuse. I couldn't leave, I didn't want to most of the time, but there were times when it all really got to me. Session after session, I stood and sat, stood and sat, stood and sat, sweat pouring off me with the exertion, as they measured and graded, talked gobbledegook and mulled over the statistical read-outs. To get me to stand, they had to try nearly four hundred different patterns of muscle sequences in each leg, each test session taking several hours.

I don't think I had ever realized how physically and emotionally exhausting the whole process would be, or how incredibly slow. It became a dreadful chore to have to do the exercises at home every day, and to make those long journeys to and from the different hospitals. I felt shattered nearly all of the time, and often wondered if I was doing the right thing by going on. I am sure Kevin did too, although he never said as much. But he was just as tired as me – driving me to my appointments, waiting and watching as I was manipulated and prodded and examined like some strange organism under a microscope.

There were some results that interested me. I learned a great deal, especially what an incredibly complex machine the human body is. The purpose of the implant was to try to send signals into my body's very core, something that had never been attempted before. One of the most amazing things to come out of it is that, in spite of my complete and irreversible spinal break, the implant has somehow enabled me to have some sensation in my lower limbs. I call it a sixth sense, an inner-core feeling similar, I imagine, to the feeling experienced by the blind and the deaf. When I am being electronically stimulated, I can somehow tell what position my legs are in, even though I still have no feeling in them. But if the current is off and I close my eyes, and my legs are manually manipulated, I have no idea whether they are straight or bent. It's intriguing.

But interesting as that may be, even to the likes of

me, the pace was still painfully slow. I discovered from Nick and Tim that it was considered quite normal for a new medical project like ours to take ten to fifteen years to get fully established. 'This is long-term research,' they would remind me. It was something they had stressed all along. But one year down the line, and with only a succession of troughs – not peaks to speak of – I couldn't help but feel frustrated. I wouldn't have been human if I hadn't. In fifteen years' time I would be positively middle-aged, and I couldn't be blamed for wanting some results well before that.

Over the course of the next few months, I came to realize that there would be little or no progress with the programme until other paraplegics agreed to have the implants, or unless I created such a fuss about what I wanted out of it that they were sparked into action for fear of losing me. Knowing that the future funding of the project was constantly at risk and that only a couple of other guinea-pigs were currently lined up, I decided to start complaining – and complain I did.

After a long weekend of hard thinking, I telephoned Nick one Monday afternoon in the late summer of 1995 and gave him an ultimatum. 'Things are dragging on and on and it feels like nothing is being achieved,' I told him angrily. 'We seem to have come to a complete halt. In many ways, we're going backwards. We're fiddling around with this, and I need something more. I need a light at the end of the tunnel to aim for – otherwise I want out.'

There was an uneasy silence at the other end of the line, while I waited for Nick's response. Finally, he blurted nervously: 'Come in next week and I'll see what I can do.'

From that moment on, it was all hands to the pump, and the project came along by leaps and bounds. Nick told the team that they were going to forget about improving my standing technique for a while and try and get me to step a few paces instead. Just by spreading my legs to the position of a stride should give me a better base, and improve my stability in any event, so there was no reason why we couldn't try it, he argued. And he was right. In a relatively short time, a few weeks or months after working on a new computer program to send the right signals to the right nerve endings, I was ready to give it a go.

Strapped into what looked like a giant baby-walker but was actually a recycled air – sea rescue harness attached to a metal A-frame on wheels that would move with me, and with the department head, Paul Taylor, hanging off a rope at the back, ready to hoist me up if I fell, I was prepared for take-off on 16 November. Duncan Wood, the electrical engineer, was lying on the floor at my feet with Tony Tromans, making sure my ankles were all right and didn't give way, Viv was clucking around as usual, and Tim sat in front of me on a stool on wheels, slider box on his lap, ready to move along with me as I prepared to take a few tentative steps.

We were all pretty hyped up, and then Tim said ominously: 'Don't hope for too much.' I could have hit him. I was only too well aware of the rawness of the work we were doing, the newness of it in terms of world advances, but right then and there I needed to hear that it was likely to have at least some limited success.

Kev, sensing the tension, made a joke. 'Hey, Tim, why don't you let me take the controls and we can have

Julie prancing all over the room, like something out of *The Wrong Trousers*?' The thought of the Wallace and Gromit cartoon, one of the children's favourites, broke the ice and made me laugh.

Feeling like a trussed-up chicken, I stood up as well as I could with the help of the A-frame, and everyone held their breath as the controls were slid into position in the attempt to make my legs move. I watched, sweating, along with everyone else, as my dead and useless legs took two tiny steps beneath me – steps so feeble that they didn't even move the frame by so much as an inch. It felt extremely odd, not in any way pleasant, and there was nothing like the highs I'd felt when I'd achieved previous milestones. Exhausted, I collapsed back down and, close to tears, told Nick: 'If I never do that again for the rest of my life, I won't be unhappy.' Poor man, he must have hankered back to the days when his patients were animals, unable to answer back.

This episode taught me what I think I had known all along – that although stepping was, in theory, possible, it was not something that was ever going to be easy. Before I could step, I would have to be able to stand, and that in itself was a long way off happening. Aware that I was feeling very downhearted by the lack of progress, the team took me at my word and decided not to push me into attempting stepping again for a while longer. Accepting that there could be no quick fix, that any glimmer of light at the end of the tunnel was extremely faint, we agreed to go back to standing trials. It would be another long and tedious year of weekly sessions in which I often felt as if I had lost the will to carry on with the project altogether.

ELEVEN

Floodlight

THE PROBLEM with my standing technique had been pinpointed to the fact that using the electrodes had somehow over-tightened the muscles in my hips, to the point that they would probably have to be cut away surgically to stop them pulling me over. The team had also discovered that stepping was much more complicated than they had ever imagined. It involved synchronizing the contraction and relaxation of dozens of muscles, while at the same time maintaining stamina and conquering my fatigue. The brain is very good at giving just the right amount of power at the right time to make each muscle move. My implant was far less sophisticated, with far less control over which muscles it stimulated and – crucially – by how much.

It was scientifically interesting, but a big disadvantage to discover that each nerve bundle controlled several different muscles – it meant that the muscles that made my knees straighten were also making my back jack-knife. It was what was known as a multimuscular response. To identify which part of which muscle was causing the problem, the team eventually decided to try something very radical. By anaesthetizing the individual muscles that ran through my groin and then switching on the electrodes, they hoped to be able to pinpoint the problem muscle. The idea was that they could then intensify the activity they wanted while weakening the one they didn't. If they blocked the activity of the problem muscle using a long-lasting anaesthetic – one that would last a week or more, to allow enough time for testing – and surgically cut the nerve that supplied it, or relocated the muscle tendons so that it performed some other function, progress might be made.

To begin with the team used local anaesthetic on the muscles, knocking them out one by one to try and identify the one that was causing the problem, but its effects were rather hit-and-miss and not long-lasting enough. On one memorable occasion, Tony accidentally plunged the needle in too deep and anaesthetized my bowel, with instant and devastating results. I don't know who was more embarrassed, me or him, but the wonderful Viv was on hand to clean things up and the incident was soon forgotten, although I do sometimes remind Tony of it.

After a lot of experimentation, it was decided that a stronger anaesthetic cocktail was needed. 'We're thinking of injecting an exotic poison into your psoas muscles,' Viv explained brightly to me one day. 'It's called botulinus toxin. Tony says it comes from dodgy rice in Chinese restaurants that's been left around too long.'

'Sounds lovely,' I grimaced. 'When can we start?'

The team had to get permission from the hospital's ethical committee before they could go ahead. Injecting a potentially lethal toxin into an otherwise healthy patient was not something they undertook lightly. But the committee agreed, and the operation went ahead. With Kev at my side and an operating theatre full of people, David Lintin, a consultant anaesthetist at Salisbury, was called in to inject the toxin with a giant syringe that would have looked more at home at a vet's. For some reason, I felt incredibly nervous. There seemed to be so much riding on the procedure's success, so many goals dependent on its outcome. The operation involved keeping my psoas muscles (the muscles used in flexing the hip joint) under constant X-ray, watched on special monitors above the operating table, so we all had to wear the heavy plastic-coated aprons that protect against radiation. I was fully conscious and lying on my left side, as Mr Lintin set to work. The most surprising thing of all was that it hurt. He had to jab the needle into my hip, hit the bone and then pull out slightly before depressing the plunger. Even though I theoretically have no feeling below my waist, each time he hit bone I winced. I was very glad when it was over.

It came as a real blow when the tests carried out afterwards failed to identify the muscle they were looking for. It seemed after all that no one muscle accounted for my problem, although the iliacus and rectus femoris muscles were chief suspects, with the smaller hip flexors such as sartorius, pectineus and tensor fasciae latae making small contributions. (Over the years, I've come to recognize the names of the muscle groups as if they were my children.) The team now also realized that electrical stimulation to the lumbar and sacral roots didn't always confine itself to activating one muscle alone – it sometimes activated two working against each other, which made it almost impossible to separate their functions.

Once again, the team had discovered that their attempts to replicate the intricacies of the human nervous system were to be thwarted. As Tim tried to explain: 'If only the original designer of the human body had made it more convenient for the likes of us to improvise and rectify, then life would be much simpler. I wish there was a magic wand, but there isn't. You only get results in the end by sheer bloody-minded persistence, worrying away at the problems until they give up out of sheer exhaustion.'

I knew he was speaking the truth, but the disappointing result, after what had been a painful and very dangerous procedure for me, meant going back to the drawing board. In future implant patients, it's hoped that the problem may be solved at the surgical stage when it may be feasible to divide each nerve bundle into its many different branches and attach an electrode to each. But for me, now, that would be far too complicated and lengthy.

The complexity of the body's nervous system, not yet fully understood, caused me and the team untold problems. It was also discovered that the larger axons feed quick-action muscles for short bursts of activity like running, while the smaller ones feed the slowly contracting muscle fibres needed for everyday tasks like holding a cup of tea. Although a typical muscle has about three hundred of these axon–muscle fibre packages, or motor units, only 5 per cent of them are usually contracted at once, so that others can rest until they are needed for intense activity.

I was encouraged to try to combat the problem myself, by spending an hour a day lying down, my feet dangling off the bed with two-kilogram weights strapped to my ankles. Setting the control unit to 'automatic', I would repeatedly lift and lower my legs, the idea being that by stimulating the fast-reacting muscles for a while every day they could be converted into slower, fatigue-resistant fibres. The team also joined forces with engineering colleagues at the University of Surrey to work on a possible pressure switch in my shoe that would provide a feedback system and stimulate a muscle just above my knee, to make it bend and to lift my feet even higher off the ground when I step. There are other plans afoot that involve the idea of harnessing my own sensory nerves by use of a telemetering implant that could pass messages from them to warn me when I was unstable or likely to fall over. It would work in a similar way to the pressure switch, only more naturally.

We tried stepping again and again and, little by little, my technique did improve. After a while, I was able to dispense with the A-frame and use a Zimmer, which gave me a better gait. But we accepted that stepping wasn't something that was going to happen overnight and that there were other, less time-consuming, things that we could concentrate on instead. In fact, we went back to basics and started all over again. With Viv and Duncan at the controls, we spent what seemed like an age working on muscle signals and trying to find out what the activation of each electrode could actually achieve. All the tweaking and tuning proved was that the computer programming still needed a lot of refining.

In spite of the ongoing frustrations of the LARSI project, my personal life was getting better and better. The boys were growing fast, Kev and I had come to a new level of understanding, and I was as busy as ever with Back-

Up. There were holidays to go on and a full and active social life to enjoy, as well as fund-raising events to organize like the annual sponsored ramble in the local country park, an event for able-bodied and wheelchair users alike which has raised more than £50,000 pounds in five years. Was there really any need to take the project any further? I've wondered more than once.

I knew that the team were all on my side, and that they were doing the best they could in difficult circumstances, but it still seemed to be taking so very long to get anywhere. I sometimes felt like they needed a bomb up their backsides, the lot of them. They couldn't even argue that I'd known what I was letting myself in for, because I hadn't, and neither had they. Although I had willingly volunteered for the programme, no one could have foreseen back then what it would be like – and if they'd told me, I'd probably never have gone ahead with it in the first place. I still found it hard to believe that after all this time they were still talking about things they'd been talking about the day after the operation. My patience was fast running out.

But in February 1996 the first television documentary on my life and the implant, called 'On My Feet Again', was broadcast in the BBC's *Inside Story* series, and it sparked off a flurry of media interest, including television and newspaper interviews. I was called the 'Bionic Woman' or the 'WalkMum', and news organizations from all over the world showed considerable interest. Articles about me appeared in everything from the *Sunday Times* to the *Mirror*. I was the 'And Finally' item on ITN's ten o'clock news the night the Maxwell brothers were acquitted, I won a special-category award in the 1996 European Women of Achievement awards, and appeared on countless television programmes including *The Big Breakfast, Anne and Nick* and the *Selina Scott Show*. I was even flown to Ireland with Kev to appear on the *Pat Kenny Live* show, after which we were mobbed by crowds of well-wishers and Kevin had a very touching encounter with a wonderful woman, the young wife of a terminally ill man, who sat him down and spoke movingly of their shared experience of having to take second place. It was a watershed moment for him.

The kids were well impressed with my new celebrity status, and although I sometimes felt like a performing seal as television crews continued to film me during standing sessions, at home with the family and in training, the mass media interest rekindled my own enthusiasm as well as my friends' and family's. I was inundated with letters from the public, ordinary people whose lives had been touched by disability or who were simply impressed with the progress I had made. It was incredibly heart-warming to read their letters, including the funny ones – like the bloke who suggested I buy a donkey to help me get about more easily. The media hype refocused both me and the team and made us appreciate just how much we had achieved, although national newspaper headlines like 'Walking Miracle' made us all laugh – we knew only too well that miracles didn't come into it.

We had also had a new breakthrough. I'd been able to make my first stable stand since the implant – I could even take my right hand off my stick and still keep my balance. Suddenly we seemed to be making headway again. I'd always thought it would work, but my patience in sticking with it surprised me – this was the only thing I had ever stuck with in my life.

As the project slowly progressed, I resolved to get on

with my life the only way I knew how – full steam ahead. I treated Kev to another holiday in the Gambia, a brilliant trip we both hugely enjoyed. For his part, he took me to the Highlands of Scotland with our friends Alan and Ann, and together we made it to the top of Anag Mor, after riding up by cable car and then Kev wheeling me up the steep path. He was on a mission – it was clearly something he needed to do – and getting to the top felt as significant to us both as if we had just climbed Everest. 'We've made it, Julie!' he panted, as we reached the summit. 'We bloody well made it!'

The children, who had never been fazed by my disability, had even asked me to come into their school and give a talk to their fellow pupils on what life in a wheelchair is like. 'They've got this other lady who comes in, and she makes it sound so depressing,' they said. 'She's not at all like you.' So I went along and braved a class full of children and tried to sweep away some of the misconceptions. The talk worked and Nathan and Daniel were delighted. Not only had I made the class feel more comfortable about disability, I had now become something akin to a celebrity. After the success of my visit to the children's school, I volunteered to give disability talks at schools throughout the region, talking to kids and answering most of their amazingly frank questions about what it's like to be disabled. 'How's your sex life?' one cheeky ten-year-old asked me as his classmates giggled.

'Fine, thanks – how's yours?' I responded, before swiftly moving on.

Almost every time I went to Salisbury, I was invited to go into the eight-bedder – the acute ward – and talk to the newly injured, to offer them the sort of support and encouragement that had meant so much to me in the earliest stages of my disability. My talks ranged from the ease of travelling abroad when disabled to getting over the problem of phobias about sex. Some of them responded well; others were still so bitter or angry about their changed circumstances that there was no way I could get through. But at least I'd tried.

One person who asked to see me on several occasions was Lady Tryon, known as 'Kanga', a close friend of the Prince of Wales, who became paraplegic after falling from a hospital window. She was amazingly animated and charming, and she wanted to know everything there was to know about self-image and how to cope with relationships once she returned to life outside the hospital. Sadly, not long afterwards she suffered a mental collapse and, after taking herself off to India to seek a 'cure', she died from septicaemia caused by untreated pressure sores.

Through contact with others less fortunate than myself, I gradually came to feel that, although I may have been dealt a poor set of cards as far as the accident was concerned, Fate had given me another chance with the implant programme. I believe that everything happens for a reason, and maybe I had to become paralysed so that I could be in the right place at the right time for the technology. Who knows? But one thing I do know is that I was keener than ever to force the programme ahead as far as I could. I wanted to get the very best out of the implant and out of those parts of my body I could use, to give myself the maximum mobility and strength. It was with a very determined effort that I decided to try to use my new momentum to push the project further than it had ever originally been intended to go.

Watching the children on the brand-new mountain bikes Kev and I had bought them for their birthdays and feeding on the memory of my own childhood cycling, an embryo idea began to hatch in my brain. The boys were growing so fast, in stature and in independence. Watching Daniel pedalling off down the drive one day, a grin on his face, I felt proud – then suddenly sad as I realized that it would be Kevin, not me, cycling out with him and Nathan at weekends and holidays, something I had always dreamed of doing with them when they were older. But a flash of inspiration nearly blinded me. Cycling! Why couldn't *I* do it? My body weight would be supported by the machine, there would be no problem with hip stability, and my legs could be programmed to turn the pedals rhythmically. Given a tricycle, or a bicycle with stabilizers to keep me from falling over, there was no reason why I couldn't go for miles, pedalling off down the road with Kevin and the boys at my side – a mother's dream fulfilled.

I could hardly wait to get inside and wheel myself to the phone to call Tim and ask him if he thought it might be possible. 'Tim, it's Julie. What's to stop me sitting on a tricycle and heading off into the sunset with my kids?' I asked him enthusiastically. 'It would rule out the need for me to stand or step and all you'd need to do is to work out a program to make my legs move the pedals.' I made it sound so simple, when the reality was that I was asking him to do something so mind-bogglingly complicated that nobody in the world had ever dared to attempt it.

Tim's reaction was typical. Steeped in the 'how do we know unless we try?' approach of Professor Brindley, he and Nick and the rest of the team would never rule out anything, even if it seemed on the face of it completely impossible. There was a long pause before Tim said cautiously: 'Well, we can certainly give it a go.'

It was by pure coincidence that a German television crew were spending a few days with me that week, filming me and my progress with the implant. The worldwide media interest in me had never really subsided, and I was quite accustomed to getting phone calls from producers and directors from all over the globe, hoping for a chance to see me 'in action'. The reality for them was often disappointing. I wasn't quite the Bionic Woman they had hoped I would be – of course, I was never bionic – I had just been fitted with some clever electronics that made my muscles and bones do the work. So for most of the time I was in my wheelchair, and although I used the implant at home regularly to exercise I wasn't about to embark on the London Marathon, as they may have been hoping.

But the Germans struck lucky. They just happened to be with me in the physiotherapy department of the Salisbury spinal unit that afternoon in the late spring of 1996, not long after my phone conversation with Tim. Viv Harper had found a small set of wheels in the physiotherapy storeroom, used to strengthen the leg muscles of people who had been bedridden, and she and Tim laid me down and bandaged my feet to the pedals. Standing at his magic slider box, fiddling with the controls while the film crew set up their camera, Tim tried to work out which combination of instructions he would have to feed into the software to make my feet turn the pedals. 'I've no idea whether this will work or not, but we'll give it a go,' he said bravely, as I lay there feeling hopeful. No sooner had the camera been switched on and Tim moved a few of the slider controls around than, hey presto, my legs jerked into life and started to make the right pedal-turning movements.

'Fantastic, Tim!' I cried, watching the pedals complete a full circle. 'Make it go round again!'

Beaming from ear to ear, Tim repeated the process and, lo and behold, I managed two or three revolutions of the pedals. Viv clapped her hands in delight, and the film crew could hardly believe their eyes. They had inadvertently filmed a moment of scientific innovation, and it had worked. It wasn't rigged or fixed in any way. It just happened, as naturally and as effortlessly as that. I was over the moon.

After that, Tim was like a terrier with a rag doll. Having seen what he could do when he was merely playing about, he resolved to sit down and work out the exact program he would need on the computer to make my legs turn the pedals. This was his baby, and he was tireless in his determination to get it right.

The first thing we needed was a tricycle. After shopping around, Tim, Viv and I went to Manchester to see a firm called the Seat of the Pants Company which manufactures recumbent tricycles – the sort that give you the most energy-efficient way of cycling – made from carbon fibre, aluminium and titanium. They had Mike Burrows working for them, the creator of Chris Boardman's Olympic-winning bicycle, who had also designed their Windcheetah Supertrike. But the seat of their trike was too low for me to get on to and, although they were extremely helpful, in the end we found another firm who were even more suitable – the Bicycle Barn Company in Lymington, Hampshire. Their trike, called a 'Trice', was just the job. Designed by Crystal Engineering of Penryn, Cornwall, the seat was higher and it was slightly less fancy and more amenable to being interfered with.

Once we had located the correct equipment, we had to work out exactly how I could use it. Devising the electronics side of things was a phenomenally complicated process, and Tim worked day and night to get it right. He fitted sensors to the pedals to send a signal back to the computer behind the seat each time they had completed a full turn. Little magnets, stuck with Blu-Tack to metal plates attached to the tricycle, tripped switches on the computer program to tell my hip and knee flexors and my thigh and calf muscles to act in a certain way. Tim likened it to a central-heating timer with four stops, bringing in a different program each time you go past the next stop. What he created was a unique talk-back system, with machine talking to machine, then to my nerves and finally to my muscles, to keep the whole system moving rhythmically.

As the chain wheel rotated with the movement of my legs, so the pedals went round, and then the magnets passed the appropriate switch, activating the next pattern of stimulation. The difficulty was getting the stimulation levels correct for the different channels, and getting the position of the magnets right too. Tim had to divide the 360-degree turn into four sections and fit angled sensors to a sprocket behind the seat. He also had to mount strain gauges to measure the pedal force, and devise a shaft encoder to relate what the pedals were doing to the implant so that my legs could know what stage they were at. There are a million combinations of possible electrical stimulations per leg, and Tim narrowed it down to ten per leg. It was all incredibly complex but, with his usual modesty, he claimed the program was actually 'very simple, once I'd worked it out'. I didn't care how he'd managed it – I was just delighted we had a system that actually seemed to work.

And the best thing of all was that it was completely portable, there were no slider boxes, no vast contraptions, just me and my trike. Never before had such a system been perfected. There had been bicycles created to turn the pedals on their own with paralysed limbs strapped to them, and surface electrode systems had been used in a similar way, but this was to be me, *my* muscles working, controlled internally, to move the pedals round. Another world first! It would really become the light at the end of my tunnel, a tangible result of all the years of boredom and hard work, a chance to go out with the boys on my own and be like any other Mum. Kevin had always joked that Nick and Tim are too intelligent for their own good. They are sometimes so closely focused on the scientific details of the programme that they can't see the bigger picture, and don't have the practicality to suggest such an idea themselves. But once I had made the commonsense connection between what I was able to do and how it could be put to a practical use and suggested it to them, they jumped at the challenge.

As the pace of progress speeded up enormously, I got very excited and just hoped and prayed that there wouldn't be another setback. It felt incredibly important to me to keep the momentum going and I didn't want anything to stand in the way. What I would not have predicted was that it would be my own foolishness that would cause the next problem, and in the most unexpected way.

In May 1997, not long into the new cycling programme, I went on a trip to the Lake District organized by Back-Up. I had been elevated by then to the lofty position of group leader, assisted by Julia, a friend and physiotherapist at Salisbury, helping those on their first ever outing to relax and enjoy themselves. It was a position I had never held before and I was very aware of the responsibility. I would be in charge of a whole new group of people who had never been in this situation before, and who were about to experience very new and very frightening challenges. I was as scared as the rest of them, especially when I found myself first in the queue to be thrown over a cliff edge on a rope on an abseiling day, sitting on that precipice, harnessed into the ropes, ready to be pushed off. I screamed as I went down, until I got a grip on myself and lowered my body weight down with the ropes. When I got to the bottom, it felt great. My job was then to encourage the rest down – having done it, I could now give them the encouragement they needed to make it happen.

We had the most wonderful trip. The most moving moment for me was talking a fellow paraplegic out of committing suicide, during a canoe hike downriver. It really brought home to me what Back-Up is all about: teaching people what their abilities are, as opposed to their disabilities. The three or four hours we spent nurturing and counselling this poor young man, who felt at that particular moment that life simply wasn't worth living, were very significant to me too. Sitting outside on a very wet night in Cumbria, talking to him, trying to sustain him, did me a power of good. I found that I really believed what I was telling him. 'Your life can still be so wonderful,' I said. 'Losing the use of your legs doesn't necessarily signify the end.' I was speaking from the heart.

The penultimate day before we left we did some more adventure sports and I went quad-biking, racing across the moors near Greystoke in stunning scenery. I was petrified at first and the slowest of the lot by far, but with the help of a gorgeous ex-SAS instructor who showed me how to use the machine properly, I spent the next two hours riding over acres of open country-side. It felt wonderful to have so much freedom; this really was the opposite of what any paraplegic expects – to be able to control a machine beneath you and allow it to carry you at speed across country. I loved it and hoped this was how being on the trike would feel.

But, although I wasn't yet aware of it, I wasn't quite as invincible as I felt. I was wearing leather boots, as advised, but they were not quite thick enough, and during the two hours I'd spent tearing around the muddy tracks the heat from the engine housing of the bike had burned through the boots and the lining, which then smouldered away against my skin. After such a long time without respite, the heat burned such a big black hole in my left foot that it created a massive blister that almost reached the bone. In the end I would have to have a skin graft. Although we tended the wound as best we could there, and then when I got home my GP tried to deal with it through constant dressing and redressing, it simply wouldn't heal.

With me out of action, all the testing on the cycling

programme came to a grinding halt. It was a terrible setback, and I was furious with myself. Seeing my frustration, Tony Tromans, the surgeon who had put my implant in, finally decided enough was enough. 'Like that, it's going to take six months to heal, Julie,' he told me after examining my festering wound. 'If I check you into the burns unit, we could get it sorted in six weeks.' So back I went to hospital, back in time and in progress.

I have never hit such a low in all the years since the accident as I did then. I was suddenly and very painfully made aware of my own vulnerability, just at the point when I had been on the greatest high. I hadn't realized that my foot was burning – I didn't have the control to stop it happening because I simply couldn't feel it, of course. I had broken a basic rule of the paralysed, which is to take very good care of yourself, particularly in those areas with no sensation. The burn had proved that my life was still a precarious balance between health and ill-health, and the fact that I could be set back by something so simple, so stupid, appalled me.

I sank to awful depths. I became tearful and non-communicative. I was shaken to the core by what had happened, and felt more bitter than ever about the frustrations of my disability. I brooded day and night, out of reach of anyone who tried to help me. Even when I came home from hospital, I was constantly reminded of my stupidity. My leg had to be permanently extended on a platform, so I became unwieldy again, crashing into walls and furniture and unable to do all the independent things it had taken me seven years to learn.

The accident also took its toll on Kevin and me as a couple. Before the burn, we had been happier than we had been in years. He had become far more tolerant of me and was gradually overcoming his prejudices about the disabled. We had faced and overcome our problems with our sex life – Kevin admitted that he had regarded me as only half a woman after the accident – and the implant programme had given us an important neutral area of discussion, on which we had slowly rebuilt our lines of communication. Also, the programme was no longer just about me. The children and Kev could see it as something constructive that they could all take a part in, especially the cycling aspect. I was the guinea-pig, but people's livelihoods were at stake and the happiness of all those others still to come. I had come to realize, perhaps rather slowly, that my obligations reached far beyond myself.

But with me off the programme while my foot healed, and as miserable as sin to boot, Kev went back to his bad old ways. 'It's your own bloody fault,' he shouted at me one day. 'If you will go off and do these madcap things, what do you expect? You're a paraplegic, for God's sake!' It was not what I needed to hear, and I resented his comments. I was also deeply hurt by the attitude of my friends and family, who didn't seem to appreciate the seriousness of my injury and actually treated it quite light-heartedly. 'If I had ignored this blister and it had set in, it would have got infected, it would have crept up my leg. I would have had poison in my body and I could have died,' I tried to tell them, but their response was pretty much that it hadn't and I didn't, so what was the problem?

I felt isolated and totally alienated for the first time in years. No one seemed to understand what bugged me really – that I was no longer in control. I fell into a dark despair and I didn't know how to pull myself out of it. I punished myself and I punished the people who didn't react the way I wanted them to. Not surprisingly, perhaps, Kev and everyone else kept well out of my way. I was a complete cow.

It was months before I felt back to normal again, months before I could resume the programme and think about the future. I felt psychologically scarred and physically drained. But the burn incident did bring one benefit with it – it prevented me from ever being complacent again. And when I did get through all the shock and depression, and come out the other side, I think I was a stronger, better person for it. The pain I had endured was something that had been suppressed inside me for years. Now that I had raged and wailed and rid myself of the hurt and the guilt and the anger, I somehow felt renewed.

It was that sense of renewal that made me finally ready for an outdoor trike ride in Stansted Forest, near to where I live. It was the most amazing experience – in many ways it was the best so far in terms of achievement. There I was lying back in my recumbent position, the children watching, their own bikes at the ready, and off I went. Cycling smoothly and rhythmically, a little yellow flag fluttering triumphantly at the back of my trike, and with Kevin and Tim running alongside me shouting encouragement, I covered a distance of just over a kilometre. It was exhilarating.

To feel the wind in my hair and the sun on my face on a glorious day, to have the children join me, cycling at my side, was a moment to savour for ever. The looks on their faces were priceless as they watched me, their paraplegic mother, moving my legs round and round on the pedals without any equipment attached. Whatever their young minds had told them about my disability, it had clearly never featured my ability to go out on a trike with them. They were thrilled, and I was amazed. All the hard work had paid off. The documentary-makers were filming me again that day, and the passers-by who stopped to stare as we passed must have wondered what all the fuss was about – we looked like a completely normal family, out cycling. I felt like screaming an explanation to them: 'But I'm paralysed! And I'm cycling!'

For Tim and Nick, that day also represented a personal achievement and a high point in their long and successful careers. Tim is especially proud of the trike, and I am really chuffed for him. Bless him. He is such a clever man. The team has invented something that can be taken out of the laboratory and used in the field – literally – helping a paralysed person to use their limbs efficiently and functionally in a fun way. Their work has finally allowed me to rejoin the able-bodied society that I was once a part of, and is a justification of all the years of frustration and effort on their part as much as mine. My moment of triumph was shared by us all.

TWELVE

Radiance

DURING THE next two years, we managed to improve my cycling technique to the point where I have now been allowed to take my tricycle home and use it whenever I like. All I do is get on, press a blue button for start and off I go, my little legs going like pistons. When I want to stop, I press a red button that activates the brakes *and* stops my legs going round. If I'm feeling strong enough, I can cycle up to a mile at a speed of ten miles per hour. It isn't as fast as the boys can go, and I think they get a bit frustrated with their slowcoach mother holding them back, but they don't really mind waiting for me to catch up with them.

The tricycle I have is going to be replaced shortly, for one with a motor on it from the same firm, which will mean that I can get home under power if I get too tired or have to climb a steep hill, or if something goes wrong with the program and I'm left in the middle of nowhere, unable to move. My first machine will become a prototype in the laboratory for future users. I wish them all the joy on it that I have had.

I now use the implant every day for aerobic exercise

in a special gym set up in a summerhouse in the garden of my home to improve my general health and fitness. I am probably one of the fittest paraplegics in the world because of it. Kevin now joins me, using his own gym equipment, and our friend and neighbour Janine comes in, too, for the regular sessions that have now become part of our social life as well as our health regime.

I have also managed to perfect my stepping technique to twenty-four steps – the exact distance between the two ends of my house. The computer program now makes my knees bend and my hips flex, and lifts my feet off the ground enough to do that. All I have to do is push a button on the Zimmer frame to start or stop. There are still problems with my knees not being strong enough to sustain the stepping, and I'm a long way off signing up for dancing lessons. But all the same, it's a major achievement.

Standing still and fully upright has proved to be more of a problem. Although my posture has been improved using the nerve blocks, I was still able to stand better before the implant operation, just using the RGO or the FES system. The team is coming slowly to the view that radical surgery will almost certainly be necessary to correct my hip alignment, although Tony Tromans is anxious not to do anything that could set me back with the cycling programme that has done so much to boost my morale. He wants to be a hundred per cent sure that any surgery he undertakes now will be the correct procedure, and that he can do it all in one go. My body has gone through quite enough already without adding any burdens. The big fear is that the very hip muscles that I need to allow me to step and cycle are the ones that keep me kinked and my back concave when I stand. To cut those muscles away could have dire consequences on my other activities. And even if they went ahead and did it – and that would probably be a world first in its own right – there would be no guarantees that it would help because there are so many other factors to consider and nobody has ever done it before. The fact is that, medically and scientifically, my body only becomes more puzzling as the years go by.

Further surgery is also planned that will allow me to be connected to a new and improved thirty-two-channel electromagnetic device, which will give me even more control. At the press of a button on the control box, I should be presented one day with an extraordinary series of choices – 'Exercise', 'Stand', 'Step' or 'Cycle' – choices that no paraplegic has ever been given before.

Whatever funding difficulties the team faces – and their Medical Research Council grant was not awarded in 1997 – they have promised they will always keep enough back to maintain my system and repair it if necessary. One other patient, an Australian called Chris Brogan, has also had the implant put in, in December 1996. But unfortunately it has not been nearly as successful, which is a shame because he had waited a very long time for it (he was one of the first volunteers for the programme before I joined). He suffered extensive nerve damage during the operation, much more than I did, and his receiver became unreliable and will need to be surgically replaced. They have been able to get him standing, though, and have gleaned some interesting information from him, such as the fact that, like me, he is not symmetrical – there are big differences between his left and right sides. I really hope they can do something for him because he is a brilliant person, a real diamond.

There are other, similar, projects ongoing around the world which have also made significant progress. One, in Cleveland, Ohio, involves fitting paraplegics with up to forty-eight stainless-steel electrodes in the legs, buttocks and lower back, and allows them to walk, climb and move from side to side. But at a cost of $200,000 per patient, it is also extremely expensive and tremendously complex, which means that more things can go wrong. The surgery needed is extensive, the infection risk is high and the computer software very complicated. People who have volunteered for it have found that it is of little practical benefit outside the laboratory.

The LARSI team currently receives its money from mixed sources which include the Wellcome Foundation and European Union grants under the BioMed initiative. University College London funds Nick; the charity Inspire pays for the Salisbury staff. There are six full-time, fully paid members of the team, with dear old Peter Donaldson still working for free. The funding issue places huge pressure on the team, having to continually scrabble around for money and justify their research through writing up papers and presenting them at medical conferences. It is all very labour-intensive, and means they can't do things as quickly as they would like to. But it's all part of the politics of scientific research these days, something biomedical engineers are not very good at.

In recent years there has also been a change in the way they are regulated. If the team wants to make my type of implant more widely available, and on a commercial basis, they now have to seek permission from the Medical Devices Agency, a branch of the Ministry of Health, and provide them with incredibly detailed documents that go into every single nut and bolt of the implant and every manufacturing stage. The trouble is that there is no one else in the country who knows more about these implants than the LARSI team, so the Agency has to try to find people who understand what they are doing and what it all means before they can even get to grips with what they're being asked to give the go-ahead to. Needless to say, the frustrations are enormous.

The television interest has helped. A follow-up programme on my progress was broadcast in the BBC's *QED* series, and warmly received by the public. A third documentary is in the pipeline, and international media interest had remained high. Four new recruits have enlisted to the programme and two of them should have their devices in place by the time this book is published. I can't wait for that to happen. I'm very excited for them, and pleased, too – purely selfishly – because it will give the boffins someone else to play with. They have learned so much from me, and I feel that I have almost come to the natural end of the trial and testing process. To be honest, after seven years, I have had enough. Now I want to be able to gain from the experience of others and use that knowledge to improve my own abilities to the maximum.

There is still a great deal of potential with the implant that I have. I feel that so much is within my grasp – the ability to stand and take a hand away, to be able to use crutches or a stick instead of a Zimmer frame. As soon as I get to the point where I feel I have reached my full potential, I will be truly happy. I have given a great deal, and although I am well aware that I have also received a great deal, at the moment I feel as if the credit is a little overbalanced on my side. It's now pay-back time – I want results, and I want them sooner rather than later. People will move on, Nick and Tim will one day retire and lead quieter, less complicated lives. But I'll still be here, still wired up and tuned in, still needing support. The implant is so resilient, in fact, that it will almost certainly outlast me – a deeply unwelcome thought. I dread to think of the idea of someone switching me on when I'm six feet under. For me, this implant is for life and beyond, not just for the duration of its inventors' careers.

Don't get me wrong. I am incredibly grateful for everything that has happened. In spite of all the pitfalls and hurdles the team have had to overcome, there is no getting away from the fact that they have allowed me to become the first person in the world to have this amazing device. Not only that – I am also the first ever implant patient to have worked so well and to have so much control. I'm in charge of it: that's the difference – the controllability. As a result of a unique collaboration between British medical experts and engineers, I now have something I can take home and use in my everyday life – the realization of a dream for Professor Brindley, Peter Donaldson, and their many able successors.

The present grant covers the neurological prostheses unit until the year 2001, and even if the team directors were to retire or die, the data has now been separately logged so that others could take their place. Nick and Tim are also hoping to train up a successor, one of the many bright young visiting Ph.D. students who pass through the unit for the duration of their studies, who

may be persuaded to stay on and carry on their work –
although they admit that the poor pay, long hours and
selfless dedication needed for the job aren't proving to
be an attractive proposition to the new generation. In
the words of Peter Donaldson: 'We need to find someone as daft as the rest of us.'

Nick and Tim are still the mainstay of the unit. Older
and wiser now, they have carried on tirelessly with their
extraordinary double act, ironing out my problems and
perfecting things for the next recipients, whoever they
may be. They have had to struggle on with my implant
while carrying on with their own lives, with all the usual
ups and downs. Tim's wife Sheila, a teacher, has recently
had a scare with cancer, and Tim, too, has had several
cancerous cells removed from his face. Living in Han-
well, west London, he still has three children at home
and one at university. He hopes that his seventeen-year-
old son Christopher may follow him into the world of
computer programming. Nothing seems to dampen his
enthusiasm for life. He is a keen cyclist and regularly
takes part in the London to Brighton bicycle race. His
passion for his work is infectious and he is the perfect
complement to Nick, who is quieter and far more
serious, but just as lovely.

It has been good for me to bear in mind that each
member of the team has had their own personal trials
and tribulations to live through while I struggled with
mine. Viv Harper has now left Salisbury District Hospital
to stay at home and look after her growing family. With
three young children, she has her hands full. I still miss
her smiling face every time I'm in for more tests. Not
only was she a true professional, she became a friend.
She has now been replaced by a lovely woman called

Anna Dunkerley, who is young and bright and full of ideas.

Peter Donaldson, whom I first met a long time after my implant operation at an FES conference in Salisbury, still works alongside his son Nick at University College London, though he is now well into his seventies. His clear-headed ability to look at a problem and take the time it needs to find a solution to it has been invaluable to the team. When he is not volunteering his services there or busy in his workshop at home, he helps his wife run their Kentish smallholding.

Professor Brindley, whom I have yet to meet, the man who started the whole implant business off, has filled his retirement years just as fruitfully. Many-talented, he is fluent in several languages and, after redesigning the bassoon, has also become an acknowledged musical instrument maker. He has always considered time-wasting the greatest sin, and neither his professional nor his personal life have ever lacked adventure. In his sixties, he resumed his teenage sports of pole vaulting and running, and he currently holds the European over-sixty-fives record for the 2,000-metre steeplechase.

He still acts as a consultant on several implant projects; among them as an idea to try to turn brain-waves into electrical impulses, which would allow the severely disabled to communicate with computers just by thinking. Professor Brindley has also set up his own surgical implant business with his wife, making and selling the implants he designs, and he has ploughed a lot of the profits back into projects that did not qualify for other funding. His two children have both followed him into the field of medicine – his son is a paramedic and his daughter a hospital administrator. He is also a devoted grandfather, twice over.

I have now, sadly, lost contact with most of the people I befriended when I first arrived at Salisbury District Hospital. Eamonn and the rest of the lads were key players in my recovery; they helped me to laugh again and to see that there was more to life than being able to walk. Becky was always going to be a lifelong friend, and has remained an inspiration to us all. In her late twenties now, she leads a full and active life, works full-time for British Telecom and lives on her own in a specially adapted flat in Milton Keynes. A very special person, the only thing missing from her life is a man. I hope she finds the right chap one day soon.

My baby brother Neil, such a pain as a child and such a brick since the accident, has remained a source of great support and encouragement to me. In 1998, he and Bridget flew to America and, in typically understated style, got married on their own in Las Vegas. They are very happy and we were all delighted for them, even though we were denied the chance to buy new hats!

My mother, Brenda, has never stopped being my best friend. She is completely recovered from her mini-breakdown and has become a much stronger person, as I think we all have. We still see each other almost daily, along with my wonderful father, Norman. I feel privileged to be their daughter. I don't know what I would have done without them. With their help, I have become the person that I am today.

Kevin and I are closer now than we were on our wedding day. Together we have been to hell and back, but we have come out the other side and ended up as soulmates. The children have been superb and are, I hope, better human beings because of what has happened to their mother and better able to cope with what life may throw at them.

Kev and the boys are also the people who keep me going, day in, day out. The boys, in particular, are my heart's pride. Funny and intelligent, they impress everyone they meet and have developed a true sense of caring and understanding. From potting up my hanging baskets to doing their newspaper rounds, they never fail to amaze me in terms of how well they have coped with all that has happened in the last ten years. Nathan has taken his GCSEs and moved on to the sixth form, and is showing great promise. He wants to go to university – which would make him the first person in my immediate family who has – and is considering a career as either a teacher or a journalist. He is a good sportsman, keen on hockey and football, and he's computer-mad. He's just beginning to take an interest in girls. Daniel is growing fast, and informed us recently that he wants to be an actor – something he would be excellent at because he's a natural comic. He has joined the Chichester Festival Youth Theatre – and who knows? – one day we may get to see him on the stage. He dotes on his father and likes nothing better than to potter around the house, doing DIY or gardening. Both boys are extremely kind and well-mannered individuals, and I am terribly proud of them.

The experiment that is me has been a journey of immense discovery for us all. Those responsible for it insist that they are not in the business of miracles. At one time they thought they could use conventional control engineering on the lower body to make it do what they wanted, and that the brain could be left to get on with its own thing. But they have learned that they could not detach the paralysed lower limbs in that way. It is all much more complicated than they envisaged, and not nearly as easy to mimic the brain as they thought. Also, the muscles of able-bodied people and animals react in a different way to those of the paralysed, which lose their strength and atrophy.

Through the systematic study that the team has carried out on me, they have discovered that I am not symmetrical. I was born with big differences in the way the left and the right sides of my body work in terms of muscle and neurological responses – a discovery which has led to the understanding that each one of us is as individual, with flaws and differences, as if we had been hand-crafted. Thorough scientific research on every millimetre of my nervous system has enabled Tim and Nick to rewrite the medical textbooks on the detail of nerve stimulation and the patterns of muscle control. But at least a decade more work lies ahead. The computer program needs much more tweaking and tuning; all the hardware is in place, but they need to do more work on the software.

And they need even more guinea-pigs, although they accept that it will be hard to find anyone quite as resilient as me. I am desperate for them to have a new 'toy', so that I can get on with my life and give up all this commuting. I joke with Nick and Tim that watching paint dry would have been more exciting than working with them, but the truth of the matter is that over the years we have become extremely fond of each other. I love them to bits and our relationship also contains a large amount of mutual admiration. Our joint dream is to get together enough funding to take the implant programme into the next century, and eventually make implants available on the NHS.

Worldwide talk of remarkable new experiments in which nerves in the severed spinal cords of rats have been regenerated through drug intervention, fails to impress me. Millions of pounds have been wasted, in my opinion, on chasing that particular rainbow, considering that it's not something that is expected to become viable in the near future. I first heard about the regeneration work in 1990, and way back then it was billed as 'a cure for paralysis within a decade'. Scientists working at the University of Zurich and elsewhere have undoubtedly made amazing progress, inducing up to four millimetres of new growth in severed nerves after treating them with antibodies and growth-promoting factors. But from what I have gathered from talking to those at Salisbury and elsewhere, the problems are numerous. The biggest fear is that newly grown nerves might wander aimlessly or make the wrong reconnections, giving the patient some sensation but no control. Because of such a frightening prospect, the regeneration of human spinal cords is not something that is likely within twenty years from now – maybe not even in our lifetimes. And the only people who will be suitable for experimentation will be the newly injured, not those with well-established breaks like me.

I would love to think that regeneration is possible, and I am sure it will be one day. In fact, I would be very foolish not to hope it could happen, even if it meant that the implant programme would become defunct overnight. But I'm afraid my scepticism rules my heart on this one. In my opinion, it's an unrealistic goal. Given the choice of having something now which will be able to help me in my lifetime, or of waiting to see if a minor success with a rat in a lab can be translated into something usable within the next twenty years, then I know which one I would go for.

Christopher Reeve has been at the forefront of the new movement. Since he fell off his horse in 1996 and became the world's most famous ventilator-dependent tetraplegic, he has probably done more for spinal injury than anyone else. As the actor who played Superman he has focused world attention on the problems facing us all, and for that we shall always be grateful. But he seems to be hanging on to a dream that one day he will walk again, and has vowed to do so within ten years. I have never met him, so I can't say if it is something he truly believes or whether the media have hyped it up around him, but they have certainly latched on to it in a big way with headlines like 'Superman Will Walk Again'. Some quarters of the spinal charity business have, understandably, grabbed on to his celebrity status and used it to promote their cause. There are hopes of raising £20 million to provide research funds for regenerating damaged spinal-cord nerves, and claims that the first laboratory trials will be ready for testing by the start of the new millennium.

The problem with all of this is that it plays on people's emotions, especially the emotions of people new to spinal injury. I feel very strongly that to offer even the idea of a 'cure' when there clearly isn't one yet, is completely wrong. People have got to be able to get on with their lives; they have got to be able to face up to their disability and move forward. If they think there might be a cure, then they simply won't bother to stay fit and healthy, or do all the boring physiotherapy they need to do to keep them in shape and alive into old age. 'Why bother?' you can hear them cry, 'We're all going to be cured in a year or two.'

All the while, millions of dollars keep pouring in to the numerous regeneration laboratories, trying to keep the flame alive. The exponents of 'the cure' have all the best equipment available, with the highest-paid technicians working in the smartest surroundings, and hold their conferences in places like Bermuda. I feel that if just some of the millions they receive was more usefully spent, then real progress might be made. The bladder-implant programme, for example, is already making a huge difference to the lives of thousands of paralysed people. And what about the further development of visual prostheses for the blind, or any number of other more *realistic* projects? Last but not least, of course, there's the LARSI programme, which operates on such a shoestring and relies so heavily on the goodwill and vocational spirit of the people behind it. With the right support, and financial backing, the LARSI system could actually make a difference, and relatively soon. It certainly has for me.

It has been an incredibly time-consuming and often frustrating process, but I can honestly say I am fitter now than I have ever been in my life. I was bone-idle before the accident, not at all self-motivated. My only exercise was running to the car, and I never once appreciated how truly wonderful it is to be able to walk, to run, to swim or jog – to do all those things that every able-bodied person takes for granted. Now that it is too late for me, I have had to learn to readjust my sights. But in many ways, I am happier for it. The implant has been the catalyst for my future, and the fringe benefits of being so fit mean that I shall now be able to have the best of the rest of my life.

Losing the use of my legs forced me to look at the positives of my situation rather than the negatives. It made me realize that life doesn't end just because you can no longer walk. There are actually many advantages to having no feeling below your waist – I can have my legs waxed without pain (or even a full bikini wax, as I was given in Kenya without even realising!), and I never have a period pain or a stomach ache. Going somewhere like Wimbledon in a wheelchair guarantees me a great seat, and we have queue-jumped all round Disneyworld. We also get special treatment on airlines and from travel companies.

Thanks to the kindness and support of others, I have been skiing, water-skiing, go-karting and quad-biking, and I've thrown myself off a cliff. In fact, I've done all sorts of things I would never have dreamed of attempting before the accident. I have been on safari, and holidayed all over Britain and the world – Switzerland, Greece, Africa, Turkey, Ibiza, America, Cyprus, Corfu and Crete – even though my implant sets off the airport security scanners every time! My disability has hardly prevented me from doing anything; on the contrary, it has given me a renewed lust for life, a realization that there is so much yet to live for.

I still have a tremendous urge to get out and be good at what I'm good at. The process of finding the real Julie Hill, the woman who was more than just a mum, was rudely interrupted by the accident. Before the crash I believed my future lay in sales; I was really enjoying my new job and saw myself staying in that line of work and developing it further. But the accident has shown me that my greatest skill is actually in dealing with people on a one-to-one basis, and it is something I would very much like to work on and make a new career out of. I took a GCSE in counselling and psychology with my friend Angie, and am currently the vice-chairman of the Back-Up Trust. I have so much more confidence, and I've developed more staying power, more determination than I would ever have thought possible. It's as if by losing the use of my legs I have somehow become a whole person at last. What happened to me has given me an empathy with other people which I can now put to good use in a new career, working with others in a similar situation. What I don't want to become is Julie the super-para, Julie who has achieved so much 'in spite of being disabled'. I don't want to be good at being disabled, I want to be good at being me, Julie Hill, the person, regardless of my disability.

Of course, I would much rather that the car accident had never happened and that I could walk like anyone else, but there is no point dwelling on the past and all the might-have-beens. Looking back is something I just don't do. I only try to think of my life after the accident. I can't allow myself to remember what it was like dancing the night away, running into the sea or kicking a football with my mates – or, if I do, I only permit it occasionally, when I'm feeling strong enough, and then I lock the memory away again for a few more years.

Who knows what the future may bring? – for me and for the two hundred thousand other paraplegics and tetraplegics in Western Europe. This amazing project that I have been so lucky to be a part of, at the cutting edge of biomedical science, may one day change *all* our lives. After all these years of painstaking research and scientific investigation, we are so close to achieving our original goals that I can almost taste the victory. After all the miles we have covered, I feel like I am just an inch away.

As soon as my hip problems are sorted out and I have built up my strength again, the dream will be just waiting to happen. Apart from the freedom it will give me, I won't have to carry round half the medical physics laboratory each time I use the implant. As crazy as it may sound, I would do it all over again; I would go through all those years of boredom and frustration and tears just to be able to be at this point again. The project has evolved from something very hit-and-miss into something quite brilliant in a typically British, self-effacing sort of way. The potential is so enormous.

Some people might look at me and say: 'Why bother about the implant? There's nothing wrong with your life. You can do everything you want to do, anyway.' And that's true – I can do all those things. But with the implant, I can also step, stand and cycle – and because it's there, because I am the only person in the world to have been given the chance to try it, then I must. I know that the implant will almost certainly never replace my wheelchair, but what it has done is give me back a lost choice. It allows me just enough extra mobility for all the little things in life that matter so much, day to day. It will let me stand at a bar and have a drink with Kev, reach the top shelves in the kitchen, sit in an armchair at a friend's house if I want to, without leaving a muddy track through their hallway or having to be constantly lifted and shifted. I want to use it to go and visit people – to stay with friends who don't have wheelchair access, to stay overnight without a huge amount of fuss and upheaval having to be made on my behalf.

Now, if I don't stand, step or cycle, it's because I don't want to, not because I can't. Unless you've been paralysed, it's hard to understand that simply having that choice is an amazing feeling, after so many years of having no choice at all and of being viewed as something alien just because of being in a wheelchair and not being at everyone else's eye level.

My worst experience of what that can mean happened while I was Christmas shopping with my parents last year, and they left me outside a store in Portsmouth while they went in to buy my present. Sitting quite happily waiting, watching the world go by, I watched quizzically as a passer-by stopped right in front of me, delved into her handbag and pulled out her purse. Before I could say anything, she had pressed a fifty-pence piece into my hand with the words 'Merry Christmas', and scurried off. I was gobsmacked. Even though I could see the funny side of it, that incident, above all others, represents to me the worst of what being paralysed can mean. The minute a previously normal, healthy, independent human being sits in a wheelchair, they are transformed in the public mind to an abnormal, unhealthy and dependent individual, the type who needs their charity. I joked with my parents that next time I'd take the kids along, and a hat!

A much better Christmas lies ahead. A decade after the accident which propelled me from my safe little world into one of such frightening limitations, I shall go for a walk in our local park with my family. Using the implant, I will stand up from my gaily painted wheel-chair and hold on to the crutches I need for balance. With Daniel and Nathan at my side and Kevin a few steps away, the Hill family – all four of us – will link hands and make footprints in the usual thin spattering of snow. Admittedly mine will be punctuated either side by little round holes where my crutches have been, and two skid marks where my feet will have dragged slightly behind, but they will not detract from this moment in any way.

Looking back at the four sets of footprints, side by side and in step, still together as a family after all we have been through, I will know at last that however hard the journey has sometimes been, it will all have been worth-while. Against all the odds, despite all the pain and the moments of despair, we will have made it.